Soldier and civilian in Roman Yorkshire

Soldier and civilian in Roman Yorkshire

Essays to commemorate
the nineteenth centenary of the foundation of York
edited by R. M. BUTLER

Leicester University Press 1971

This volume is published with the help of a grant from the Yorkshire Philosophical Society

First published in 1971 by Leicester University Press
Distributed in North America by Humanities Press Inc., New York

Designed by Arthur Lockwood

Set in Monotype Plantin
Printed in Great Britain by Western Printing Services Ltd, Bristol

ISBN 0 7185 1095 X

Preface

In 1967 it was suggested by Mr L. P. Wenham to the Council of the Yorkshire Philosophical Society that, since the year 1971 would mark the nineteenth centenary of the coming of the Ninth Legion to York and the beginning of the city's recorded history, the occasion should be marked by the publication of a new survey of Roman York compiled by local archaeologists. The Society agreed that the centenary should be celebrated by a book of commemorative essays to be written by scholars of local and national repute. It therefore invited several learned societies and other bodies to send representatives who could form a committee to pursue this matter. This volume is the result of that committee's meetings and has been made possible by the initiative and generosity of the Yorkshire Philosophical Society.

The committee met under the chairmanship of Mr L. P. Wenham, representing the Yorkshire Philosophical Society and St John's College, York. Its other members were Dr R. M. Butler (Secretary), Miss M. C. Cross (Department of History, York University), Mr B. R. Hartley (Roman Antiquities Section, Yorkshire Archaeological Society), Professor A. F. Norman (East Yorkshire Local History Society), Mr H. G. Ramm (Royal Commission on Historical Monuments (England)), Mr J. Shannon (York Civic Trust), Mr O. S. Tomlinson (City of York), Mr G. F. Willmot (Yorkshire Archaeological Society), and Miss F. E. Wright (Yorkshire Architectural and York Archaeological Society).

A distinguished group of scholars has contributed essays and Leicester University Press has agreed to publish the resulting work. The committee is indebted to all of these and is glad that the outcome of its deliberations has been so satisfactory. It is hoped that the following volume will make a useful contribution to knowledge of Roman York and Yorkshire in the city's centenary year, consisting as it does of original studies, whether of unpublished material or based on further consideration of that already known.

R. M. BUTLER

Contents

Line illustrations

Plates

between pp. 104–105

Abbreviations

Ant. J.	*Antiquaries Journal*
Arch.	*Archaeologia*
Arch. Ael.	*Archaeologia Aeliana*
Arch. Camb.	*Archaeologia Cambrensis*
Arch. Cant.	*Archaeologia Cantiana*
Arch. J.	*Archaeological Journal*
A.N.L.	*Archaeological News Letter*
B.M.	British Museum
CIL	*Corpus Inscriptionum Latinarum*
Cos.	Consul
Cos. suff.	Consul suffectus
*CW*²	*Transactions of the Cumberland and Westmorland Antiquarian and Archaeological Society* (new series)
FC	*Fasti Consulares*
Gents. Mag. Lib. R.B.	G. L. Gomme (ed.), *Gentleman's Magazine Library, Romano-British Remains* (1887)
Geog.	*Geography*
H.M.P.	Hull Museum *Publications*
ILS	H. Dessau, *Inscriptiones Latinae Selectae* (1892–1916)
J.R.S.	*Journal of Roman Studies*
Leg.	Legio
Med. Arch.	*Medieval Archaeology*
Not. Dig. (occ)	*Notitia Dignitatum (occidens)*
O.R.L.	E. Fabricius, F. Hettner, O. von Sarwey, *Der Obergermanisch-Raetische Limes des Römerreichs* (1894–1937)
O.S.	Ordnance Survey
*PIR*²	E. Groag and A. Stein (eds.), *Prosopographia Imperii Romani* (2nd ed. 1933)
P.P.S.	*Proceedings of the Prehistoric Society*
Procs. Arch. Inst.	*Proceedings* of the Royal Archaeological Institute
P.S.A.S.	*Proceedings of the Society of Antiquaries of Scotland*
R.C.H.M., *Roman London*	Royal Commission on Historical Monuments (England), *London III, Roman London* (1928)

R.C.H.M., *York*	Royal Commission on Historical Monuments (England), *City of York I, Eburacum* (1962)
R.E.	Pauly-Wissowa, *Realencyclopädie*
RIB	R. G. Collingwood and R. P. Wright, *Roman Inscriptions of Britain I* (1965)
RIC	H. Mattingly, E. A. Sydenham, C. H. V. Sutherland, *The Roman Imperial Coinage* (1923–1967)
S.H.A.	*Scriptores Historiae Augustae*
V.C.H.	*Victoria County History*
W.A.M.	*Wiltshire Archaeological Magazine*
Y.A.J.	*Yorkshire Archaeological Journal*
Y.A.Y.A.S. *Procs.*	*Proceedings* of the Yorkshire Architectural and York Archaeological Society
Y.M.H.	*Yorkshire Museum Handbook*
Y.P.S.R.	Annual *Reports* of the Yorkshire Philosophical Society

Notes and references are printed at the end of each article. The pages on which the notes appear are given, in diamond brackets, on the headline to each text page.

S. S. FRERE

Introduction

A volume designed to celebrate the safe passage of 1900 years since the foundation of York, by inviting a variety of scholars to discuss aspects of its Roman past, is to be welcomed since it provides an opportunity to stand back from the busy tasks of the moment to take stock of what we really know. Archaeologists proceed from the particular to the general, by proposing hypotheses to account for observed facts; but there is a human tendency for these hypotheses, once accepted, to become dogmata into which later observations are expected to fit, unless a conscious effort is made to think afresh. On the other hand, there is also a tendency for a new generation of workers to reject the conclusions of the past, not always on adequate grounds or with a full consideration of all the facts. For both these reasons the provision of an opportunity to reassess evidence and to write in a general way, summing up the evidence for conclusions, and pointing the way ahead, is likely to be useful.

The present volume deals not only with Roman York itself, but with its context in the Iron Age background and in the succeeding Romano-British environment of the surrounding region. On the first Dr I. M. Stead throws much new light in his study of the Iron Age inhabitants of eastern Yorkshire; his paper by implication shows how minimal is our present knowledge of the nature, background and origins of the Brigantes of the western part of the county. Here there is obviously a need for much more work.

York itself is one of the outstanding examples in this country of that genius of Roman commanders for choosing a site which, once established, excellently fulfilled not only their own requirements but also those of very different subsequent generations. But we have only to remark the moments when the place entered recorded Roman history – two emperors died at York, at least one was proclaimed there, and its bishop attended the Council of Arles – to realize how little archaeology has yet revealed of its essentials.

At many Romano-British sites today it can be said that the most interesting problems relate to the beginning and the end: the origins and cause of settlement on the one hand, and on the other the question of survival into and/or continuity through the migration period, and the modes of doing so. But naturally this emphasis presupposes also some knowledge of the growth and history of the place during the period of Roman rule itself. On sites which, like York, have been fully occupied by medieval and modern successors the acquisition of this knowledge is in itself a major task, and much remains to be done by modern excavation both in the fortress and in the colonia at York. To take only two examples, an examination of the defences of the colonia is an undertaking too long postponed; while the problems posed by the restoration of a fortress of full legionary size in the early fourth century, and the subsequent use of the space within, also call for large-scale excavation, which would provide much-needed control on current theories of late Roman military organization. All this calls for co-operative work, well organized and on a large scale. The foundation of an Excavation Committee charged with all these matters, and loyally supported by local workers, is overdue.

Mr L. P. Wenham describes the evidence, tentative perhaps as yet, for a pre-Flavian phase at York. It seems highly likely, indeed, that a pre-Flavian auxiliary fort may one day be proved to occupy the site. The most promising position for this would seem to be north-west of the bridge, in the area of St Mary's Abbey; there suggestive pottery has been found, and it would seem to be the focus of some of the approach roads. Yet a curious fact is the wide distribution of recorded pre-Flavian sherds: they have been found at places too far apart to fall within the area of a conceivable early fort.

Here, too, it is well to remind ourselves of the important paper published by Dr Stead in 1968 (*Y.A.J.*, xlii (part 166), 151–64), in which he shows how flimsy is the strictly archaeological evidence for the traditionally accepted defensive stages of the York fortress, when divorced from deductions and speculations, however reasonable in themselves these latter may be in the context of a military site, with its presumption of method and completeness. We need not, perhaps, be too worried over the question whether the Trajanic wall went all round the circuit. This is so probable, even if it was not finished until Hadrian's reign, as to be virtually certain; and Dr Stead's scepticism took no account of the dismantled turves and pottery filling the first-century ditch below Tower S.W.5.

The evidence, however, for a legionary fortress at York under Petillius Cerialis must be admitted to be still very weak. A pre-Agricolan rampart can be proved beyond reasonable doubt at only one point, below the south-west wall of the fortress at Coney Street (*J.R.S.*, xlvi (1956), 79, fig. 11; R.C.H.M. *York*, fig. 15). And even here the reinterpretation by the R.C.H.M. of the 'palisade-slot' as a mere marking-out trench introduces the possibility that the clay and timbers sealing it in front of the clay core may only be the foundation of a turf front applied in a second stage of the same operations, and thus that the entire rampart is really of a single phase and the work of Agricola. The marking-out trench would no longer be needed once the rampart itself began to take shape, and it is hard to see how it could have remained open.

A claim that the rear turf-revetment of the Cerialian rampart was found near Tower S.W.5 has been made by Mr Wenham (M. G. Jarrett and B. Dobson, *Britain and Rome* (Kendal, 1966), 8, fig. 3, section A–B: this section is repeated in R.C.H.M. *York*, fig. 13, but with an important discrepancy). Two turf-stacks were found on this site with a sandy filling between. These three elements would normally be taken as composing a single rampart. Wenham, however, interpreted the front turf as the *rear* revetment of the Cerialian rampart, and the rear turf as defining a widening of the rampart under Agricola, and quoted the removal of the topsoil below this rear stack as evidence of different date. But, (i) his drawing, section A-B, clearly shows topsoil continuing beneath this turf, though the R.C.H.M. redrawing has dutifully removed it; (ii) the north-east face of the 'Cerialian' turf-stack, which should be its external rearward face and ought therefore to present an unbroken slope, is in fact interleaved with sand from the central core, an indication which clearly shows that it is the front revetment of the visible rampart and not a rear one as suggested. At another site, too, in Davygate, also on the south-west front, the Cerialian rampart is conspicuous by its absence; this can hardly be explained by removal in order to insert an Agricolan timber tower, for the tower is only 11ft wide while the hypothetical gap has a width of at least 30ft. On other sides of the fortress the Cerialian rampart can be restored only by re-interpreting S. N. Miller's results. This may or may not be justified. But when we remember the possible large site at Malton and the newly discovered 23-acre fortress at Rossington Bridge, we would do well to pause before committing ourselves, on existing evidence, to a Cerialian regular fortress of full legionary size at York. A supply base, an enclosure of 'half-legionary' size, or even an auxiliary fort are all still possibilities.

Certainly under Agricola, if not before, York became the base of Legio IX Hispana; and when that legion departed, under circumstances here for the first time fully set out and discussed in relation to all the recent evidence by Professor E. Birley, its place was taken by Legio VI Victrix. York became the seat of the British northern command, the hub of all military activity on the frontier. It is appropriate, therefore, that the central core of this book should contain Mr B. R. Hartley's paper on Roman campaigns in northern Britain and Mr A. R. Birley's historical account of the Sixth legion. They deal with events central to the wider history of York, as does Dr R. M. Butler's study of the fourth-century defences of the fortress.

Much of the book relates to Yorkshire in the later Roman period. This is as it should be, for the reassessment of the state of Britain in the fourth century, made possible by discoveries since the Second World War, has been one of the most remarkable achievements of recent years, and is not yet complete. Notable in this connection is Mr J. S. Wacher's paper on the Yorkshire towns in the fourth century, in which he demonstrates the exceptional character of some of them. In Britain we have not yet reached the stage where we can illuminate outstanding problems of late Roman military supply, as has been done on the Continent with the discovery of the Trier *horrea*, the Veldidena supply-base, or the curious store-buildings at Nieder-Mumpf and Sisseln. Such sites are still to seek. But are we perhaps moving towards a solution of another problem, that of the field-army of the *Comes Britanniarum*? I myself recently discussed the problem briefly (*Britannia* (London, 1967), 237–8), discarding the theories of Bury and Collingwood and suggesting that there had been a comitatensian army commanded by the Count in these islands at least from the intervention of Stilicho and possibly earlier. "We may bear the possibility in mind that the command was actually established earlier, perhaps by Magnus Maximus, the list as we have it merely reflecting a later situation." Perhaps the most valuable part of this suggestion is the possibility of detaching the date of the *creation* of the command from the date of its sole appearance in a written source (*Notitia Dignitatum Occ.*, vii and xxix). More recently the matter has been taken further by K. M. Martin (*Latomus*, 1969, 408ff.) with his suggestion that the *comes maritimi tractus* killed in A.D. 369 was the commander of comitatensian troops, and that *maritimus tractus* is merely a synonym for the south of Britain. It is never easy to trace the stations of units of the field-army, since they are not given in the Notitia. In Britain their non-appearance has strengthened the idea that there was no field-army here before the opening years of the fifth century, whereas the earlier existence of the *Dux Britanniarum* and *Comes Litoris Saxonici*, who are equally attested by name only in the Notitia, has been given substance by known forts. But the Theodosian Code (e.g. VII 9) provides evidence for the billeting of troops in towns, and since the force was mobile its stations may have changed from time to time. It is certain that Count Theodosius introduced many changes into the military organization of Britain, and it is valuable to be reminded of the coincidence of date in the changes recorded at Catterick and Malton. If Catterick became a garrison-town under Count Theodosius, but is not listed in the Notitia as such, can we suggest that it held part of the field-army? If so it is to be hoped that further such stations may be recognized. They will only be identifiable by divergencies from normal development (like those which led J. S. Wacher himself to postulate Brough-on-Humber as a naval base), or by bulk finds of military equipment. There are no sites which have yet produced the latter; but in the former category we may venture to propose Clausentum and Great Chesterford for further investigation.

The evidence adduced by H. G. Ramm shows that already a substantial body of facts is amassing with which to illustrate the continuity of life at York in the fifth and sixth centuries. It is not surprising that many of these facts concern the cemeteries, in which York is rich, though unfortunately many of them were explored in the nineteenth century. Indeed, the scientific excavation of urban cemeteries is a task which is still in its infancy in Britain. They have been strangely neglected, but recent work at Winchester, Dorchester and Cirencester shows that much can be expected once the correct techniques have been mastered and background services organized.

In conclusion, therefore, it may be hoped that the essays included in this book will enjoy wide circulation. Combining, as they do, so much that is germane to the history and archaeology of Roman Britain and to the Roman Empire at large with so much that is significant to future work in York and its region, it will be strange indeed if this volume is not extensively circulated. Our gratitude must be expressed to the organizers who conceived the volume, and to its editor, Dr R. M. Butler, who faced the thankless task of extracting contributions as punctually as possible from busy colleagues, and who welded them into what is now before us.

I. M. STEAD

Yorkshire before the Romans: some recent discoveries

York was a Roman foundation. It is true that there are prehistoric remains from the city, and from its immediate neighbourhood – Mesolithic flints from St Mary's Abbey,[1] a hoard of Neolithic implements from Holgate,[2] a beaker from the railway excavations in 1840,[3] and several Bronze Age weapons and tools[4] – discoveries reflecting the position of York on a moraine which provided a route across the Vale in prehistoric times. That prehistoric finds are more concentrated in York than elsewhere along the moraine is due no doubt to disturbances caused by occupation here in more recent times, and to the early foundation of a museum and an active Yorkshire Philosophical Society. It may well be that the Green Dykes on the east side of the city belong to the Early Iron Age,[5] and artifacts of that period may yet be found, but there is no major settlement here. The Romans selected this site with a view not only to local factors, but to a plan envisaging the conquest and control of the north of England,[6] and it is this wider context, which had no relevance in pre-Roman times, that determined the site of the largest Roman and medieval settlement in northern England.

The Vale of York, too, was of little importance in the Early Iron Age. Sherds of pottery have been found at Roomer Common and Grafton,[7] towards the north-west edge of the Vale, and south of York there are two cemeteries of barrows at Skipwith which seem to be outlying sites of the Arras Culture.[8] But there is nothing more, and the Romans must have found the Vale but sparsely populated.

A denser population would have been encountered at the start of Cerialis' campaign in A.D. 71, when the invading army moved north from the end of Ermine Street on the Humber bank, into the territory of the Parisi. Not only was the native population greater there than in the Vale of York, but much more is known about it, and in several ways knowledge has been advanced in recent years.[9]

This part of Yorkshire had been settled four centuries or so before the Roman conquest by Celtic peoples whose peculiar burial rituals can be compared with rites found on the Continent, particularly in eastern France. Unrecorded in history, this pre-Roman population is known only through archaeology. It takes its name, the Arras Culture, from a site some two miles east of Market Weighton, where a large cemetery of small barrows included some covering cart-burials, and others surrounded by square-plan ditches. These rites, and their Continental analogies, have been discussed elsewhere;[10] the present paper will outline more recent developments which are gradually extending our knowledge of this Early Iron Age culture.

Although Arras is still the richest La Tène burial site in Yorkshire, it is not the earliest. The Arras cemetery belongs, apparently, to the third or second century B.C., and the large cemeteries at Danes Graves and Eastburn are later. Other sites, such as Pexton Moor, Hunmanby, Huntow and Sawdon, may have been contemporary with Arras, or even earlier. Uncertainty about chronology is a major problem, because most of the grave-goods cannot be compared in detail with Continental forms on which the divisions of the La Tène period have been based. But there is one site whose grave-goods can be matched exactly on the Continent, and as a result it can be securely dated – to an early stage in La Tène I, in the fourth century B.C.[11] That site is at Cowlam, and an opportunity to re-examine it was recently taken, as part of a programme of excavating plough-threatened barrows on the Yorkshire Wolds.

A group of five barrows at Cowlam was excavated by Canon Greenwell about a century ago,[12] but only three have ever been plotted by the Ordnance Survey, and they were the only mounds still visible in 1969. Greenwell did not publish a plan showing the relative positions of his barrows, nor can a plan be extracted from his descriptions. It was hoped that re-excavation would locate sufficient features described by Greenwell to identify the individual barrows, but after the three mounds had been excavated, at Easter 1969, there was still a lack of correlation. The other two barrows will have to be located and excavated before the evidence can be fully assessed.

One important discovery of the recent excavation was that the three barrows were each surrounded by square-plan ditches (plate 1a). The largest, Barrow A, had a fairly square platform about 46ft across, surrounded by a ditch about 6ft wide and a little over 3ft deep below the present ground level. The mound was only 10in. high, and hardly anything of its structure survived. It had been built on a layer of reddish-brown earth, which here covered the surface of the chalk, whose surviving area, together with the pattern of silting in the filling of the ditch, indicated that originally the barrow had been about 30ft in diameter and surrounded by a berm. Barrow B, now only 8in. high, was on a platform about 32ft square, and there had been no berm. The ditch was nearly 10ft wide and about 3ft 6in. deep. The third barrow, C, had had a slight berm, and its ditch resembled that round Barrow A. Its position was scarcely perceptible – it was no more than 6in. high – and its square platform measured about 34ft across (plate 1a).

Greenwell's excavation was recognized in each barrow – although its extent could not be defined accurately because so little survived of the mounds, and consequently very little of Greenwell's disturbance. It seemed that he had tackled these barrows in his usual way – approaching from the south and stopping a little beyond the middle.[13] Particular attention seems to have been paid to Barrow B, which had traces of closely-spaced trenches across the centre. Near the middle of each barrow human bones were scattered within the area of the earlier excavation, but nowhere was there a grave. This confirms Greenwell's observation that at Cowlam the bodies had been buried on the old ground surface.

There can be little doubt that the largest surviving mound, Barrow A, was the largest barrow excavated by Greenwell, Barrow LIV. For some unrecorded reason Greenwell assigned this mound to the Bronze Age; perhaps its very size (he measured it as 50ft), larger than any known Early Iron Age barrow in Yorkshire, was regarded as a sufficient argument. But the recent excavation has located a square-plan ditch round the barrow, so it surely belongs to the Early Iron Age. No doubt the five mounds were more or less contemporary.

The burial rite is interesting, for not only were the central inhumations on the old ground surface, but all five skeletons were crouched, and one of them "had been quite tightly contracted, and only occupied, measuring from the ends of the toes to the back of the head, a space of 35in."[14] The crouched or contracted skeleton is a departure from the practice of extended inhumation universal in the La Tène areas of western Europe, and it is interesting to find it at such a very early stage of the Arras Culture. Such burials are common in Yorkshire in the Early Bronze Age, but none can be dated to the millennium 1400 to 400 B.C. The rite of contracted inhumation also occurs in La Tène contexts in parts of eastern Europe.[15]

It has been argued elsewhere, on the basis of similar grave-goods, that Cowlam was not only the site of the earliest La Tène burials in Yorkshire, but was also the earliest site of the Arras Culture.[16] Thus the initial date of the Arras Culture in Yorkshire should be no later than the fourth century B.C. The discovery of square enclosures round the barrows at Cowlam – a feature virtually unknown in Britain outside the Arras Culture[17] – not only emphasizes this, but quite seals the argument. Cowlam and Arras belong to the same culture.

A second discovery, scarcely less important, was that the Cowlam barrows had been built on the site of an Early Iron Age settlement. Greenwell had found some potsherds in the bodies of his barrows, on the old ground surface and in pits sealed by the mounds. In the recent excavations a further collection included some from Neolithic and Bronze Age vessels, but they were mainly Early Iron Age sherds. This pottery is evidence for an Early Iron Age settlement which has unfortunately been ravaged by recent ploughing. The occupation level survives only under the barrows, but a geophysical survey has suggested that there are several pits between the mounds and this warrants further investigation. An Early Iron Age settlement securely sealed, and thus dated, by fourth-century B.C. barrows would indeed be a fascinating discovery.

One of the main obstacles to the study of the Arras Culture is amply illustrated at Cowlam – important sites were found by antiquarians whose methods fell far short of modern standards. But Cowlam is by no means the worst example – William Greenwell published a fairly detailed account and the finds survive and can be correlated with his report. No account of the 1815–17 excavations in the Arras cemetery was published for 30 years – when Edward Stillingfleet gave his "recollection after a lapse of years".[18] Furthermore, the Arras finds were divided by the excavators and only Stillingfleet's collection survives, along with tantalizing references to lost grave-goods: "we found several much finer bracelets; but they did not fall to my share".[19] There are severe limits to the study of a small number of indifferently recorded objects, and in order to further research on the Arras Culture the thorough investigation of new sites is essential.

One new site, another cemetery, has been identified during air surveys by J. K. S. St Joseph, who in 1962 noticed typical small square enclosure ditches in the same field as a Neolithic henge monument, and in several fields to the south.[20] Two years previously in the same area J. E. Bartlett had excavated five crouched skeletons, each at the centre of the small circular ditch of a plough-flattened barrow. Both discoveries belong to an enormous cemetery whose burials extend, perhaps intermittently, for at least two miles in the parishes of Burton Fleming (North Burton) and Rudston.[21] The site is on gravel, in the valley of the Gypsey Race, and it seems that there are more than 500 burials in the vicinity, on both sides of the stream.

Two areas of the Burton Fleming cemetery, about 200 yards apart, were excavated in 1968 and 1969 with a view to sampling the extent of plough damage as well as comparing the burials and grave-goods from different parts of the site. The first area (fig. 1, and plate 1b) was excavated entirely by hand, and the trenches were positioned initially on the information provided by a resistivity

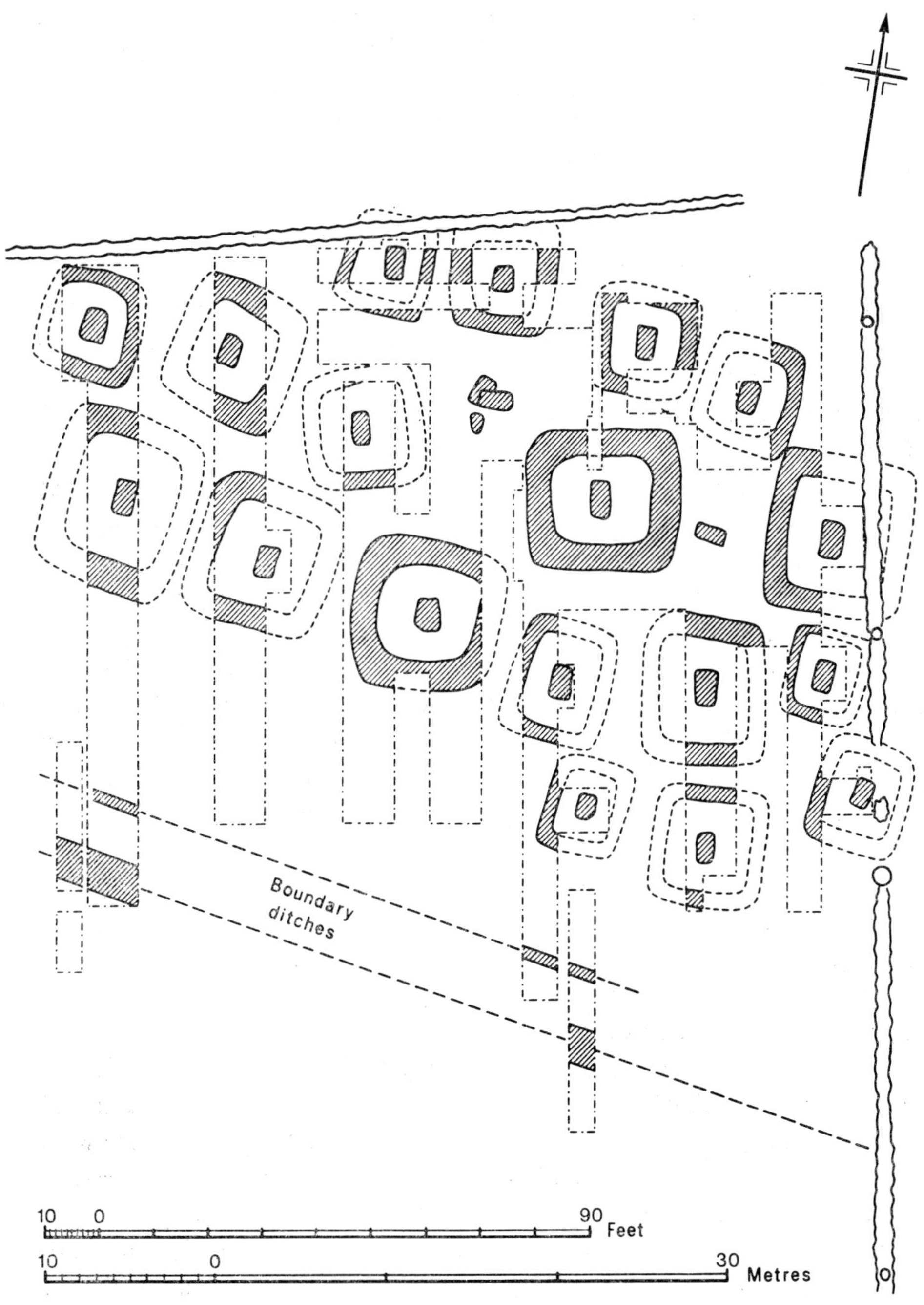

Figure 1. Burton Fleming: field 1.

survey which defined the barrow ditches with striking accuracy.[22] On the south side of the area a boundary ditch, 4ft deep below ground level, measured 8ft wide at the bottom of the plough-soil. To the north the barrows had been fairly closely packed, with some ditches virtually touching, but where there were spaces between barrows thorough stripping revealed four flat graves. The entire area was quite flat, with no hint of a mound, although on excavation one or two of the barrows had a higher level of gravel towards the centre than the level beyond the ditch. Eighteen barrows were excavated, and their platforms varied from 12ft to 22ft square. Each barrow had a fairly large central grave, on average 6ft long and 4ft wide, and without exception these graves were orientated north–south. The orientation of the square-plan ditches was based on the graves, and the excavated barrows were arranged in four lines (the southern line incomplete) which were orientated with the boundary ditch.

The majority of the burials were crouched or contracted, more rarely flexed; on their left sides, with their heads at the north end of the grave and facing east (plate 2a). One had the head facing west, although the legs were drawn up on the east side; and another was completely inverted from the normal position, with the head at the south end facing west. Three of the four flat graves held peculiar burials – two were orientated west–east (one of them extended), and the third was an adolescent whose skull alone had survived. The only odd position occupied by a burial which had been covered by a barrow was one where the skeleton appeared to have fallen into the grave – possibly an accident at the funeral.

Some of the skeletons were very tightly contracted, so much so that the corpses must have been bound. This rite is curious in view of the comparatively large size of the graves. At least three skeletons had been buried in some kind of wooden coffin, measuring between 1ft 6in. and 2ft wide and up to 3ft 6in. long (plate 2b). The shape of the coffins survived merely as a slight dark stain, occasionally emphasized by a sharp contrast in the grave filling.

Over half of the burials had grave-goods, including ten each with a single pot, and ten with pig bones – eight burials had both pot and pig bones (plate 2a). The pots were invariably simple jars of the type well known from Danes Graves and Eastburn where they also frequently held joints of pork.[23] Seven brooches were found near the chest, neck or head, where they had apparently been used to fasten some kind of garment. The only bronze piece was a small penannular brooch with expanded terminals and a humped pin (fig. 7, no. 1); whilst two long 'flattened bow' brooches and four involuted brooches were made of iron. Two small glass beads were found each by the side of a skull, and they might well have been used as ear-rings. One of these beads was found in the same grave as a fine shale bracelet, worn on the left fore-arm, and as this skeleton also had a brooch and a pot it provided the richest grave-group found so far (fig. 5).

The second area excavated at Burton Fleming (fig. 2 and plates 3a and 3b) was on higher ground where ploughing had caused more damage – little or nothing survived of some of the barrow ditches, and the graves were shallower. Here the plough-soil was removed by a Drott Tractorshovel, and a larger area was then excavated. But the density of burials was less than in the first area – 19 graves were excavated, and each one had probably been covered by a barrow. Most of the graves were orientated north–south, but there was no overall linear arrangement of barrows, due in part perhaps to the distance from the boundary ditch. Instead these barrows seemed to fall into three groups, but the significance of this grouping will have to await the excavation of adjoining areas. The barrow platforms varied in size from 11ft to 28ft across.

The positions of the skeletons resembled those found in the first area, although there was slightly more variety in their orientation. The normal position was repeated – ten skeletons were crouched or contracted (one was flexed) on the left side, with the head at the north end facing east. Six other skeletons were in a similar posture but differently orientated – two of them with west–east orientation; two extended inhumations were orientated west–east; and there was one skeleton on its back with the head at the north end and legs flexed. In this area similar wooden coffins were recognized in five graves.

Compared with the first area there were fewer pots, but one more brooch. The five pots were similar in type and three of them were associated with pig bones. Of the eight brooches the finest, involuted and made of bronze, had fine moulded ornament and a knob of 'enamel' on the foot (fig. 6, no. 4; and p. 36). The iron brooches included a large piece decorated with a bead of reddish material, which resembles a Continental La Tène I brooch (fig. 6, no. 3 and p. 36), but the others were typical Yorkshire forms: a very short 'flattened bow' brooch, three complete involuted types, and fragments of two others. Other iron objects await radiographs before they can be identified.

There are certainly some differences between the two areas so far excavated at Burton Fleming, but other areas will have to be sampled and more burials excavated before the significance of these differences can be assessed. This site is important in part because it is the first modern excavation of an Arras Culture cemetery, but beyond that the air photographs show that to some extent there is a linear arrangement of barrows. There is a possibility that this pattern will provide a sequence, with one end of the cemetery earlier than the other, and if this sequence covers a sufficient period of time it could be of great importance for the chronology of the Early Iron Age in England. Such a 'horizontal stratification' at Münsingen forms the basis of the classification of the La Tène period in Switzerland.[24]

Another Arras Culture cemetery is currently being destroyed by gravel working at Garton Slack, four miles west of Driffield. More than 30 Early Iron Age burials there have been rescued by C. and E. Grantham, and also, on behalf of the Inspectorate of Ancient Monuments, by T. C. M. Brewster. The cemetery resembles Burton Fleming in having had small barrows, now flattened, some with square enclosure ditches, as well as several flat graves. Grave-goods (fig. 6, no. 2; and pp. 36–7) can be matched at both Burton Fleming and Danes Graves, and weapons were absent but for a broken spear-head which may have been lodged in the shoulder of a corpse.

The burial rite, and particularly the use of square enclosures, is sufficient to demonstrate the relationship between Cowlam and the later cemeteries at Burton Fleming and Garton Slack. But these later stages of the Arras Culture cannot be tied to any exact chronological scheme, and there is insufficient material to construct even a comparative chronological framework. For the moment it must suffice to place these sites within La Tène II and III. Over the years there may have been a tendency to reduce the size of barrow platform, for the earlier sites at Cowlam (32ft to 46ft) and Arras (35ft and 41ft)[25] had barrows considerably larger than those found at Burton Fleming (11ft to 28ft, with an average of 17ft). And there may be some significance in their situations, for Cowlam and Arras are on the top of the Wolds, whereas the later sites tend to be further east, on or near the more recent geological deposits which border that edge of the Wolds.

Settlements of the Arras Culture have never received the attention devoted to the cemeteries, and no site can certainly be assigned to the same period as the burials. An extensive occupation area at Driffield has been sampled,[26] but as yet there is nothing to link it positively with the adjoining Eastburn cemetery. Two other promising sites have been located recently, but they also await detailed investigation. The first, in a field to the east of Little Thorpe Farm, Rudston, was found when several querns and some Early Iron Age potsherds were dragged to the surface during deep-ploughing, and this might be the site of a settlement connected with the nearby Burton Fleming cemetery.[27] The second site was also noticed after deep-ploughing – in a field at Kilham, to the south of Woldgate and not far from Harpham Roman villa. Excavations here by C. and E. Grantham produced an iron penannular brooch (fig. 7, no. 3) and a bronze swan's-neck pin (fig. 6, no. 1) as well as a collection of pottery.

The only Early Iron Age settlements in eastern Yorkshire to have been extensively excavated either defy close correlation because of the paucity of artifacts (Grimthorpe);[28] or date earlier than the Arras Culture (Scarborough; Staple

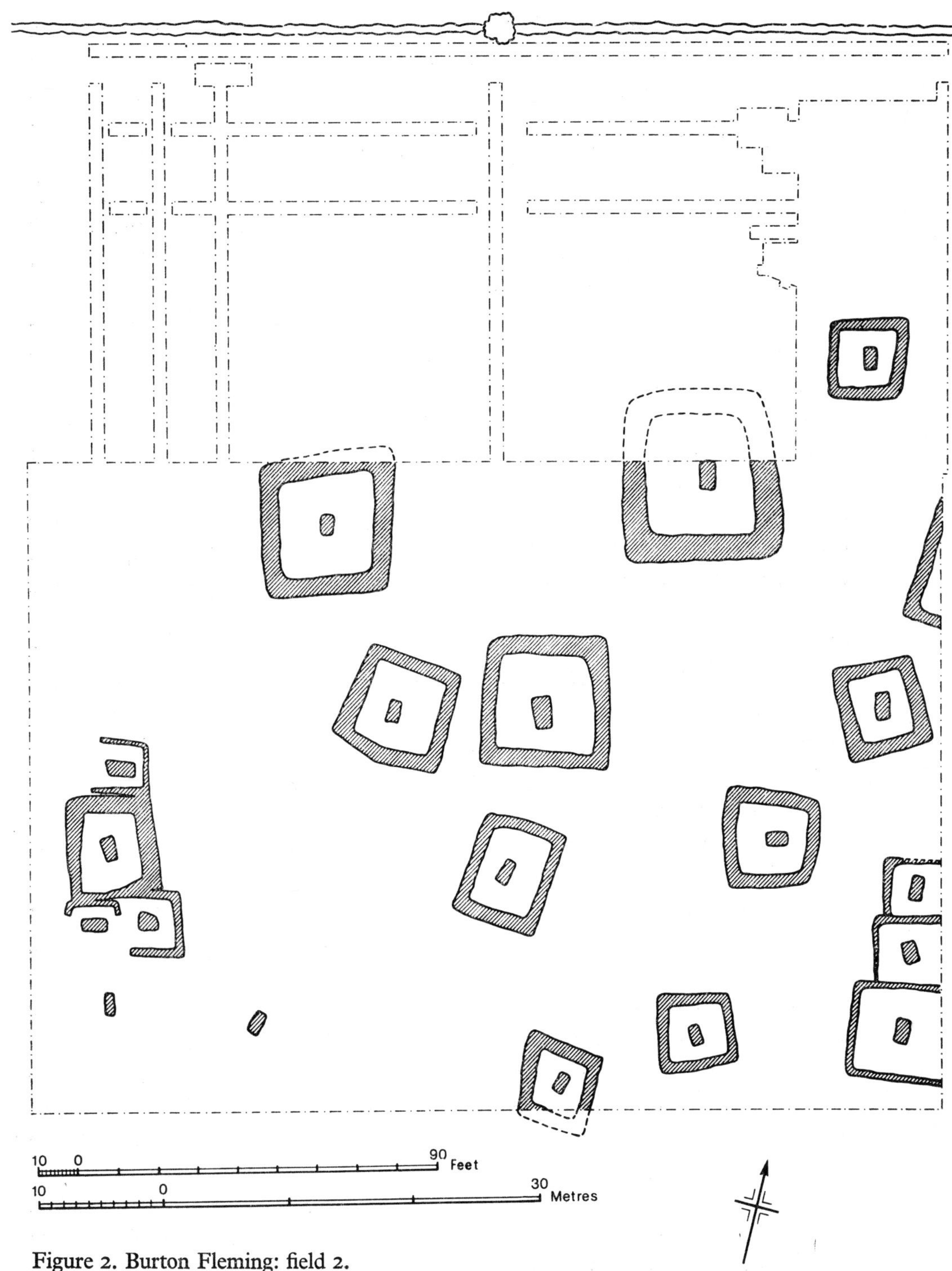

Figure 2. Burton Fleming: field 2.

Howe);[29] or belong to the period shortly before the Roman conquest, after the main floruit of the Arras Culture (e.g. Rudston). Perhaps the Rudston settlement belongs to a late phase of the Arras Culture, but there are some notable differences, especially formal burials in domestic ditches in contrast to the barrow cemeteries, and pre-Flavian brooches which have never been found with Arras Culture burials.

Attention was drawn to the Rudston site, in 1839 and again on its re-discovery in 1933, by the remains of a Roman villa – mosaic pavements and hypocausts. Excavations between 1933 and 1937[30] showed that these more spectacular features belonged to the end of the Roman period, but the site had been established for centuries before that. The earlier phases were further explored during excavations following the removal of the mosaic pavements to Hull Museum in 1962.

Undoubtedly some of the large ditches at Rudston were excavated in the first century A.D., and some might well belong to the pre-Roman period. These ditches were found in the 1930s and several more sections across them were excavated recently, but their pattern is complicated and a few trenches will not elucidate it. The only published plan[31] is inaccurate because ditches found in different trenches have been wrongly linked. So far a single enclosure has been identified, defined by a very deep V-section ditch into which the Venus mosaic pavement had subsided; but Antonine samian was found near the bottom of that ditch. In the filling of another ditch, under the 'Workshop', graves had been excavated for three skeletons – one accompanied by an early Roman iron brooch and another with a bronze penannular brooch of a type found in pre-Roman contexts (fig. 7, no. 4, and p. 39).

However, perhaps the most interesting pre-Roman discovery of the recent excavations was traces of a series of circular huts, immediately to the east of the fourth-centnry house (fig. 3). The huts had been bordered by curved drainage ditches which had been cut through the surface clay into the top of the chalk. These ditches enclosed areas between 16ft and 26ft in diameter and defined at least six different huts. But they had not all been occupied at the same time, for several of the curved gulleys overlapped one another and in one place provided a sequence of three successive huts. Within the drainage gulleys it proved impossible to distinguish the plan of any one hut from a pattern of post-holes, but this is not an unusual experience in the excavation of Early Iron Age huts.[32] Five burials of new-born infants were found in the vicinity of these huts and might have been contemporary; and six pits with articulated skeletons or cremated remains of young animals might best be regarded as 'ritual'. No metalwork was found in the vicinity of the huts, and the pottery from the gulleys was of un-

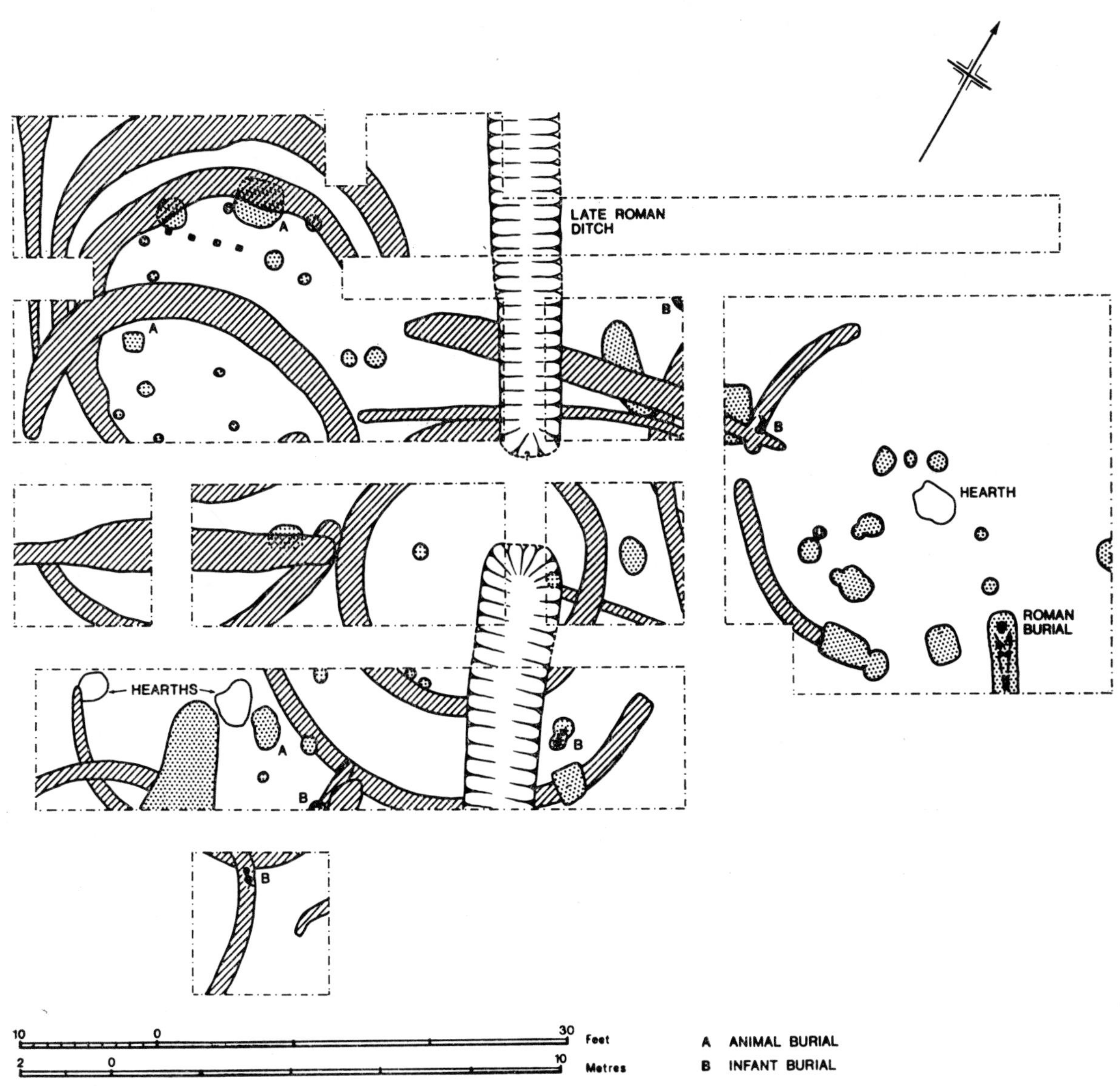

Figure 3. Rudston: circular huts.

distinguished 'native' ware, apart from sherds from a white flagon which suggests a date in the first century A.D.

Elsewhere on the Rudston villa site, 80 yards to the west of these huts, slight curved drip channels defined other circular buildings but there were no associated post-holes. Near by a curved chalk wall and a curved band of clay might belong to other huts of the early Roman period, but they had been cut by the modern road. 'Native' pottery was also found in chalk-cut rubbish pits – some perhaps grain storage pits in origin – on three different parts of the site, but no useful dating evidence was associated. The earliest metalwork from Rudston – Colchester, Hod Hill and Aucissa brooches – should date before the Roman conquest of Yorkshire (fig. 8, nos. 4 and 5; and p. 40).

Rudston is not the only site in eastern Yorkshire to have produced pre-Flavian brooches. So far there are 13 examples from the area (pp. 39–40) – a collection not impressive in itself, but unmatched elsewhere beyond the Claudian frontier of Roman Britain. This list of brooches, although it is not supplemented by imported pottery – North Ferriby remains the only site with any significant imported wares,[33] is an indication that peaceful contact with the peoples to the south was maintained despite the presence of the Roman army in Lincolnshire.

Indeed, the archaeological evidence suggests that during most of the Early Iron Age the inhabitants of eastern Yorkshire lived at peace with their neighbours. Certainly for about three centuries from the inception of the Arras Culture there is little sign of warlike activity, and only from the start of La Tène III are there hints that life was more troubled. On the western edge of the Wolds there are warrior burials at Grimthorpe and North Grimston, and a sword probably from a burial at Bugthorpe. Further east there is a sword, shield fragments, and a spearhead from the cemetery at Eastburn, and the sword from Thorpe Hall also belongs to this period.

But the most fascinating suggestion of war – possibly but not certainly La Tène III – lies in the remarkable collection of chalk figurines from Garton Slack (fig. 4, and plate 4). Each figure is wedge-shaped, with narrow shoulders and a flaring 'skirt'; belts are indicated but the profile is not waisted. There are no legs or feet, but hands and arms are crudely marked and two figures each have a sword on the right side (fig. 4, no. 4 and plates 4a and 4b). The surviving height, from the shoulder to the bottom of the skirt, varies between 3in. and 6½in. There are fragments from at least 13 figures, but only one is complete (fig. 4, no. 3); the rest have been decapitated and some broken into smaller pieces, but only one other head survives (fig. 4, no. 1; plate 4c). Another carving, found in the same place, is a model of an oval shield (plate 4d), which is consistent with the evidence of the associated pottery in suggesting an Early Iron Age date. These

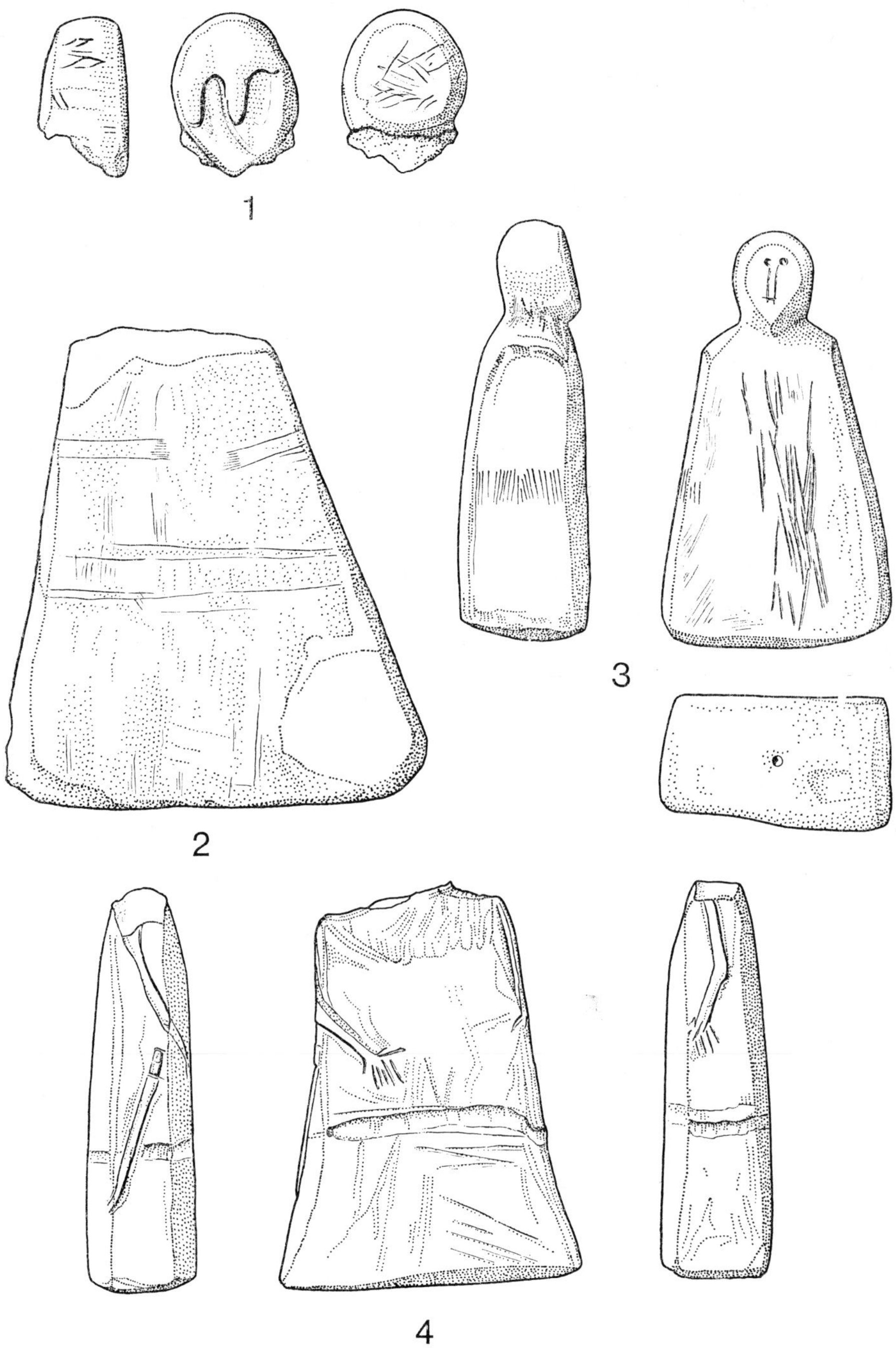

Figure 4. Chalk figurines from Garton Slack ($\frac{1}{2}$ size).

pieces owe their survival to the sharp eyes of C. and E. Grantham, who rescued them from a ditch on the edge of the Garton Slack gravel quarry. But they are not unique in Yorkshire, for the same excavators found a very similar, slightly heavier, headless figure on the site of Harpham Roman villa, and J. R. Mortimer discovered another with Romano-British pottery in a ditch at Blealands Nook.[34] They are not dissimilar from the slightly larger chalk figurine, also lacking the head, found in a Neolithic pit at Maiden Castle.[35] Of course it could be that the Garton Slack figurines were toys, and that their heads were broken by accident, but it is tempting to see them as images of warriors, beheaded in a magical attempt to immobilize the enemy. The shield may also have had a 'ritual' use, for slightly smaller models, made of bronze, are usually regarded as 'votive'.[36]

This evidence for military activity in La Tène III, although slight compared with the rest of southern England in the Early Iron Age, is nevertheless in marked contrast to the earlier La Tène phases in eastern Yorkshire. It may indicate no more than local conflict, but there were major developments outside Yorkshire which must have displaced populations and caused repercussions throughout England in La Tène III – the development of the Aylesford Culture; the Roman conquest of Gaul; and indeed Caesar's invasion of Britain.

When the Romans eventually reached the Humber, and then crossed it a generation later, there seems to have been little immediate effect on the archaeology of eastern Yorkshire, and the predominantly peaceful image of the area remains. No native defences of that period have been discovered, there are no war cemeteries or signs of massacre, and no hint of the Roman military presence near the native population centres along the eastern borders of the Wolds. Unfortunately the relevant books of Tacitus have not survived, and history tells us nothing about the Roman conquest of Yorkshire.

Catalogue: some recent finds[37]

a. *A grave-group from Burton Fleming* (fig. 5)

1. A small jar, 5.5in. high, whose pinched rim has a slight internal bevel. Variegated from buff to dark grey, it includes some quite large pieces of calcite grit. It was found at the feet of the skeleton – a long way from the pig bone, which was next to the skull.
2. A small blue glass bead, 0.25in. diameter. It was found between the right shoulder and the skull and may have been an ear-ring from the right ear.
3. A fine deep shale bracelet. Its internal diameter varies from 2.3in. to 2.5in. and it is 1.3in. to 1.5in. deep. It was found on the left fore-arm, just above the wrist, and is the only bracelet found so far at Burton Fleming.
4. An iron 'flattened bow' brooch, 3in. long. It appears to have had a three-coil spring – obscured by corrosion – but it probably includes a swivel mechanism similar to that employed on the bronze brooch from Sawdon.[38]

   Two other iron 'flattened bow' brooches have been found at Burton Fleming: one, 3.8in. long, has a disc and drum mechanism, and the other, only 2in. long, might fall between the 'flattened bow' and involuted series.

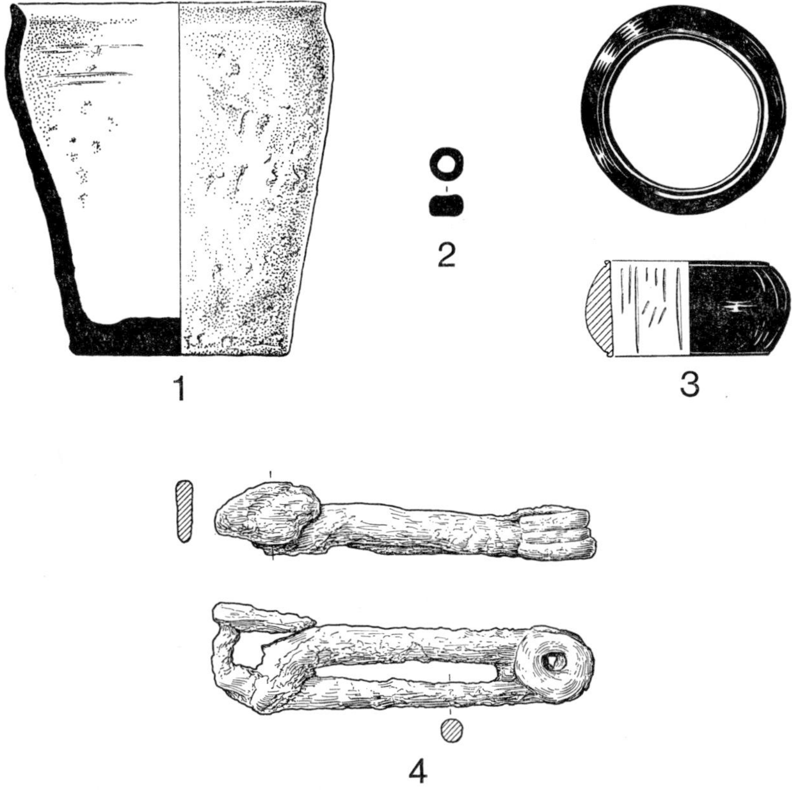

Figure 5. A grave-group from Burton Fleming. 1 and 3 ($\frac{1}{3}$); 2 and 4 ($\frac{2}{3}$).

b. *Swan's-neck pins* (fig. 6)

1. Simple bronze pin, 3.4in. long, with a swan's-neck kink in the stem, and the head curved back to form a ring. There is a slight groove near the top. Found on a domestic site at Kilham (p. 28), in the same pit as an iron penannular brooch (fig. 7, no. 3). Grantham Collection.
2. A small but beautiful swan's-neck pin, 2.8in. long, with a fine patina. The large head has been hollowed to a surface diameter of 0.32in. and a depth of about 0.4in., and this cup presumably held a paste, enamel or stone bead. Around the outside of the head is a fine relief ornament – six pointed oval eye-like motifs arranged diagonally as a zig-zag band. The pin was found with a burial in the Garton Slack cemetery. It was at the back of the skull, which had been stained green by its contact, in a position which corresponds to that of the wheel-head pin from Danes Graves,[39] and which leaves no doubt that they were used as hair-pins. Grantham Collection.

c. *Fibulae from Burton Fleming and Garton Slack* (fig. 6)

3. A large brooch, 4.5in. long. It is unique among the finds from Burton Fleming in being typologically an Early La Tène brooch. The bow is fairly low and long, and is touched by the foot which is ornamented by a large reddish disc, 1.3in. diameter, attached by a single iron pin. Very little of the red disc's outer surface survives, but there is sufficient to show that it was once decorated. The head of the brooch is obscured by corrosion: there seems to be an external chord, and radiographs appear to indicate a large coiled spring, whilst at both ends domed rivet-heads betray the position of a bar through the centre of the 'spring'. This brooch has been treated and examined by V. R. Rickard, Ancient Monuments Laboratory, who reports that the red disc is made of iron oxide.

   Similar disc-ornamented fibulae were popular on the Continent, and many have been found at Münsingen in La Tène Ib and Ic contexts.[40] Unfortunately the condition of the Burton Fleming brooch prevents detailed comparison, although the shape of the bow may be compared with the bronze brooch from Münsingen grave 49 – which also has a bar through the spring.[41] Comparison with these Swiss examples suggests that the Burton Fleming brooch could date as early as the third century B.C.
4. A fine bronze involuted brooch, 1.9in. long. The foot, from the underside of the catch-plate to the disc, bears a sweeping asymmetrical moulding with a projecting lip-motif. The disc, whose edge is neatly notched, is covered by a red dome attached by a bronze pin, and the upper surface of the bronze has been deeply scored to assist in securing it. The head of the brooch is formed by an open ring with a small barrel-like projection at the end and low moulding above. The lower part of the head-ring is thickened and conceals a slot in which the pin is very loosely pivoted on a small bar. V. R. Rickard reports that the applied red dome seems to have been moulded in a quartz clay fabric and its surface then glazed.

   This brooch is in the same class as the very best bronze ornaments with plastic decoration found in Yorkshire graves – the involuted brooches from Danes Graves[42] and the pin from Garton Slack (fig. 6, no. 2).

   Nine iron involuted brooches have been found at Burton Fleming, but they require radiographs and treatment before they can be classified. From Garton Slack there is an iron involuted brooch, 2.65in. long, with solid disc mechanism resembling Eastburn 2;[43] a shorter and more curved iron brooch, 1.7in. long, with drum mechanism and a very wide flat foot like that on the Beckley brooch;[44] and fragments from two other iron involuted brooches with similar wide feet.

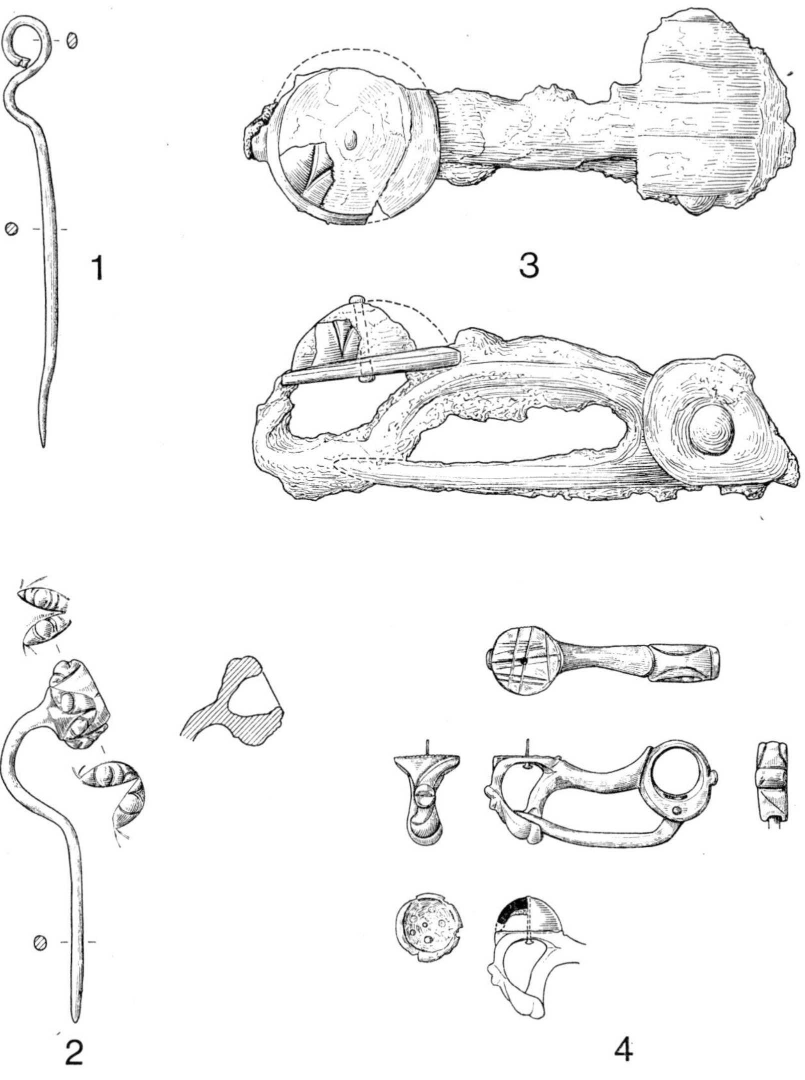

Figure 6. 1 and 2, bronze pins from Kilham and Garton Slack; 3 and 4, brooches from Burton Fleming ($\frac{2}{3}$).

d. *Penannular brooches* (fig. 7)

The penannular brooch is an interesting type whose appearance in the British Early Iron Age has provided a great deal of discussion including theories of independent development.[45] But attention has now been drawn to two bronze examples in Marnian graves[46] which provide a possible source for the British brooches – although the type is still extremely rare in La Tène contexts in France. Certainly the Burton Fleming brooch (no. 1, below) is quite similar to that from Trugny, Aisne,[47] and if the latter is as early as Rowlett suggests (early fourth century B.C.) this type could have formed part of the original equipment of the Arras Culture. If the introduction of the penannular brooch to Britain can be thus explained, its popularity here, in contrast to its rarity in France, is in keeping with those other hinged pin devices which British craftsmen preferred to the spring mechanisms of Continental La Tène brooches.

1. A small bronze penannular brooch, 0.9in. diameter, with slightly expanded terminals and a humped pin. Found in a grave at Burton Fleming.
2. A corroded and broken iron penannular brooch, 1.2in. diameter. The circular terminals are obvious on radiographs, but on the object they cannot be distinguished amidst the corrosion. The pin is broken but may possibly have been humped. Found with a burial at Arras,[48] and now in the Museum of Archaeology and Ethnology at Cambridge.

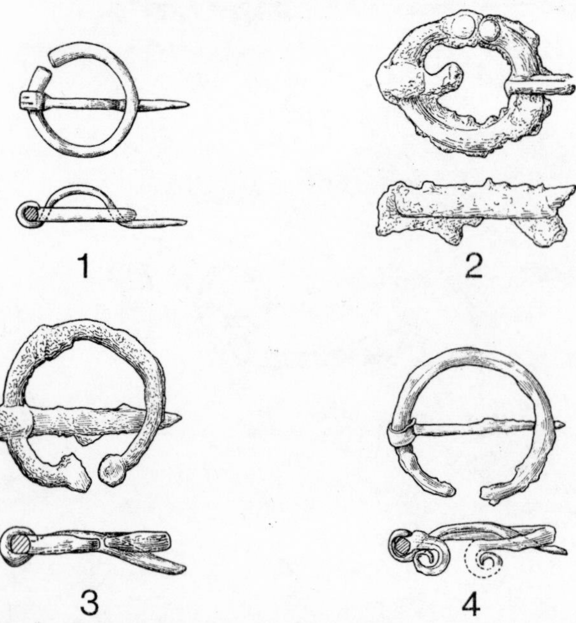

Fgure 7. Penannular brooches (⅔).

3. Iron penannular brooch, 1.4in. diameter. It has flattened circular terminals and a curved, but not humped, pin. Found with the bronze pin (fig. 6, no. 1) at Kilham. Grantham Collection.
4. Bronze penannular brooch, 1.3in. diameter. The terminals are tapered and curved spirally – set at right angles to the plane of the ring – and the pin is slightly humped. Found with an inhumation in a grave cut into a ditch at Rudston (p. 30). This type has been found in Aylesford Culture contexts[49] and may be compared with the other pre-Flavian brooches from Rudston.

e. *Pre-Flavian brooches* (fig. 8)

The Colchester brooch is the most common type from cemeteries and settlements of the Aylesford Culture, and it continued in use into the early Roman period.[50] Aucissa and Hod Hill brooches belong to the same period, and they seem to have fallen out of use by the end of Nero's reign.[51] With the exception of the brooches listed below, these types are restricted in distribution to that part of southern England occupied immediately after the Claudian conquest.

Colchester brooches

1. A bronze brooch, 3.85in. long. The catch-plate is solid, and has been decorated with engraved La Tène ornament – unfortunately it is corroded and some of the details of the design have been lost. No other Colchester brooch is decorated in this way, and the knob which terminates the catch-plate is also very unusual. The top of the bow is decorated with engraved lines, and ribbed side-wings cover a 12-coil spring. This brooch was found at North Ferriby in 1967 and is now in the Hull Museum. (M. R. Hull confirms that the North Ferriby brooch resembles the Colchester type, and is unique in having a catch-plate decorated in this way; but there is rather similar decoration on the catch-plates of certain brooches of the Backworth type.[52])
2. A typical Colchester brooch, 3.1in. long, whose pierced catch-plate has been broken. The top of the bow is undecorated, but the side-wings are ribbed and they cover a 10-coil spring. Said to have been found at Hessle, it was until recently in the Scarborough Museum but has now been exchanged and is in the Hull Museum. No other Romano-British or Early Iron Age remains are known from Hessle, but it is only two miles east of North Ferriby.
3. A small bronze Colchester brooch, 1.8in. long. It has three perforations in the catch-plate; the side-wings are undecorated; and the spring – broken and replaced in antiquity – has six coils. It was found in a ditch at Garton Slack. Grantham Collection.

   A similar brooch, only 1.5in. long, was found during the recent excavations at Rudston Roman villa, and another is said to have been found in the grounds of Watton Priory. Beyond this area there is an outlying Colchester brooch from Glenluce, Wigtownshire.[53]

Aucissa brooches

4. Bronze brooch, 2.1in. long, inscribed with the name 'Aucissa' in a plate near the head. It has a high arched bow with a moulded band of decoration; a short catch-plate with a large knob at the end; and a hinged pin which pivots on an iron bar. Found during the recent excavations at Rudston Roman villa.

Two other Aucissa brooches have been found north of the Humber: one in eastern Yorkshire, at Thornton-le-Dale;[54] and the other from the West Riding, at Aldborough.[55] There is also a related brooch from North Ferriby.[56]

Hod Hill brooches

5. A bronze brooch which has been silvered, 2.2in long. Broad short bow with projecting knobs near the head and longitudinal mouldings; the lower part, over the catch-plate, has a series of cross mouldings. The catch-plate has been mended by the addition of a plate fixed by two rivets. The hinged pin has not survived, but what appears to be its tip (? iron) is corroded onto the back of the catch-plate. Found during the recent excavations at Rudston Roman villa.

Another example, found during the earlier excavations at the same site, has a shorter bow with central projecting knobs.[57] A third specimen was found during the recent excavations at Brough.[58]

P-shaped brooches

Pre-Flavian examples of this type (Collingwood Group T) are not common in Britain, but one has been found recently by W. J. Varley at Ousethorpe, near Pocklington, East Riding, which can be matched by an example from Stainburn Moor, near Otley, West Riding.[59]

Notes

1. information from G. F. Willmot.
2. *Y.A.J.*, xlii, part 166 (1968), 131–2.
3. *A Hand-book to the Antiquities . . . of the Yorkshire Philosophical Society*, 8th ed. (1891), 200. *York: A Survey*, 1959 (British Association Meeting), 86, and fig. 11, no. 3.
4. *A Hand-book . . .*, 1891, 203–5.
5. *Y.A.J.*, xli (1966), 587–90.
6. R.C.H.M., *York*, xxix.
7. *Y.A.J.*, xxxviii (1955), 383–97.
8. I. M. Stead, *The La Tène Cultures of Eastern Yorkshire* (1965), 22–3.
9. Much of this information has been gathered by the Inspectorate of Ancient Monuments, Ministry of Public Building and Works, who organized the excavations at Burton Fleming, Cowlam, Rudston, and some of the work at Garton Slack. For help in the preparation of this paper the writer is particularly grateful to two of his colleagues, Miss G. D. Jones, who drew all the line illustrations, and A. L. Pacitto who, apart from

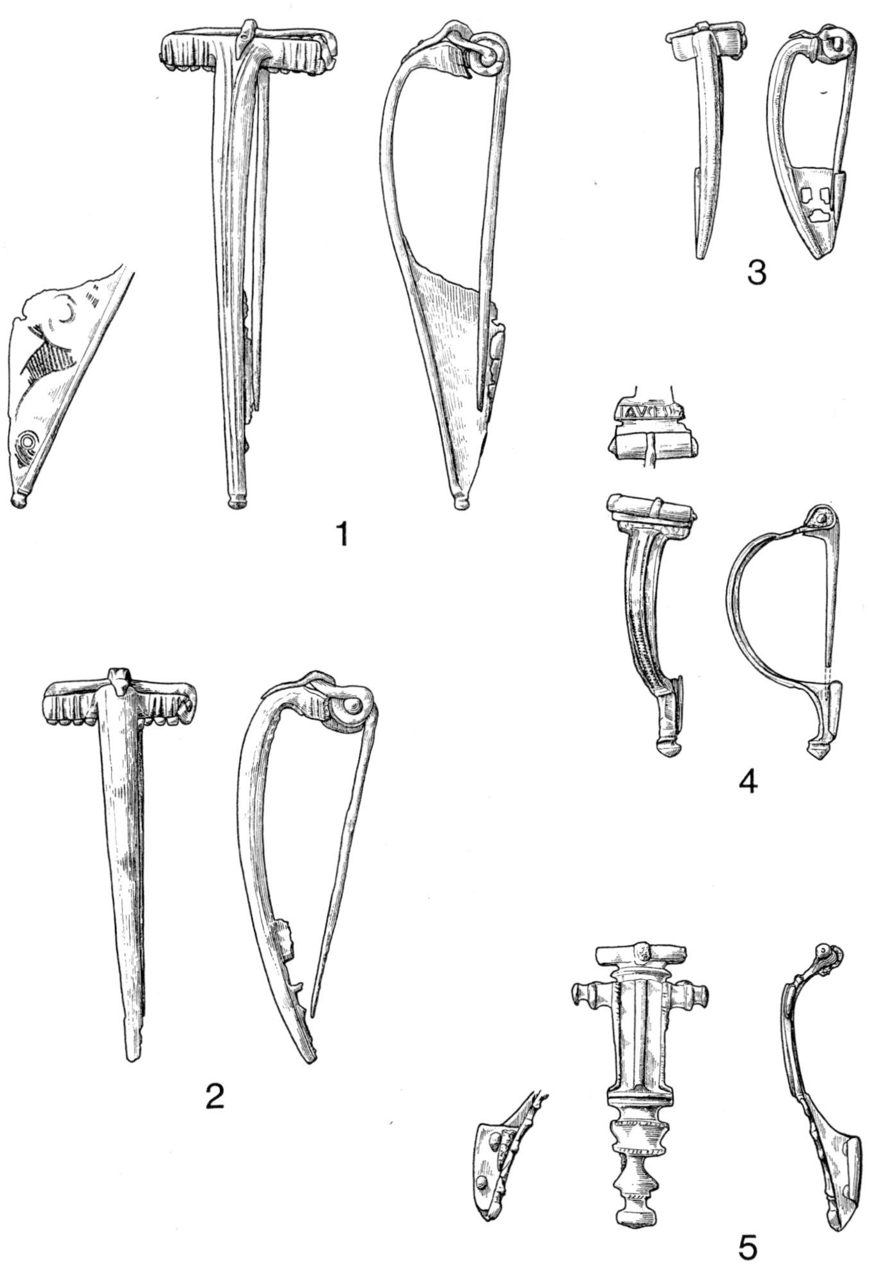

Figure 8. Bronze brooches ($\frac{2}{3}$).

assisting in the direction of the Burton Fleming and Cowlam excavations, also took the photographs from which the plates (except plate 1b) have been prepared.

10. I. M. Stead, *op. cit.*, 1965.
11. *Institute of Archaeology Bulletin*, no. 4 (1964), 137.
12. W. Greenwell, *British Barrows* (1877), 208–13.
13. *ibid.*, 27, note 1.
14. *ibid.*, 210.
15. J. Filip, *Celtic Civilization and its Heritage* (1960), 180.
16. Stead, *op. cit.*, 1965, 81–2.
17. *Ant. J.*, xli (1961), 44–62.
18. *Procs. Arch. Inst.*, York meeting (1848), 27.
19. *ibid.*
20. *Antiquity*, xxxviii (1964), 217, and pl. xxxvii, a.
21. Its extent may be illustrated by published photographs: the fields with the henge monument and adjoining barrows (*ibid.*) are almost a mile north-north-east of the site shown in plate 1b, and more than a mile north-east of that another group is shown in M. W. Beresford and J. K. S. St Joseph, *Medieval England* (1958), 263, fig. 111.
22. The resistivity survey was carried out by A. J. Clark, Ancient Monuments Laboratory, and it is reported in *Prospezioni Archeologiche*, 3 (1968), 113–14, and fig. 40.
23. e.g. British Museum, *Guide to Early Iron Age Antiquities* (1925), 118, fig. 129.
24. F. R. Hodson, *The La Tène Cemetery at Münsingen-Rain* (Acta Bernensia, V), 1968; also *Celticum*, vi (1963), 75–80, and *Institute of Archaeology Bulletin*, no. 4 (1964), 123–41.
25. *Ant. J.*, xli (1961), 45–6.
26. *Y.A.J.*, xl (1962), 183–91.
27. found by W. Gatenby, and part of the site then excavated by J. E. Bartlett.
28. *P.P.S.*, xxxiv (1968), 148–90.
29. Scarborough: *Arch.*, lxxvii (1927), 179–200; Staple Howe: T. C. M. Brewster, *The Excavation of Staple Howe* (1963).
30. Published in a series of interim reports, *Y.A.J.*, xxxi (1934), 366–76; xxxii (1936), 214–220; xxxiii (1938), 81–6, and 321–38; and xxxiv (1939), 102–3.
31. *Y.A.J.*, xxxiii (1938), 320, fig. 1.
32. e.g. S. S. Frere (ed.), *Problems of the Iron Age in Southern Britain* (1958), 21–6; Sir Mortimer Wheeler, *The Stanwick Fortifications* (1954), 8.
33. *Ant. J.*, xviii (1938), 262–77.
34. J. R. Mortimer, *Forty Years Researches* . . . (1905), 198, and pl. lxiv, fig. 492.
35. Sir Mortimer Wheeler, *Maiden Castle, Dorset* (1943), 181–3, fig. 49, pl. xxv.
36. Miniature bronze shields have been found on the sites of Romano-Celtic temples at Worth, Kent (*Ant. J.*, viii (1928), 79–81), and Frilford, Berks. (*Oxoniensia*, iv (1939), 14); and there is another from Hod Hill, Dorset (*Ant. J.*, ii (1922), 97–9).
37. The writer is grateful to J. E. Bartlett (Hull Museum) and C. and E. Grantham (Driffield) for permission to publish objects in their custody.
38. *Ant. J.*, xxvii (1947), 178–9.
39. *Ann. Rep. Yorks. Phil. Soc.* (1897), 2–3, and pl. iii.
40. Hodson, *op. cit.*, 1968.
41. *ibid.*, 96, pl. 22, no. 797.
42. *Arch.*, lx (1906), 267, figs. 13 and 14.
43. Stead, *op. cit.*, 1965, 47, fig. 26, no. 6.
44. Sir Cyril Fox, *Pattern and Purpose* (1958), 13, fig. 9B, and pl. 12a.
45. *P.P.S.*, xxvi (1960), 149–71.

46. *Antiquity*, xl (1966), 133–4.
47. *ibid.*, fig. 1.
48. *Ant. J.*, xli (1961), 46.
49. C. F. C. Hawkes and M. R. Hull, *Camulodunum* (1947), 326–7; *P.P.S.*, xxvi (1960), 165–6, and fig. 9; see also *H.M.P.*, no. 214 (1963), 29–30.
50. C. F. C. Hawkes and M. R. Hull, *op. cit.* (1947), 308–10.
51. *ibid.*, 321–4.
52. British Museum, *Guide to the Antiquities of Roman Britain* (1922), 55, fig. 62.
53. *Ulster Journal of Archaeology*, xxiv–xxv (1961–2), 29, fig. 4, no. 4.
54. *Y.A.J.*, xxx (1931), 166–7, and fig. 3, no. 5.
55. *Arch. J.*, lx (1903), 243.
56. *Ant. J.*, xviii (1938), 277.
57. *Ant. J.*, xxiv (1954), 73–4, no. 2.
58. J. S. Wacher, *Excavations at Brough-on-Humber 1958–1961* (1969), 92–3, fig. 39, no. 32.
59. *Ant. J.*, viii (1928), 526–7.

L. P. WENHAM

The beginnings of Roman York

In A.D. 43 the Roman conquest of Britain began. The invading army consisted of some 30,000–40,000 men made up of four legions together with a complement of auxiliary regiments. Three of the legions came from Germany – II Augusta from Strasbourg, XIV Gemina from Mainz and XX Valeria Victrix from Neuss, while the fourth, IX Hispana, came from Pannonia. The commanding officer, Aulus Plautius, also came from Pannonia.

Roman conquest took two forms – subjugation by the sword and the formation of alliances with native princes prepared to accept Roman overlordship, making their territories into what it is convenient to term 'client kingdoms'. By such alliances the invaders secured "a maximum of peace with a minimum expenditure of Roman military strength".[1] Soon after the initial landing in Britain two important native kingdoms entered into such a relationship – the Regnenses in Sussex under their king Cogidumnus and the Iceni in East Anglia under their king Prasutagus. A little later, but still under the first governor, Aulus Plautius,[2] the Brigantes under their queen, Cartimandua, entered into a similar arrangement.

As the early history of Eburacum is closely bound up with that of Brigantia and of its queen, a brief reference to what was happening there will help in an understanding of the beginnings of Roman York. According to Tacitus, the Brigantes were numerically the largest tribe in Britain. They certainly covered the whole of Yorkshire (except the East Riding which was controlled by the Parisi), Lancashire, Westmorland, Cumberland and County Durham with the Solway–Tyne line as their approximate northern boundary. Their southern boundary was probably on, or near, the Humber–Trent–Mersey line. This vast territory consisted of many different tribes and subdivisions and the queen's power, especially in the outlying districts, was doubtless of the flimsiest. I. A.

Richmond[3] has described Brigantia as a "coalition of isolated groups in an uneasy balance, united by the marriage connections of the great families and explaining both the ever-changing face of Brigantia and the basic reliance of Cartimandua, *pollens nobilitate* (Tac. *Hist.* iii, 45), upon her family connections. . . Conditions among the Brigantes varied greatly, from primitive savagery at the barest subsistence level among scattered cow-herds inhabiting the bleak uplands, to a certain barbaric splendour among their chiefs."[4]

It seems that in Brigantia itself two widely differing views were held about this Roman alliance. The queen herself was clearly pro-Roman. Her consort, Venutius, at first supported her, though probably with doubts and reservations which later hardened into open opposition. Sometime about A.D. 48 when the governor Ostorius Scapula was campaigning against the Deceangli in North Wales he had to abandon operations for a time in order to suppress a rising amongst some of the Brigantes against their queen. It seems that when Cartimandua (apparently assisted by her husband on this occasion)[5] tried to suppress them she nearly precipitated civil war in her realm. Scapula marched into Brigantia and crushed the hostile forces (Tacitus, *Annals* xii, 32). Cartimandua was left in power though she doubtless received a reprimand from the governor about keeping a firmer hold on the insubordinate elements in her dominions.

The supreme test of her loyalty came in A.D. 51, when after his defeat in Wales by Scapula, Caratacus fled to Cartimandua for succour. She showed her loyalty to Rome by handing him over to the Romans (Tacitus, *Annals* xii, 36).

About A.D. 57 the differences between Cartimandua and her husband flared up into an open quarrel and Venutius raised an army from among the discontented elements in Brigantia and from allies outside Brigantian territory in an attempt to depose his wife. The queen appealed to the Romans for help and the governor, Didius Gallus, sent troops into her realm to her aid. Tacitus gives two accounts of this incident, viz.:

> i. *Agricola*, 14
> Didius Gallus, the next governor, kept a firm hold on what his predecessors had won, and even advanced some few forts into outlying [or remoter] districts, so that he could say that he had extended his sphere of duty.
>
> ii. *Annals* xii, 40
> . . . some cohorts were sent to her aid and a sharp contest followed, which was at first doubtful but had a satisfactory end. A legion under the command of Caesius Nasica fought with a similar result.[6]

The inference is that, as a result of the breach between Cartimandua and Venutius, the Romans had entered Brigantia and restored order in those areas immediately under the queen's control. It seems that now the kingdom was virtually split in two, the queen holding on precariously with Roman aid to the south,[7] while Venutius, leading the anti-Roman forces, controlled most of the north. For some years the latter maintained a sullen, watchful truce from headquarters at (?)Stanwick or still further north, beyond the immediate reach of intervention. The climax came in A.D. 69, 'The Year of Four Emperors'. In the autumn of the previous year Nero committed suicide and after that no less than four emperors (Galba, Otho, Vitellius and Vespasian) wore the purple in the space of less than 12 months. Vespasian, the founder of the Flavian dynasty (A.D. 69–96), had commanded Legio II in Britain under Claudius. After some initial hesitation[8] the British legions accepted him. However, as far as Cartimandua was concerned, the confusion and divided loyalties of that nightmare year brought her reign to an abrupt end. Tacitus (*Histories* iii, 45) gives this graphic account of the events:

> Inspired by these differences between the Roman forces and by the many rumours of civil war that reached them, the Britons plucked up courage under the leadership of Venutius, who, in addition to his natural spirit and hatred of the Roman name, was fired by his personal resentment towards queen Cartimandua. She was ruler over the Brigantes, having the influence that belongs to high birth, and she had later strengthened her power when she was credited with having captured king Caratacus by treachery and so furnished an adornment for the triumph of Claudius Caesar. From this came her wealth and the wanton spirit which success breeds. She grew to despise her husband Venutius, and took as her consort his squire Vellocatus, whom she admitted to share the throne with her. Her house was at once shaken by this scandalous act. Her husband was favoured by the sentiments of all the citizens; the adulterer was supported by the queen's passion for him and by her savage spirit. So Venutius, calling in aid from outside and at the same time assisted by a revolt of the Brigantes themselves, put Cartimandua into an extremely dangerous position. Then she asked the Romans for protection, and some of our auxiliary troops, cavalry and infantry, after meeting with indifferent success in a number of engagements, finally succeeded in snatching the queen from danger. The throne was left to Venutius, the war to us.

The governor who sent in auxiliaries to rescue Cartimandua was almost certainly Bolanus.[9] One of Vespasian's first acts after becoming emperor was to replace him by Cerialis. The latter moved Legio IX up to York from Lincoln, led his forces against the Brigantes under Venutius and ultimately crushed them. Tacitus (*Agricola*, 17) records these events thus:

> Petillius Cerialis at once struck terror into their hearts by attacking the state of the Brigantes which is said to be the most populous in the whole province. After a series of battles, some not uncostly, Petillius had operated, if not actually triumphed over, the major part of their territory.

Excavation has shown that Stanwick, near Scotch Corner, was the scene of one of these battles – possibly the last – which Tacitus mentions.[10] The exact date is unknown but as it was under Cerialis it must fall between the years A.D. 71 and 74, probably towards the beginning rather than the end of that period.

It will be seen from the above that there is literary evidence pointing to Roman intervention in Brigantia at least three times[11] during Cartimandua's reign – in A.D. 48 under Scapula, in A.D. 57 under Gallus and again in A.D. 69 under Bolanus when she was rescued and brought back to safety into Roman-controlled territory. The generally accepted view[12] is that on all these occasions the Roman troops merely went into Brigantia, dealt with the particular emergency which had arisen and then withdrew immediately afterwards. However, it is possible to put another interpretation on the literary evidence and, in particular, on the first of the two passages quoted above relating to Didius Gallus. Tacitus says that he "even advanced some few forts into outlying [or remoter] districts" (*paucis admodum castellis in ulteriora promotis*). If these 'outlying/remoter' districts were, in fact, Brigantia itself and if 'advancing' forts is interpreted as meaning that these were built and then held, permanently or semi-permanently, by the Romans it is possible to postulate a revised timetable for the Roman advance into the north of England. One of the obvious places for one of these "few forts" (doubtless auxiliary forts, as no Roman general worth his salt would place a legion or part of a legion in hostile territory far in advance of his main forces) is York, "the key-position . . . for the control of the Brigantes".[13]

Archaeological evidence is accumulating for such a pre-Flavian occupation at York. The Yorkshire Museum contains a sizeable collection of both Roman coins and Roman pottery of a Claudian-Neronian date. These have been accumulated over the past century and a half mostly as a result of chance finds; only a few have come from controlled scientific excavations. No detailed account of the pottery has been written[14] though a short, but important, paper has been published on the coins.[15] The two relevant excavations are those conducted by Mr G. F. Willmot beneath St Mary's Abbey in 1951–4[16] just outside the south-west corner of the legionary fortress – and by the writer in the garden adjoining St William's College,[17] only a stone's throw from the east end of the Minster (i.e. in the *retentura* of the legionary fortress). The former produced, among other early pottery, sherds of St Rémy-en-Rollat ware (see Appendix, no. 4). In the St William's excavation the writer found in a sealed layer among some 200 sherds of rusticated ware, carinated bowls and flagons in self-coloured red ware,[18] two sherds of Firnisware ('varnished ware') of Claudian date which, up to the time of writing, represent the earliest Roman pottery so far found in York. They have only been identified on four other sites in Britain – Richborough, Colchester, Wroxeter and Exeter[19] – all of which are known to have been founded before A.D. 69. This ware is of German origin, apparently being manufactured in the

Rhineland approximately *c.* A.D. 40–50. On the German evidence this ware is clearly pre-Flavian and was being made in the decade mentioned: how long it continued after that date is not certain. In Germany, the largest and most important find of such pottery came from the fort of Hofheim.[20] The two York sherds are from different cups. They are quite fragile and it is difficult to imagine vessels of this fabric surviving long in a military area. To have survived complete – and in use – after A.D. 71 they would have to be between 20 and 30 years old. It seems more reasonable to explain them as representing sherds from pots long broken during an earlier pre-Flavian occupation. They may, of course, have come to York in the way of trade and have been used by native Britons rather than by Roman soldiers, though it must be stressed that, hitherto, no Iron Age occupation whatsoever has been found there. They – and the next find – represent the only pre-A.D. 71 finds so far made in Eburacum on the site of the fortress.

In 1968 a sewer collapsed in Ogleforth opposite no. 2. A trench 14ft deep was dug to repair it. Some four dozen sherds of unstratified Roman pottery were found by the workmen in the trench fill and given to the writer. One was another sherd of Firnisware. The find-spot was approximately 42 yards due north of the St William's excavation.

The writer is only too well aware that three sherds of Firnisware (and only two of them stratified) do not prove the existence in York of a Claudian auxiliary fort! Actual structural remains or occupational debris in much greater quantity must be found before that is an established fact. However, the cumulative evidence from the literary sources, from these sherds and from the other early archaeological material (numismatic and ceramic) noted above suggests that such a possibility at least demands serious consideration. In a letter which he has given me permission to quote, Professor E. Birley wrote as follows: "To my mind, you have a very strong case now for pre-Flavian occupation of the site – whether by a Roman outpost, a Roman military mission to Cartimandua, or Roman material reaching one of her residences. What is needed (and this article should serve to focus attention on that need) is an investigation of the earliest levels at York in the hopes of finding structural evidence."

Space forbids exhaustive treatment of another aspect of this problem. If Gallus did establish forts in Brigantia we must look for other sites in the southern Pennines in addition to York. Some, or all, of the following might suggest themselves – Melandra, Buxton, Brough-on-Noe, Templeborough, Manchester, Castleshaw, Slack, Ribchester, Elslack, Ilkley, Castleford and Doncaster. All except the last two are known to have been in existence by the time of Agricola[21] (they may be earlier) while Templeborough was certainly Neronian.[22] With springboards such as these established in Brigantia before his time, the conquest by Cerialis of the whole of the north, at least up to the Carlisle-Newcastle line, becomes a reasonable assumption. Tacitus's statement, quoted above, that "Petillius had operated, if not actually triumphed, over the major part of their territory" would certainly bear such an interpretation.[23] At least some of the marching camps built by Cerialis in his advance over the Stainmore Pass into the Eden Valley have been identified.[24] Early Flavian pottery has long been noted at forts on the Stanegate frontier,[25] has been found in some quantities at Carlisle[26] and Corbridge[27] and also in south-west Scotland.[28] A Cerialian occupation as far north as the Tyne–Solway would, in turn, make better sense of Agricola's great push forward into Scotland. His advance may well have been from a Tyne–Solway, rather than a York–Chester, springboard; his campaigns would otherwise have been perilously far from secure bases. In 1958 J. Clarke[29] wrote: "The roads and forts of northern England are commonly attributed to Agricola, but the construction of a first strategic network must have been begun by Cerialis immediately after his conquest and may indeed have been substantially completed by him, since his successor, Frontinus, was able to turn his whole attention to Wales."

Appendix

References to pre-A.D. 71 occupation at York

1. C. H. V. Sutherland, *Romano-British Imitations of Bronze Coins of Claudius I*, American Numismatic Society (1935), 8 and 23:

   Yorkshire
   York. Of the surprising number of Claudian coins of local provenance, a third are copies (Yorkshire Museum).

   The proportion of copies [of bronze coins of Claudius I] at Lincoln is remarkable enough: it is still more remarkable at York, which lay outside the conquest boundary. By the time that Petillius Cerialis moved Legio IX from Lincoln to York (A.D. 71), Flavian coinage and the preceding issues of Nero were presumably circulating regularly in Britain, and perhaps the Claudian copies at York indicate an earlier occupation, by some kind of expeditionary force, than has hitherto been deemed the case.[30]

2. D. Atkinson, *Wroxeter 1923–1927*, Birmingham Archaeological Society (1942), 20:

   [Atkinson is discussing Sutherland's paper quoted above and, in it, a particular passage relating to Wroxeter]. On the following sites for which no statistics are available Mr Sutherland (p. 57) notes or implies that Claudian copper occurs freely: London, Silchester, Winchester, Dorchester, Gloucester, Cirencester, Lincoln and York. In all cases except York there is evidence of pre-Flavian occupation. How the "astonishing number of Claudian coins" came to York is beyond conjecture, but in spite of this exception, these data, may, I think, fairly be taken to imply that a free occurrence of Claudian copper is evidence of a pre-Flavian occupation.

3. A. R. Burn, *Agricola and Roman Britain* (1953), 18–19:

With Caradoc [Caratacus] at large in Wales, the Romans were in no position to fight at the same time the great northern tribe of the Brigantes, in Yorkshire and Durham; but fortunately for them this tribe also had its internal dissensions. The queen-regnant, Cartimandua, and her consort, a great warrior named Venutius, had opponents at home; and to secure their position they were not above accepting Roman assistance. Tacitus' account of Plautius' governorship is lost; but when he next mentions Venutius, in the time of Plautius' successor, he reminds us that Venutius had *earlier* accepted Rome's alliance and armed Roman aid. Finds of apparently Claudian pottery at York are perhaps a tangible relic of this episode. Plautius was thus able to neutralize, with small forces, the most powerful tribe in Britain.

4. G. F. Willmot, Y.A.Y.A.S. *Procs. for 1953–54*, 13 (reporting on his excavations[31] under St Mary's Abbey, York, 1952–3 – some 30 yards outside the south-west corner of the legionary fortress):

The pottery discovered in some quantity suggests an earlier occupation than A.D. 71. A stamped Gallo-Belgic Platter, sherds of St Rémy ware, and marbled ware in comparatively considerable quantities, hitherto unknown in the north, suggest an occupation about A.D. 60, and the possibility of an auxiliary fort prior to the legionary fortress must be kept in mind.

5. Grace Simpson, *Britons and the Roman Army* (1964), 11–12:

York may have been Queen Cartimandua's capital because there is Roman pottery in the Yorkshire Museum of earlier periods than Vespasian's reign, including, among other kinds, some marbled samian pottery, the only fragments known in northern Britain: Roman traders could have brought such goods and other luxuries to her court. Her loyalty to the Roman treaty had brought her wealth. No pre-Roman site has been identified, but York is the natural control-point for Brigantia. The Romans chose it for its strategic position on the River Ouse; as Collingwood wrote "it is a position from which to strike".

6. Mr Brian Hartley of the University of Leeds is compiling a *corpus* of the samian potters' stamps found in Britain. He has examined the large collection of these in the Yorkshire Museum, York and has kindly supplied the following information about them. Seventeen stamps are pre-Flavian: 11 of these have also been found at Caerleon. The provenance of most of the stamps is unfortunately unknown, but assuming that all were, in fact, found in York, the percentage of pre-Flavian ones is 1.8 per cent. The following are the names recorded: ABITUS, ACUTUS, AQUITANUS, BILICATUS, CASTUS, FELIX, FELIX-SEVERUS, GALLICANUS, MASCLUS(2), MODESTUS, NIGER(2), PASSENUS(3), SCOTNUS.

Notes

1. I. A. Richmond (ed.), *Roman and Native in North Britain* (1958), 32.
2. E. B. Birley, *Roman Britain and the Roman Army* (1953), 5. As many of the early governors of Britain are referred to in this work it will be useful to include here a list of their names and dates up to the time of Agricola:

Aulus Plautius	A.D. 43–47	M. Trebillius Maximus	A.D. 63–69
P. Ostorius Scapula	47–52	M. Vettius Bolanus	69–71
A. Didius Gallus	52–57	Q. Petillius Cerialis	71–74
Q. Veranius	57–58	Sex. Julius Frontinus	74–78
G. Suetonius Paulinus	58–61	Cn. Julius Agricola	78–85
G. Petronius Turpilianus	61–63		

3. Sir Mortimer Wheeler, *The Stanwick Fortifications* (1954), 62. Cf. I. A. Richmond, 'Queen Cartimandua', *J.R.S.*, xliv (1954), 43–52, and Birley, *op. cit.* (where references to other pertinent works are quoted).
4. Richmond, *op. cit.*, 32.
5. see Appendix to this article, no. 3.
6. A. R. Burn, *Agricola and Roman Britain* (1953), 30, considers that on this occasion Nasica may have been operating "beyond the Border", i.e. as far north as the Lowlands of Scotland.
7. Her headquarters were probably the hill fort of Almondbury near Huddersfield, though G. Simpson, *Britons and the Roman Army* (1964), 11–12 (see Appendix, no. 5) has suggested that they might be York itself. Cf. Birley, *op. cit.*, 33, 36.
8. Birley, *op. cit.*, 12.
9. For what it is worth the Roman poet Statius (*fl. c.* A.D. 100), *Silvae* v. ii, 145–6, says that Bolanus set up in Britain "watch-towers and forts far and wide". Cf. Birley, *op. cit.*, 13–15, who discusses this and other evidence bearing on military operations in the North during Bolanus's governorship.
10. Wheeler, *op. cit.* The Venutio of the Ravenna Cosmography, somewhere in south-west Scotland, has been suggested as another. Cf. Birley, *op. cit.*, 45–6.
11. Birley, *op. cit.*, 47 would make it four, the first being earlier during A. Plautius's governorship.
12. but see Appendix for some contrary opinions.
13. I. A. Richmond in R.C.H.M., *York*, xxix.
14. but see Appendix, nos. 3–6.
15. C. H. V. Sutherland, *Romano-British Imitations of Bronze Coins of Claudius I*, American Numismatic Society Notes and Monographs, No. 65 (1935), 23 (see Appendix, no. 1).
16. Y.A.Y.A.S. *Procs.* (1953–4), 1.
17. report unpublished.
18. These types of pottery – rusticated ware, carinated bowls and flagons – are of a type and fabric which until recently would have been described as 'Flavian, post A.D. 71'. There is, however, no reason why they too should not be pre-Flavian. Once the possibility of occupation in York before A.D. 71 is admitted, there is no reason why some of the 'Flavian' coarse pottery found there should not be pre-Flavian. For rusticated ware see F. H. Thompson, *Ant. J.*, xxxviii (1958), 15–51, esp., 48–9.
19. for the Richborough, Colchester and Wroxeter finds, see A. Fox, *Roman Exeter* (1952), 65, 77, figs., 9, 12 and pl. Xc.
20. E. Ritterling, 'Das Fruhrömische Lager bei Hofheim in Taunus', *Annalen des Vereins für nassauische Altertumskunde* (1913), 252: taf. xxxii, Type 22A^2, where it is dated A.D. 40–50.

21. Simpson, *op. cit.*, 20, fig. 4 and endpaper.
22. Forty years ago T. May, *The Roman forts at Templeborough near Rotherham* (1922), 6, wrote that "Templeborough was probably one of these [forts of Gallus]" as some of the samian pottery he examined there was clearly Neronian. Simpson, *op. cit.*, 11 and endpaper, agrees as does G. D. B. Jones, 'Romans in the North-West', *Northern History*, iii (1968), 2.
23. Burn, *op. cit.*, 74, 75, holds the same opinion: "The years 72 and 73 saw the Roman columns penetrate to the far north of the Brigantian country, perhaps even into Scotland . . . How far Cerialis finally penetrated is uncertain; his advanced columns may even have entered Scotland, but he certainly did not consolidate as far as that." Birley, *op. cit.*, 13–14, supports this view and quotes a reference from Pliny's *Natural History* which mentions campaigning, probably under Cerialis, in the "neighbourhood of the Caledonian forest", which he would place "within measurable distance at least of the Forth–Clyde line".
24. *CW*[2], xxxiv (1934), 57; *J.R.S.*, xli (1951), 54; and *Procs. of the British Academy*, xli, 298, n. 2.
25. J. P. Bushe-Fox, *Arch.*, lxiv (1913), 293–314. Cf. Birley, *op. cit.*, 40.
26. See *inter alia* R. Hogg, 'Excavations at Tullie House, Carlisle', *CW*[2], lxiv (1964), 14–62. Pottery found (*ibid.*, 33) included a sherd of early St Rémy-en-Rollat ware, which has also been found at York (Appendix, no. 4). Bushe-Fox, *op. cit.*, 311, suggested that Cerialis built a fort at Carlisle.
27. B. Dobson, *Durham Archaeological News Bulletin*, li (Sept. 1968), demonstrates that there are no less than four pre-Hadrianic periods at Corbridge, one at least of which is likely to be Cerialian.
28. Richmond, *op. cit.*, 38. Cf. Birley, *op. cit.*, 41n.
29. Richmond, *op. cit.*, 43–4.
30. However Richmond (R.C.H.M., *York*, xxx) interpreted their presence at York differently: "They may represent the old savings deposits of the Ninth [Legion], brought to York on removal".
31. No detailed report of these excavations has been published, but in a short summary (R.C.H.M., *York*, 61b) the early finds are referred to thus: "Associated with it [a wooden hut] was abundant late 1st-century pottery, including some that, out of this context, might have been considered pre-Flavian, though insufficient to suggest a pre-Flavian date for the occupation here."

    Examination of this pottery in the Yorkshire Museum shows that it consists of a sherd from a Belgic butt beaker; samian marbled ware: one complete bowl (Dr. 18) and fragments from seven other vessels, including three cups of Dr. 27; *terra nigra*: sherds from the bases of three vessels; St Rémy ware: the base and wall of a small cup with green glaze.

    These sherds represent at least 13 different vessels. While it could be argued that the collection was Flavian, it is reminiscent of finds from North Ferriby in Lincolnshire from the pre-Roman native site there. (*Ant. J.*, xviii, 262f.)

B. R. HARTLEY

Roman York and the northern military command to the third century A.D.

It is a commonplace of Romano-British history that the strategic position at York was seized upon early in the campaigns of the Flavian governor Petillius Cerialis and that from then on York virtually remained, for the rest of the Roman period, the headquarters of the northern command. The assumptions usually made are that York was the permanent station of Legio IX Hispana from A.D. 71 or 72 until that unit somehow disappeared from the scene, to be replaced at York about A.D. 122 by Legio VI Victrix,[1] which then remained there until the end of Roman control. This general picture cannot be far removed from the truth, but it remains a generalization which may be questioned here and there on points of detail, and it implies a much more static situation than the true complexities of northern history allowed. In order to appreciate York's true position more fully, it is necessary to look beyond it to the fields of command falling to its successive legions, to consider the parts played by them in the campaigns in the North, and to survey such shifts in the balance of frontier policies as may be disentangled from our meagre literary sources and our, frequently equivocal, archaeological evidence.

In dealing with the history of Roman Britain nothing is more difficult than keeping in mind the distinction between received tradition, derived from the writings of modern scholars, and the relatively few certain facts. Search for novelty for its own sake can be tempting but ought to be avoided, but the plain fact remains that the truth has to be sought amongst evidence which is often difficult to assess, frequently fragmentary, and not seldom capable of being interpreted in more than one way. This certainly applies to many of the topics touched on here, and the writer is more concerned to put some views which seem to him worth considering than to claim any finality for them.

An initial chronological approach is demanded by the question of the establishment of York as a Roman site. Is it conceivable that a garrison of auxiliaries existed there before the Flavian period? The general position of the Brigantes as Roman clients under Cartimandua would not necessarily exclude the possibility, since Roman troops were occasionally stationed in client kingdoms in special circumstances.[2] The struggle between Cartimandua and her consort, lasting from the governorship of Didius Gallus (A.D. 52–57/8) to A.D. 69 offers a possible context. But there is no positive evidence for occupation under Gallus, and a study of the potters' stamps on samian ware from York (p. 131) does little to encourage the belief: the chronological pattern of the York stamps is strikingly close to that for Caerleon, where the fortress was undoubtedly established by Julius Frontinus about A.D. 74, though there is admittedly just a slight possibility of the existence of an auxiliary fort at Caerleon before the fortress.[3] However, even if pre-Flavian occupation could be claimed for York, there would be no reason to assume a Roman garrison. And after all pre-Flavian samian was used at Stanwick in Neronian times.[4] The chances of it appearing at York, if there were a native site there, would be even greater, in view of York's ease of access to Roman traders operating to the Humber. The probability of such contact would be increased by the likelihood that Cartimandua's seat is to be expected in the Vale of York or its vicinity.[5] And indeed the very name of York during the Roman period suggests strongly that there was an existing settlement: if the site had not already been named, then it should surely have been named from one of the rivers, according to the common Roman practice.[6] One other piece of negative evidence should be noted. Any fort at York could hardly have been held in isolation, and a chain of posts linking it to the headquarters of Legio IX would be expected. There is no sign as yet of anything of the sort north of the Don. Even if we are prepared to accept the large fort at Templeborough and the even larger one at Rossington as pre-Flavian,[7] they fall into place as the watch on the Brigantian borders after the intervention of Gallus in support of Cartimandua. If the date is right, then it is particularly interesting to note that the policy of establishing them was singularly justified by the absence of Brigantian intervention at the time of the Boudiccan revolt.

As for the possibility of the existence of a military post at York under Vettius Bolanus (A.D. 69–71), the archaeological evidence must necessarily remain inconclusive. Professor Frere has tentatively suggested that Bolanus may have been active in east Yorkshire, but he can only adduce the evidence of a Roman poet, who was not necessarily thinking of east Yorkshire or the York area.[8] Despite Statius, this is really a most unlikely time for the founding of new forts, and certainly our only historical source paints a very different picture, clearly admitting a reverse for Rome.[9]

That a large military site appeared at York in A.D. 71 or, more probably 72, is certain. What is less certain is that this was intended for Legio IX as a whole.[10] The question is only to be resolved by much more work on the defences of York and by the elucidation of the precise nature of the large, early site at Malton.[11] However, it does seem extremely likely that York would have housed the legionary command from the beginning, and it must surely have been the base for operations against Venutius and his allies. Legio IX will surely have been the spearhead of the advance under Petillius Cerialis (A.D. 71–4), but as we know from Tacitus, Legio XX was also involved in the campaign, though the very fact that Julius Agricola, then legate of that unit, was only sometimes given independent command by the governor suggests that basically they were operating together.[12] As has been remarked elsewhere,[13] there is no evidence that Agricola was responsible for an advance on the west side of the Pennines at this time, and it is a moot point which of the two legions was involved in the advance over the Stainmore Pass after the presumed defeat of Venutius at Stanwick. The Stainmore marching camps of the Rey Cross series, as has often been observed, are only fit for one legion.[14] Both the legions would, however, have had to leave holding forces, probably at least a cohort strong each, in their bases, thus leaving room for some auxiliaries in the Stainmore camps, unless vexillations of the two legions were encamped in them.

Under Julius Frontinus (A.D. 74–8) the main scene of activity in Britain shifted to Wales, however thin the details which have come down to us.[15] Whether any part of Legio IX took part in the Welsh campaign is quite unknown. At most it could not have been more than a token force, since a firm watch on the North would have been needed, even with the main Brigantian resistance crushed. Frontinus, however, is notable for his energy and attention to detail elsewhere,[16] and it may be thought unlikely that he would now allow the greater part of Legio IX to lie idle in its base or bases. We might well expect some evidence of road- and fort-building. The one thing which seems certain is that the main series of Pennine forts belongs to the governorship of Julius Agricola (A.D. 78–85).[17] But York itself must now, if not earlier, have been linked with the south. A fort is obviously to be sought at Tadcaster at the crossing of the Wharfe (Newton Kyme will not do, as it is certainly related to the Rudgate, which is a secondary addition to the road system),[18] but the Ermine Street and the forts at Castleford and Doncaster ought now to have appeared.[19] Similarly, on the route north from York forts might well be expected now. Considerations of spacing require one at the crossing of the Nidd close to Kirk Hammerton; Aldborough,[20] Healam Bridge[21] and Catterick Bridge[22] ought to have followed. So far as can be seen at present, there is nothing in the records of the pottery from Aldborough or

Catterick which helps to settle the choice between Frontinan and Agricolan foundation, and perhaps it is not to be expected, since it would be extremely difficult to decide whether A.D. 75–7 or 79–80 was the more likely on that kind of evidence. Further north, however, it seems that Binchester is more likely to have been Agricolan than earlier.[23] But what of the Stainmore forts? It is at least worth asking whether the Cerialian line of advance might not have been consolidated now. The site at Carkin Moor has yielded no evidence of date.[24] Greta Bridge poses a problem, since it is too close to both Carkin Moor and to Bowes for normal spacing. Before the recent excavations it was permissible to wonder whether Bowes might not have been a late addition to the chain of forts, but now that Flavian pottery is known there,[25] it is possible to suggest that Greta Bridge is the addition. The earliest material recorded there so far is the latest class of South Gaulish samian ware belonging to the period A.D. 90–110, though admittedly it comes from the *vicus* rather than the fort itself, which has yet to be investigated. Domitianic or Trajanic foundation seems most likely, however. At Bowes one curious detail of the fort's defences calls for some comment. The original south rampart had a cheek of fine turfwork at the back, but its front was revetted by vertical timbers. No certainly Agricolan fort in the north of England or in Scotland is known to have been treated in this way, and for parallels one must turn to Lincoln[26] and, possibly, York.[27] It is impossible to avoid wondering whether this does not hint both at the work of Legio IX and at Frontinan date. If the earlier date could be accepted, we may have a possible solution to a well-known crux, namely the date of the first occupation at Carlisle, variously taken as Cerialian or Agricolan.[28] Neither the one nor the other, but intermediate? Unfortunately we still know far too little about the forts between Bowes and Carlisle.[29]

Another point which might well be considered is whether the north Yorkshire moors could have been garrisoned at this time. The most that can be said at present is that the site at Lease Rigg would be worth further examination.[30] Its proportions seem strange at first sight, but the presence of a stone bottoming to the rampart is evocative of the Roman army, though best paralleled in early days by the treatment of the Agricolan fort at Ilkley.[31] At the very least one would expect the army to have shown some interest in the lower Tees, especially as it would offer a useful harbour for shipping supplies.

Legio IX obviously played a major part in the Agricolan campaigns, initially presumably helping with the penetration and consolidation of the Dales south of the Stainmore. What part it took in building forts there is a matter which can never be settled, since the relevant inscriptions will have been on wooden tablets. It is perhaps likely that the auxiliary regiments were left to look to their own building for the most part. In A.D. 81 the Legion will no doubt have been advancing north of the Tees east of the hill country, and soon building or supervising the building of the forts in Durham and Northumberland. That it was later operating in Scotland north of the Forth in Agricola's sixth season is well-known, and there is no need to retell the story of its misfortune.[32] That York was Agricola's northern headquarters for his campaign is clear, if we may accept the equation of the Scrib(onius) Demetrius of the famous York dedications with Plutarch's informant, and it is certainly difficult not to do so.[33] It is suggested that the governor's *praetorium* of the tablets was outside the fortress on the opposite side of the river, since that is where they were found, but one may legitimately wonder whether this is likely. It would seem more in character for Agricola to have used the legionary *praetorium* as his headquarters, and it is not inconceivable that the bronze plates reached their find-spot fortuitously.

During the Agricolan campaigns the Legion was obviously absent from York for much of its time, for each fighting season would necessarily be followed by constructional work. Even allowing for this, we tend perhaps to think of most of the Legion returning to York to winter. One matter suggests that this was not necessarily so, however. Among the many forts founded by Agricola in the North is a surprising number which stand out because of their size.[34] Many are large enough to house *alae milliariae*, but obviously did not all do so, since there was only one unit of the type in Britain, if it indeed already existed. But it is equally difficult to believe that all the large forts could have been held by smaller auxiliary units stationed together, since Agricola had to spread his troops very wide and needed more units than he had for the logical completion of his system north of the Forth. It is perhaps more likely that the large forts held legionary vexillations or mixed forces of legionaries and auxiliaries, such as were used later, it seems, in the Flavian II fort at Newstead. With the bulk of Legio XX at Inchtuthil, as is likely, and with Legio II Augusta and Legio II Adiutrix needing considerable forces in reserve against the newly conquered tribes of Wales, one might expect the task of holding the large northern forts to fall more heavily to Legio IX. And this would have been a continuing state, for some of the forts were held long after the end of Agricola's stay in Britain.[35] It may perhaps be this situation which accounts for the curious drop in the quantity of stamped samian ware of the later Flavian period from York (p. 129).

The attested rebuilding of the defences, or at least of one of the gates of the York fortress under Trajan, is slightly later than the work involving internal buildings at Caerleon.[36] It is perhaps not out of the question that the later date was determined by the absence of out-stationed vexillations, which would have been returning to York after the evacuation of Scotland, A.D. 105 being the latest possible date. But it is very curious that more intense activity is not suggested by the record of stamped samian ware for this period. In fact the quantities continue to drop throughout the whole period down to A.D. 130. This is understandable for the later part of the range, but the drastic drop in about A.D. 110 makes one wonder whether the Legion as a whole could have been at York much after 108. The Scalesceugh tilery remains a problem.[37] Since legionary tiles do not normally seem to have been used in auxiliary forts in Britain, it ought to imply the presence of a fortress for Legio IX somewhere in the north-west, or at least a large fort or forts for a substantial part of the Legion. A possible context might come slightly later (p. 76), but perhaps we ought to ask whether the Trajanic frontier on the Stanegate needed stiffening in the west, just as Hadrian's Wall did in a few years' time. Otherwise, the only site which could have held part of the Legion at this time is the large fort at Malton, which has produced legionary tiles.[38] The possible alternative explanation that the Legion had already left Britain at this time seems most improbable.

Whatever precisely happened in Britain at the end of Trajan's reign must have involved the York command, whether it carried with it the destruction of Legio IX or not.[39] The scene of action may now be defined a little more closely. The Hadrianic evacuation of almost all the forts east of the Pennines and of much of the Pennines themselves shows conclusively that no general Brigantian uprising occurred as was once thought. The choice therefore lies between action in the north of England west of the Pennines or in Lowland Scotland. On balance, the latter seems more likely, and is now often accepted as one of the reasons for the building of Hadrian's Wall, where Legio VI was primarily engaged down to A.D. 128, though it has left fewer records than Legio II and Legio XX.

The fate of Legio IX is still, of course, a matter of debate.[40] It will not be discussed here except to say that it would be surprising if the Legion was still in Britain after the arrival of Legio VI about A.D. 122. Had it been here, it must surely have left some record of building on the Wall. The Stevens-Frere hypothesis that it was building the Turf Wall, and so using wooden inscriptions, seems to break down in the face of the variation of turrets (and milecastles?) on the turf sector.[41] Such variation elsewhere on the Wall is satisfactorily explained in terms of building by different legions. That it should have been assigned the monotonous task of digging the whole of the Wall ditch is most implausible: the reaction of the legionaries would have been predictable. Nor could it have been set to guard the outfield: that would be work for the auxiliaries. On the whole, it seems easier to envisage the Legion as having left Britain by A.D. 122. If it had not done so, then a new legionary fortress, either for it or the new legion, has to be postulated. As Professor Frere has spotted, Carlisle would be virtually the only possible choice, unless division between Carlisle and Kirkbride is invoked. The most to be said is that this situation would give a context for the Scalesceugh tilery.

That York itself was more fully garrisoned after about A.D. 130 is suggested by the record of stamped samian ware (p. 129), and this is entirely reasonable. What still has to be settled is whether there was any major action in the North in the governorship of Julius Severus (*c.* A.D. 130–3). There are relatively strong hints, but nothing is quite conclusive.[42]

What is clearer, however, is the area of the York command at this period. After the withdrawal of the Inchtuthil legion in A.D. 87 or thereabouts York must have been responsible for an enormous area for a time, eased eventually by the Trajanic retirement to the line of the Stanegate. From then until the end of Hadrian's principate York will have controlled the frontier zone as well as some of the north-western forts, since the Chester command will have had responsibility for part of Wales, as well as the southern Pennines and some of the Lancashire forts. In the Pennines the division between the two commands probably lay along the Chester–York road.[43] As for York's involvement with the Wall, Professor Richmond's suggestion of the Stainmore signal stations as forming part of the chain of command from legionary headquarters to the senior officer on the Wall at Stanwix is still very attractive.[44] It should be noted though that none of the posts has yet been dated, but the renewed activity at Bowes under Julius Severus might be significant, since Bowes must have controlled much of the system. On the other hand, it is perhaps not impossible that the system could have been connected with links between headquarters at York and the large forts at Carlisle(?) and Kirkbride originally.

Complication of the York command followed once more at the beginning of the Antonine period. A vexillation of Legio VI was building at Chesters, it seems in A.D. 139.[45] But soon after the Legion must have been engaged in the reconquest of Scotland under Lollius Urbicus (139–42), though details of the campaign have not survived. Soon its vexillations were building on the Antonine Wall, probably forts and certainly the turf wall itself, the barbarians 'having been driven back'.[46] As in the Flavian period, legionary vexillations were used in garrison in the northern forts. Newstead, housing part of Legio XX, is the most satisfactory example,[47] but it is commonly held that some at least of the forts on Hadrian's Wall were now occupied by legionary vexillations.[48] The evidence is not in fact conclusive for this date, since the only closely dated inscriptions are the Chesters ones already mentioned, and those could obviously be earlier than the decision to evacuate the Wall as a frontier. As the Wall system was undoubtedly wrecked deliberately under Urbicus, it seems curious that the forts should have been garrisoned at all, and another possible context for the presence of legionaries will be suggested shortly. One minor problem which occurs at this time, though it is probably also relevant both earlier and later too, is the exact relation of the legionary vexillations from other units to the York command. The Newstead vexillation under Pius was evidently one from Legio XX, probably commanded by one of the senior centurions.[49] In the absence of their legate, such units as the Newstead one, or those suggested for the large Flavian forts earlier, or for the works-depot at Corbridge later, would presumably have come under the orders of the legate of Legio VI, whose command now no doubt extended to the Scottish forts. It is odd that no coherent system for transmitting signals swiftly, comparable to the Stainmore one, has yet been detected.

On the conventional view, to which the writer subscribes, this extension of the York command will have lasted down to about A.D. 155, when the Antonine Wall and Scotland were evacuated, and a serious crisis in northern England led to the despatch of reinforcements for all the three British legions from the two Germanies. The result of the trouble was the return of garrisons to the forts in the hinterland which had been evacuated by Hadrian, and also the decision to recommission Hadrian's Wall, where Legio VI was working by A.D. 158.[50] At present we can only point to the destructions of the Antonine I forts at Birrens[51] and Lancaster[52] as possible indications of the troubled area.[53] But major events had clearly been afoot, and it would not be surprising if the action had been more widespread, in view of the decision, taken at about this time, to reoccupy forts as widely separated as Brough-on-Noe, Malton[54] and the Wall system. One might almost wonder whether the apparently certain destruction of the *principia* of the fortress at York itself could belong to this time rather than the end of the second century.[55] But we must await publication of Mr Ramm's evidence.

It is at this point that a crucial question of major concern not only for the York command, but for the whole history of Roman Britain obtrudes itself. If Hadrian's Wall and the hinterland forts were now all occupied, how could it have been possible to reoccupy Scotland soon as well? Recent verdicts on the length of the intermission between the first and second Antonine occupations of Scotland have been in favour of a short break.[56] It is true that the arguments deduced from Newstead and Bar Hill could be explained away,[57] though this will not prove quite so easy for Crawford.[58] But the plain fact remains that their cumulative evidence is strong, and the general consideration that not one of the building inscriptions from Scotland is certainly later than the reign of Antoninus Pius is very striking indeed, especially as it should be the latest stones which come from the fillings of the wells in the Scottish *principia*. The 'short break' hypothesis ought to be right on this evidence, but the problem of the required manpower still has to be faced. Professor Frere returns to the old view of the simultaneous holding of the two frontier systems, in itself a curiosity of military history, if true, but also wants not only the zone between the two walls to be held but the hinterland forts in England too.[59] This will not do: it would have been impossible without drastic reinforcement of the army of Britain, for which there is no evidence. A recent study of the potters' stamps and decorated samian ware from the two main zones, Scotland on the one hand, the southern wall and its hinterland on the other, strongly suggests that there was no overlap in their occupation. All the most typical late-Antonine potters, whose work is abundant on Hadrian's Wall and in the Pennine forts, are entirely lacking from the Antonine Wall and, with the possible exception of Newstead, from Lowland sites too. In other words, unless their garrisons used no samian ware, the Scottish forts were not occupied after A.D. 170 at the latest. The writer can here only give a brief summary of what seems to him the most likely explanation, realizing some of its difficulties, but feeling that the suggested outline accounts for more of the facts than others which have been canvassed in recent years.

By the end of the governorship of Julius Verus the situation in the north of England had been retrieved. Antoninus Pius was, however, committed to the occupation of Scotland, and by A.D. 161 at the latest it had been undertaken once more. This time, however, the structures of Hadrian's Wall were not wrecked when it was evacuated, and legionary holding-units may have been placed in some of the forts.[60] By A.D. 162 further trouble was threatening in Britain, and it may be that the Antonine Wall forts or some of them were now destroyed, if indeed the second Antonine occupation ended in destruction. Calpurnius Agricola (A.D. 162/3–165/6) was sent to deal with the situation.[61] He must soon have realized that the only possible solutions would be either to bring in considerable reinforcements, so that the recently rebellious hinterland could be garrisoned fully at the same time as Scotland, or to evacuate Scotland and return to the Hadrianic system, but with the hinterland firmly held. The former course might well have appealed to Marcus Aurelius, judging by his reaction to frontier troubles elsewhere, but this was just the moment when forces could not be spared from the likely source, the Rhine-Danube frontier.[62] Accordingly, the second alternative was chosen and Scotland was evacuated. Calpurnius Agricola then consolidated the north of England,[63] which was held continuously thereafter down to the removal of troops in A.D. 196. On this view Hadrian's Wall will once more have been the frontier of the province, but the new system may have made use of longer-ranging patrols in Scotland, as was done in the third century, it seems. Newstead may have played a part in this suggested system; Birrens, the only fort in Scotland quite certainly producing samian ware of the period A.D. 180–200, definitely belonged to it.

The difficulties about this suggested scheme cannot adequately be discussed here, but some mention must be made of Commodus's 'greatest war', since that will have involved Legio VI. The first and most obvious comment is that it has left singularly little archaeological trace for a war in which the governor of the province was killed.[64] At the most, it could only be seen in forts on the Antonine Wall, if we accept for the moment that they could have been occupied at the time. In fact there seems to be a choice open to us to accept either the (abandoned) Antonine Wall or Hadrian's Wall as the one which "divided the barbarians from the Roman garrisons" and which was crossed in the war. It may be observed here that the breaking of a frontier work would not necessarily involve more than one point along its line. The scene of the ensuing campaign under Ulpius Marcellus (*c.* A.D. 183–5) will have been in Scotland surely, and it would presumably have been more in the nature of a punitive expedition than a matter of driving invaders out of areas of the province which they had held for some months. Soon the British legions were involved in mutiny (p. 88), but otherwise so far as we know the province remained quiet until the time when Clodius Albinus (A.D. 192–7) removed much of the army to Gaul. That this led to widespread damage to forts in the north in A.D. 196–7 seems certain. Many of the forts will certainly have suffered at the hands of the Brigantes. Two problems need further discussion. There has been a tendency in recent years to doubt whether the fortress at York was involved in the disasters.[65] Mr Ramm may have us change our minds on that. If it was now destroyed, its attackers are perhaps more likely to have been inhabitants of the province than barbarians from the north. Secondly there is the question of the Wall and what happened to it. No one doubts that some forts on the Wall were destroyed at about this time.[66] The question is whether it happened in A.D. 196–7 or later and whether the Maeatae were responsible. The orthodox view, well summarized by Professor Frere, is obviously perfectly possible, but it does leave some facts unexplained or in doubt. The recovery of the Pennine area and the re-establishment of the forts there in A.D. 197–8 and the following years is not in doubt.[67] But it also seems certain that Virius Lupus (A.D. 197–202) was building at Corbridge.[68] Why, then, should the restoration of the Wall have to wait until A.D. 205 or later? Further difficulties in the hinterland may be postulated, and it is possible now to point to an intermission in the rebuilding at Bainbridge with completion of the new fort coming only in A.D. 205/6.[69] The reliefs on the Bainbridge stone of A.D. 205 may tell us that both Legio VI and Legio II had been active in the area.[70] Nevertheless, it still seems a little difficult to visualize a situation in which the frontier of the province could have been allowed to lie in ruin for so long. The writer still wonders whether the destruction on the Wall may not have come either in the governorship of Valerius Pudens (A.D. 202–205/6) or early in that of Alfenus Senecio (205/6–207). The need for expeditions into Scotland from A.D. 208 onwards would then make better sense. Furthermore, it was not against the Maeatae that the first campaign was directed, but the Caledonii.[71] This makes one wonder whether the Maeatae had attacked the Wall at all in A.D. 196–7. Their threat at that time, and the buying of them off by Lupus, might perhaps have been connected with the outposts beyond the Wall.

The imperial expedition into Scotland, led by Severus in person at first, will have involved the use of Legio VI. As is well known, Severus chose York as his headquarters and there lived in a *domus palatina*,[72] with his praetorians no doubt installed close by. The marching camps of the expeditions in Scotland, now being so clearly illuminated by Dr St Joseph, imply very large forces indeed.[73] The first campaign was evidently largely a sea-borne one with landings on the Firth of Forth. But it appears to have been followed by operations in Lowland Scotland, where there are some probable Severan marching camps.[74] There seems too to have been some provision for an overland operation at Corbridge.[75]

The Severan intention was clearly full-scale occupation of Scotland once more, and Legio VI comes into the picture firmly with the establishment of a large fort at Carpow at the mouth of the Tay, where it was building with Legio II.[76] However soon it may have been evacuated, this fort was meant to be permanent. Similarly with Cramond[77] and, probably, Newstead.[78] One may wonder too whether the enigmatic third period on the Antonine Wall, if it exists at all,[79] is not simply the preparation for the Severan recommissioning of that frontier. However that may be, Caracalla soon withdrew his forces to Hadrian's Wall, which then remained the basic frontier for the rest of the Roman period, though with much activity by patrols far into Scotland.[80]

After the final version of the Severan division of Britain into two provinces,[81] York became the seat of the praetorian governor of Lower Britain, since that office was combined with legateship of Legio VI, at least initially. Apparently soon after the division a vexillation of Legio VI was at Piercebridge with soldiers from the two Germanies, oddly enough under the command of a centurion of Legio II from Upper Britain.[82] On the whole, as Professor Birley concludes, it is unlikely that this situation was connected with campaigning, since there is no other evidence of internal disturbance of the province at this time, and indeed for the York command much of the third century was obviously peaceful. Vexillations of Legio VI might be detached from time to time, as at the works-depot at Corbridge,[83] again in association with soldiers from Upper Britain, but the fortress at York was probably held now by a fuller garrison than ever before.

Notes

1. Sheppard Frere, *Britannia* (1967), 126 and A. R. Birley, p. 82, below.
2. Tacitus, *Ann.* xii, 15, curiously enough involving Didius Gallus.
3. V. E. Nash-Williams, *The Roman Frontier in Wales*, 2nd edition revised by M. G. Jarrett (1969), 29. The chance of a pre-existing fort being held more than very briefly is diminished by the presence of Coed-y-Caerau near by, *ibid.*, 81.
4. Sir Mortimer Wheeler, *The Stanwick Fortifications* (1954), 31f.
5. In view of the rebellion in south-west Brigantia in A.D. 48 (Tacitus, *Ann.* xii, 32) Cartimandua's control there must have been weak, and now that the coins formerly assigned to the Brigantes are seen to be Coritanian (D. F. Allen, *The Coins of the Coritani*, 1963), there is no case for Almondbury at all.
6. cf. Isca, Deva, Derventio and a host of others.
7. T. May, *The Roman Forts at Templeb(o)rough* (1922): note, however, Dr Grace Simpson's caution – *Britons and the Roman Army* (1964), 11. For Rossington, see *J.R.S.*, lix (1969), 104 with pl. II.
8. Frere, *op. cit.*, 97f.
9. Tacitus, *Hist.* iii, 45.
10. *Northern History*, i (1966), 12.
11. P. Corder, *The Defences of the Roman Fort at Malton* (n.d.), 11.
12. Tacitus, *Agr.* 8.
13. *Northern History*, i, 12.
14. *CW*[2], xxxiv (1934), 50ff.
15. Tacitus, *Agr.* 17.
16. as his activity when *curator aquarum* at Rome shows only too clearly.
17. The combination of Tacitus, *Agr.* 20 with the archaeological evidence seems conclusive.
18. I. D. Margary, *Roman Roads in Britain*, 2nd edition (1967), 417.
19. Some of the pottery found recently at these two sites would fit better with construction during the 70s rather than about A.D. 80.
20. *Y.A.J.*, xl (1959), 52f.
21. A fort is demanded here by the spacing, and its probable platform is to be seen. The few finds, in the Yorkshire Museum, include, as Katharine Hartley tells me, an undoubted Flavian mortarium, an early variant of Bushe-Fox form 14/18.
22. The structures, as opposed to the position, of the forts are not known.
23. with a coin of A.D. 76 from the rampart, as Mr J. P. Gillam reminds me.
24. Recent examination by Professor Frere and the writer suggest that it was a normal fort, not a fortlet, as the Ordnance Survey Map of Roman Britain has it.
25. Including several sherds of South Gaulish bowls of form 29, a useful criterion for distinguishing earlier Flavian sites from late-Domitianic and Trajanic ones.
26. *J.R.S.*, xxxix (1949), 63f, though there with a vertical timber back, too.
27. R.C.H.M., *York* (1962), 22, fig. 15 and *Northern History*, i (1966), 11.
28. *Arch.*, lxiv (1913), 295ff.; E. Birley, *Roman Britain and the Roman Army* (1953), 10.
29. The reported stamp of the pre-Flavian potter Lupus from Brough-under-Stainmore (*CW*[2], lv, 320) turns out on autopsy to be a stamp of Rufus of La Graufesenque, though probably belonging to A.D. 70–80.
30. R. H. Hayes and J. G. Rutter, *Wade's Causeway* (Scarborough and District Arch. Soc. Research Report no. 4, 1964), 69ff.
31. *Proc. Leeds Phil. and Lit. Soc., Lit. and Hist. Section*, xii (1966), 25. The shape of the enclosure at Lease Rigg recalls Fendoch.

32. Tacitus, *Agr.* 26.
33. *RIB* 662–3: for the background see Tacitus, *Agr.* ed. R. M. Ogilvie and Ian Richmond (1967), 32–3.
34. Malton (8.4 acres), Corbridge (about 9 acres), Kirkbride (30 acres? – *CW*² lxix, 78), Dalswinton (8.6 acres), Newstead (12.6 acres), Castledykes (8.1 acres), Ardoch (7.2 acres), Dalginross (certainly large), Bertha (large), Cardean (more than 6.9 acres) and Camelon (8.0 acres).
35. Namely Malton, Corbridge, Kirkbride, Dalswinton and Newstead.
36. Caerleon, *RIB* 330 (A.D. 99–100); York, *RIB* 665 (A.D. 107–108).
37. *CW*², xvi (1916), 290. For a full discussion, J. E. Bogaers in *Studien zu den Militärgrenzen Roms* (Vorträge des 6. internationalen Limeskongresses in Süddeutschland, 1967), 68ff. Note tiles of Legio IX from Carlisle, too.
38. Corder, *op. cit.*, 38, fig. 7.
39. S.H.A. *Hadrian*, 5 . . . *Britanni teneri sub Romana dicione non poterant.* Possibly Fronto (ed. Naber, 228) too: *avo vestro imperium obtinente quantum militum ab Iudaeis quantum ab Britannis caesum*, though some would connect this with later events (Frere, *op. cit.*, 139).
40. E. Birley, *Roman Britain and the Roman Army* (1953), 20–30; J. E. Bogaers, *loc. cit.*
41. C. E. Stevens, *The Building of Hadrian's Wall*, rev. version (1966), 87. Frere, *op. cit.*, 138.
42. Mr Stevens (*op. cit.*, 52–3) would put the Hadrianic *expeditio Britannica* in A.D. 125 and have a war then in which Legio IX disappears.
43. *RIB* 624 (Slack) gives a centurion of Legio VI on undefined business. The recent excavations have confirmed evacuation of the site by A.D. 140, and increase the probability that the Chester–York route was replaced by the Blackstone Edge route then or soon after (I. A. Richmond, *Huddersfield in Roman Times* (1925), 89ff.). This explains why Slack was not reoccupied about A.D. 160. It is unthinkable that the Chester–York road was then left undefended: Slack's successor is to be sought at Greetland after all, Castleshaw's, if it had one, near Littleborough.
44. in W. F. Grimes (ed.), *Aspects of Archaeology in Britain and Beyond* (1951), 293–302.
45. *RIB* 1460–1.
46. *S.H.A. Antoninus*, 5, 4, where *summotis barbaris* is surely a reminiscence of Tacitus, *Agr.* 23. It is usually believed that it was the Lowland tribes which now threatened the province. But suppose that it was the Caledonii who had been interfering, say, with the Votadini: they would then have to be driven back, and a new frontier in contact with them would then make good sense. R. G. Collingwood's interpretation of *summotis barbaris* (Collingwood and Myres, *Roman Britain and the English Settlements*, 2nd edition (1937), 146) is difficult, and it is now doubtful whether the *numeri Brittonum* did first appear on the German *limes* under Pius (D. Baatz, *Saalburg Jahrbuch*, 25 (1968), 191).
47. *Proc. Soc. Ant. Scot.*, lxxxiv (1952), 19–21.
48. Frere, *op. cit.*, 151.
49. *RIB* 2122–4.
50. *RIB* 1389.
51. *Trans. Dumf. and Galloway N.H. and Ant. Soc.*, 3rd ser., xli (1964), 135–55.
52. *J.R.S.*, xlix (1958), 108.
53. Bowes, if it was held under Pius, should provide a crucial test.
54. Reoccupation at about this time may be deduced from the pottery published by Corder (*op. cit.*), and is confirmed abundantly by the unpublished material in the Roman Malton Museum.

55. *RIB* 582 must surely, as Macdonald saw, have been looted from the fortress at York, and presumably from its *principia* (*J.R.S.*, xvi (1926), 9).
56. K. A. Steer, *Arch. Ael.*, 4th ser., xlii (1964), 1–39; Frere, *op. cit.*, 155.
57. e.g. by suggesting that the Antonine I defences at Newstead were demolished *c.* A.D. 155 by the evacuating troops, and that at Bar Hill part of cohors I Hamiorum was in garrison with the Baetasians.
58. *J.R.S.*, liii (1963), 128, supplemented by information from Dr Steer.
59. Frere, *op. cit.*, 156. Collingwood believed at the time he was writing that the inner and outer *limites* in Germany were held simultaneously (*op. cit.*, 143). This is now known not to be so (*J.R.S.*, lix (1969), 167ff.).
60. *RIB* 1583 (Housesteads; soldiers of Leg. II *agentes in praesidio*); *RIB* 1330 (Benwell, Leg. II) and *RIB* 1725 (Great Chesters, Leg. XX). Katharine Hartley points out that the extraordinary ditches between the north wall of the fort at Great Chesters and the Wall ditch are explicable only if the fort was held as an isolated unit when the Wall was not held as a system. It may also be observed that the reoccupation of Scotland at this time should have led to withdrawal of some of the Pennine garrisons. Evidence of discontinuity is not yet forthcoming for any of the Pennine forts, however.
61. *S.H.A. Marcus Aurelius*, 8.
62. The Chatti invaded Raetia in A.D. 162, and the whole Danube frontier was in chaos for many years. *Bayerische Vorgeschichts-blätter*, 30 (1965), 154–75; A. R. Birley, *Marcus Aurelius* (1966), 162ff. for recent discussions.
63. Which explains why all his inscriptions are there: Ribchester (*RIB* 589, involving Legio VI as builders – virtually inconceivable if it still had Scotland in its command); Hardknott (*RIB* 793, probably Calpurnius Agricola); Carvoran (*RIB* 1809); Chesterholm (*RIB* 1702) and Corbridge (*RIB* 1137, 1149), where there was now a legionary vexillation in garrison. The building of the new fort at Chester-le-Street (*Arch. Ael.*, 4th ser., xlvi (1968), 75ff.) might be due to him, or perhaps came slightly earlier.
64. Cassius Dio, lxxiii, 8.
65. *Proc. Leeds Phil. and Lit. Soc.*, ix (1961), 118; *Gnomon*, xxxvi (1964), 88; *Arch. J.*, cxviii (1963), 257.
66. In recent years Halton Chesters is a certain example: *J.R.S.*, li (1961), 164; lii (1962), 164.
67. Frere, *op. cit.*, 169.
68. *RIB* 757, undated.
69. *J.R.S.*, lix (1969), 207 with fig. 30. The builders of A.D. 205 put one of their main walls over a deep demolition pit of A.D. 197–8, with predictable results.
70. The bull of Legio VI and the capricorn of Legio II both appear in the margins (*Northern History*, i, 19).
71. Cassius Dio, lxxvi, 13.
72. *S.H.A. Severus*, 22, 7.
73. *J.R.S.*, lix (1969), 113–19.
74. *ibid.*, 116, 118.
75. *RIB* 1143.
76. A. R. Birley in *Studien zu den Militärgrenzen Roms*, 1–5 for the latest summary, with corrected plan in *J.R.S.*, lix (1969), 110 and 203 (the latter mislabelled 'Antonine').
77. *J.R.S.*, lii (1962), 161.
78. Note *RIB* 2313, linking Cramond and Newstead at this time, if the restoration is correct, and also the presence of late Rheinzabern ware at Newstead.
79. *Arch. Ael.*, 4th ser., xlii (1964), 36f.
80. K. A. Steer in I. A. Richmond (ed.), *Roman and Native in North Britain* (1958), 91–111.

81. *J.R.S.*, lvii (1967), 61–4 for a convincing reassessment by J. C. Mann and M. G. Jarrett.
82. *Epigraphische Studien*, iv (1967), 103ff.
83. *RIB* 1125; *Arch. Ael.*, 4th ser., xxi (1943), 127ff., for a brilliant study of the works-depot by I. A. Richmond.

E. B. BIRLEY

The fate of the Ninth Legion

Legio IX Hispana formed part of the standing army retained after the battle of Actium in 31 B.C. Its title *Hispana* presumably proclaims that it took part with distinction in the Spanish campaigns of the following decade, but we first get word of it as part of the garrison of Illyricum in A.D. 14.[1] From Illyricum it was transferred to Africa in A.D. 20, to take part in the operations against Tacfarinas, returning in A.D. 24 to what by now was known as the province of Pannonia. Aulus Plautius was governor of that province when he was selected to command the army of invasion in A.D. 43, and he took the Ninth Legion with him. Its British record, as recounted by Tacitus, was unfortunate. In Boudicca's rising its legate, Petillius Cerialis, led part of it against the insurgents, only to lose two thousand infantry, escaping back to his base with the handful of mounted men;[2] and during Agricola's sixth campaign, described as *maxime invalida*, it had a narrow escape from disaster at the hands of the Caledonians.[3] As it happens, the career record of a young man of senatorial family who was serving as *tribunus laticlavius* of IX Hispana shows that in that year, A.D. 83, he was commanding a detachment of the legion on the Continent, taking part in Domitian's war against the Chatti, and winning the military decorations appropriate to his rank.[4] Tombstones of soldiers of the Legion, still without mention of *cognomina*, attest its presence at Lincoln early, most probably before the death of Claudius.[5] So much by way of introduction to the problem of its fate.

Nobody has ever questioned that the Ninth was the first legion to occupy the new fortress at York, when Cerialis – back in Britain as consular governor – began the annexation of Brigantia and moved his old legion forward, replacing it at Lincoln by the recently raised Legio II Adiutrix, which he had brought with him from Lower Germany. But there has been a wide variety of opinion and of conjecture as to the fate of the Ninth. It has for long been common ground that an inscription of A.D. 108 (strictly speaking, to be dated between 10 December 107 and 9 December 108, by the mention of Trajan's twelfth regnal year), attesting its erection of some building in the fortress,[6] is the latest dated record of its existence. John Horsley, writing before the discovery of that inscription, was aware that Legio VI Victrix crossed to Britain in Hadrian's reign, and deduced that the Ninth "might possibly be broke, or incorporated with the Legio sexta victrix", bearing in mind that inscriptions of both legions had been found in York, and that York was "the stated and lasting quarters" of the Sixth, as shown by Ptolemy's Geography and, in effect, by the Notitia Dignitatum.[7] But it was the general view of nineteenth-century scholars that IX Hispana had been destroyed in a British war, and that the Sixth had been brought over to fill the void created by its loss.

Huebner, commenting on the inscription of A.D. 108 (*CIL* VII 241) may be taken as a typical exponent of that view; his Latin may be rendered as follows: Since it is agreed that the Ninth Legion was not removed to another province, it is not improbable that Borghesi was justified in inferring that it had been destroyed in Britain, by the Brigantes, bearing in mind the testimony of two ancient writers. The Augustan History's Life of Hadrian, chapter 5, relates that on that emperor's accession, in August 117, *Britanni teneri sub Romana dicione non poterant*; and Cornelius Fronto, writing to Lucius Verus in A.D. 162, after Roman disasters in the opening stages of a Parthian war, consoled him by pointing out that in earlier reigns the Romans had lost battles before winning wars: *quid? avo vestro Hadriano imperium optinente quantum militum ab Iudaeis, quantum ab Britannis caesum.*[8] The most extreme statement of the view is to be found in the *Cambridge Ancient History*, xi (1936), 313, from the pen of the Berlin Professor Wilhelm Weber: "next came the crushing of the Britons, who had destroyed the Legion IX Hispana in the camp of Eburacum, and the *expeditio Britannica*, which ended in 119". Small wonder that many English and Scottish writers have evolved an even more delightful myth, which I have found still cherished as an article of faith in Roxburghshire in 1969 – that the Legion marched north, on some unspecified campaign, and was never heard of again, even by the Romans!

Weber's account, repeating in essence what he had written in his *Untersuchungen zur Geschichte des Kaisers Hadrianus* (1907), 110, took no cognisance of the doubts which had been expressed by Emil Ritterling in his monumental article *Legio*, in Pauly-Wissowa's *Realencyclopädie* xii, 2 (1925), 1668f. To Ritterling the career records of a couple of senators whose early military service had in each case been as *tribunus laticlavius* in the Ninth, and who rose to consular rank under Antoninus Pius, seemed incompatible with the idea that the

Legion had ceased to exist so soon; he felt that a date in the mid or even the late 120s must be posited, though he still assumed that it was in Britain that the Ninth was lost.[9] I myself have adduced some further evidence, in a paper first printed in the *Durham University Journal* in 1948 and reprinted in my *Roman Britain and the Roman Army* (1953), 25–8; and I was led to suggest the possibility that the Sixth Legion was brought to Britain to reinforce the skilled men needed to build Hadrian's Wall, not to fill a gap caused by the loss of the Ninth – and even to speculate that IX Hispana might have been moved to an eastern province, "on the completion of the building programme, when it was no longer necessary to have four legions in the province."

It was therefore something of a surprise to me when the late Sir Ian Richmond committed himself to writing, in his *Roman Britain* (Pelican History of England, i (1955), 47; 2nd edition (1963), 40f.):

> That the Legion was cashiered, there is no doubt, and it seems evident this fate, at the hands of the disciplinarian Hadrian, followed an ignominious defeat. But the unit was not annihilated. Some of its officers at least survived and nothing whatever is reported of the circumstances or place of the trouble. The steps which Hadrian took to repair the damage suggest, however, that the seat of disturbance lay in south-western Scotland.

A few years later, in the stimulating essay which he contributed to the Royal Commission's volume on *Eburacum* (1962), Richmond modified and enlarged upon his view of what happened:[10]

> No ancient source describes how the Ninth Legion came to disappear from the Roman army list, and the matter has given rise to varied conjecture. The circumstantial evidence, such as it is, may be summarised as follows. There was successful Roman campaigning in Britain in A.D. 119, important enough to be commemorated on Hadrian's coinage with the types of *Iuppiter Victor* and *Roma Victrix*, and *Britannia*. This is all consequent upon a state of affairs at his accession in which 'the Britons could not be held under Roman rule'. The conditions are adequate to cover a disgraceful defeat of the Ninth, meriting at the hands of the disciplinarian Hadrian the cashiering of the unit. The later the event is placed the more difficult it is to account for, and no strain is involved in associating the disbandment of the unit, whose staff officers at least survived, with the visit of Hadrian to Britain in A.D. 121–2. To assume, as has been done, that the legion was annihilated or that it continued to exist, toiling in unrecorded obscurity upon the works of Hadrian's Wall, is an unnecessary postulate.

So confident a statement, by a writer of such authority, might seem to close the affair. But it is only right that I should report a dissenting view, put forward by Mr C. E. Stevens in his learned monograph on *The Building of Hadrian's Wall* (1966),[11] 53: accepting Ritterling's reasoning, he guessed that there had been a second British war in A.D. 125, and that it was only then that the Legion was destroyed – "Hadrian's Wall", he concluded, "may have been built in the shadow of a Trajanic withdrawal: it was not built in the shadow of a Hadrianic defeat."

It so happens, however, that further evidence has come to light, from across the North Sea and from a cave in Palestine, and it is necessary to reopen the dossier, for it is no longer possible to assume that the Ninth "was not removed to another province".

The eminent Dutch archaeologist, Professor J. E. Bogaers, has drawn attention[12] to the fact that the legionary fortress at Nijmegen in Holland, which from A.D. 70 to *c.* 104 is held to have been occupied by Legio X Gemina,[13] has produced a good many tiles attesting the presence there of a *vex(illatio) Brit(annica)*, which ought to mean a task-force drawn from a plurality of units of the army of Britain, and he has suggested that that task-force formed the garrison of the fortress after the Tenth had left for the Danube. But Nijmegen has also produced a tile stamped LEG VIIII[and a mortarium with the rim-stamp]G VIIII HIS and on the assumption that the British war which was already in being in August 117 had brought heavy casualties to the Ninth, Professor Bogaers has suggested that VI Victrix was sent to Britain to replace it, IX Hispana being transferred to the Lower German fortress to rest and refit. He has also adduced an inscription from Misenum[14] which, if it is genuine (it depends on a written record), since it commemorates a soldier of the Ninth named Aelius Asclepiades, recruited in Cilicia and dying after eight years' service, ought to imply that the Legion was in fact serving in an eastern province later in Hadrian's reign;[15] and he concedes that if it was not destroyed in the serious war against the Jews, in which on any showing the Romans sustained heavy casualties – as that sentence of Fronto's shows – it might even have continued in an eastern garrison, to be identified as the legion destroyed by the Parthians in A.D. 161, according to the historian Cassius Dio (lxxx 2, 1):

> Vologaesus began the war by besieging a Roman legion under Severianus in Elegeia (a place in Armenia), and shot down and destroyed the whole force, officers and all.

At least, no other legion can be produced to fill the bill, unless indeed one were to adopt the solution of despair put forward by E. Nischer, that it was a newly raised legion, which did not exist long enough to leave any record of itself.[16]

Lower Germany has recently produced one further inscription which may have some bearing on the case, namely an altar to Apollo found in Aachen, the watering-place almost certainly known in Roman times as *Aquae Granni*, after the Celtic god of healing, Grannus, who was regularly equated with Apollo and portrayed on sculptures (as in this case) as Apollo with his lyre – though his frequent association with a goddess Sirona shows that he was not an exact counterpart of the Roman deity. The Aachen altar[17] was dedicated by a *praefectus castrorum*, formerly *primus pilus* of IX Hispana and by a reasonable inference still serving, in the higher rank, with that Legion. Professor Nesselhauf, in his discussion of the inscription, has accepted as logical that the officer had been visiting the spa from the Legion's base fortress at Nijmegen, for the *praefectus castrorum* could not have been serving with a mere vexillation, and *Aquae Granni* was the health-resort apparently reserved for the army of Lower Germany, just as Bath for the army of Britain. But he has put forward a different suggestion as to the occupation of Nijmegen, and the period of the Ninth's stay there. He cannot accept Ritterling's view[18] that X Gemina left for the Danube as early as A.D. 104, and suggests that, on the contrary, it was moved – to Vindobona (the modern Vienna) – as part of the general troop movements occasioned by Trajan's preparations for his war against Parthia, which began in A.D. 114. That would provide an occasion, he argues, for its fortress to be allocated to IX Hispana, on the assumption that Lower Germany still needed a three-legion garrison and that Britain could now be reduced safely from three legions to two. Then, he continues, a year or two later the development of a critical situation in the East – including a widespread Jewish rising and Roman defeats in the Parthian war – made it necessary for the Ninth, too, to be moved eastward, so that when the war in Britain broke out it was no longer available to reinforce the army of Britain and VI Victrix had to be sent instead, from its fortress higher up the Rhine frontier, at Vetera (near the modern town of Xanten), and that the move of VI Victrix to Britain took place as early as A.D. 119.

I find it difficult, however, to suppose that Trajan would have felt it safe to remove one legion from Britain; and if one legion had had to leave, surely the Ninth would have been least likely, in a period when archaeological evidence indicates that there was trouble brewing in the north of the province. To the archaeological evidence we may add the hints provided by epigraphy. I have referred elsewhere to the fact that *coh. I Cugernorum*, appearing in that simple form in the British diploma for A.D. 103 (*CIL* XVI 48), has become *coh. I Ulpia Traiana Cugernorum civium Romanorum* by 122 (*CIL* XVI 69), evidently gaining the titles of distinction from Trajan.[19] There is also the curious parallelism between the careers of two, or perhaps even three, legionary centurions who were transferred from the Danube front, after a Dacian war, to Britain;[20] Ti. Claudius Vitalis (*ILS* 2656) and L. Valerius Proclus (*ILS* 2666b) both began as centurions in V Macedonica in Moesia, Vitalis by direct commission and Proclus after service in the ranks; their movements were as follows:

Vitalis	*Proclus*
1. V Macedonica	V Macedonica, decorated in a Dacian war
2. I Italica, decorated in a Dacian war	I Italica
3. I Minervia, decorated in a Dacian war	XI Claudia
4. XX Valeria Victrix	XX Valeria Victrix
5. IX Hispana	IX Hispana
6. VII Claudia	*missus honesta missione*

In the third case, a centurion named Tuccius (*CIL* VIII 3005), after serving as centurion in one of the cohorts named III Bracaraugustanorum,[21] like Proclus was centurion successively in I Italica, XI Claudia and XX Valeria Victrix. If I am right, the implication is that after two Dacian wars (and it is attractive to assume that Trajan's two Dacian wars were in question) it was found necessary to send battle-tried reinforcements to Britain, at first to the Chester Legion and then to the Ninth: and that would have come conveniently after the Ninth's building project of A.D. 108.

If there was indeed warfare in Britain, beginning soon after A.D. 108 and still in being in A.D. 117, or renewed shortly before that year, that would seem to eliminate the likelihood of IX Hispana having been withdrawn as early as Professor Nesselhauf has suggested. Nor do I find it easy to accept the very close timing which, on his view, allows the Ninth to be moved further east and the Sixth to reinforce Britain, all within the period 114–19. By contrast, it still seems attractive to suppose that Platorius Nepos brought VI Victrix to Britain with him from Lower Germany, early in 122 (just as Cerialis had brought II Adiutrix half a century earlier), to enlarge the skilled labour force required to build the Wall and its forts – particularly if we accept the attractive suggestion advanced by Mr Stevens,[22] that the building of the Wall had begun under the previous governor, Pompeius Falco, and if we attribute to Hadrian himself the decision to add new forts to the scheme. In any case, Hadrian had one or two legions to spare, now that Trajan's new provinces in the East had been given up.

Just as II Adiutrix had occupied the Ninth's old fortress at Lincoln when IX Hispana was moved forward to York, so now, one might conjecture (as Professor Frere has recently hinted[23]), the Sixth was installed at York and the Ninth was intended to build itself a new fortress still further north, at Carlisle. After all, Carlisle and the tile and pottery works at Scalesceugh, half a dozen miles to the south of it, have produced tiles of the Ninth, not unlike that tile from Nijmegen in their reading LEG VIIII HIS – in contrast to the Legion's York tiles, all reading LEG IX HIS, as Mr R. P. Wright and Mr H. G. Ramm have been good enough to confirm to Professor Bogaers.[24] But with the new frontier works in sight of completion, it may be suggested, it was found sufficient to place the milliary *ala Petriana* at Stanwix, just across the River Eden from Carlisle; and now that VI Victrix was comfortably installed at York, and the fortress at Nijmegen was vacant, it might be simplest to suppose that IX Hispana was transferred to Lower Germany, *c.* A.D. 126. Four or five years later the Jewish war broke out, and Sextus Julius Severus, governor of Britain, was summoned to the East to take command against the insurgents;[25] that might provide an appropriate occasion for the Ninth to have been transferred to an eastern province, if not to the Jewish war itself.

But what about that cave in Palestine? It has produced a papyrus, the contents of which have been summarized in the *Israel Exploration Journal*, xii (1962), 259, and brought to wider notice by Sir Ronald Syme in a paper printed in *Historia*, xiv (1965), 355f. The papyrus attests as governors of the province of Arabia three successive senators: Julius Julianus in A.D. 125, Aninius Sextius Florentinus in 127, and Haterius Nepos in 130. Now the governor of A.D. 127 had long been known, all but the initial letter of his first *nomen*, from an undated inscription set up in his memory at Petra,[26] the metropolis of the province. It sets forth his career, with one or two omissions for which the stone-cutter must be held responsible, and shows that before his appointment to Arabia he had been proconsul of Narbonensis (the modern Provence), and before that legate of IX Hispana. Unless there had been a lengthy period of unemployment, he must surely have commanded the Ninth after, rather than before, A.D. 120; and if the Legion had indeed disgraced itself while under his command, he could hardly have been expected to receive from Hadrian the governorship of Arabia and concurrent command of its legion, III Cyrenaica, a post normally carrying with it the justified expectation of the consulship – if death had not supervened.

This evidence for a Hadrianic legate of the Ninth brings me back to Richmond's dictum that "staff officers at least survived". It must be borne in mind that there was only one *tribunus laticlavius* to each legion, holding that post on an average for some three years, as I have argued elsewhere;[27] so that the two officers cited by Ritterling, L. Aemilius Carus and L. Novius Crispinus, cannot have been serving simultaneously in IX Hispana, as might have been supposed from Richmond's statement. Nor need it be assumed that one was the immediate successor of the other: in view of their later careers it might be thought more likely that there was at least one intermediate holder of the post. As it happens, we have full details of those careers, and in each case a precise date for one later stage; that is why Ritterling was in a position to cite them. Carus[28] was governing Arabia in A.D. 143, and he became suffect consul late in that year, or just possibly in 144; his service with the Ninth might well have come before the death of Trajan, as witness the case of Claudius Maximus,[29] suffect consul in 144, who while *tribunus laticlavius* of the Syrian Legion IIII Scythica had been decorated by Trajan, evidently in his Parthian war (A.D. 114–17). But Novius Crispinus,[30] who rose to the consulship as late as A.D. 150, and had been holding the senior praetorian appointment as *legatus Augusti pro praetore* of Legio III Augusta in Numidia since 147, can hardly be supposed to have become consul as many as 30 years after his service with IX Hispana, to judge by the details of his career. A date nearer A.D. 130 than 120 seems most likely in his case.

To sum up: there is sufficient epigraphic evidence (cited, for convenience, in full in the Appendix to this paper) to indicate that the Ninth Legion was still in existence well after A.D. 120, and none to support the old conjecture that it was destroyed in a British war – let alone that it had suffered a disgraceful defeat and was disbanded by Hadrian. On the contrary, there is some ground for thinking that it was transferred from Britain, first to Lower Germany and then to an eastern province (though the dates of those movements are still matters for conjecture), finally perhaps to be destroyed in Armenia by the Parthians in A.D. 161.

But even so, some readers may perhaps prefer to accept the verdict propounded by a member of the Eighth Congress of Roman Frontier Studies, early in September 1969:

The fate of the Ninth still engages
The minds of both nitwits and sages;
  But that problem, one fears,
  Will be with us for years
And for ages and ages and ages!

Appendix: Some inscriptions referred to above

1. *ILS* 1025 (Tibur): L. Roscio M. f. Qui. Aeliano Maecio Celeri cos., procos. provinc. Africae, pr., tr. pl., quaest. Aug., Xvir. stlitib. iudic., trib. mil. leg. IX Hispan. vexillarior. eiusdem in expeditione Germanica, donato ab imp. Aug. militarib. donis corona vallari et murali, vexillis argenteis II, hastis puris II, salio – C. Vecilius C. f. Pal. Probus amico optimo – l. d. s. c.
2. *CIL* VII 241 = R.C.H.M., *York*, p. 111 and pl. 41, no. 1 = *RIB* 665 (York): [i]mp. Caesar / [divi N]ervae fil. Ne[rva / Trai]anus Aug. Ger[m. Dac/icus po]ntifex maximu[s tribu/niciae po]testatis XII imp V[I cos. V p. p.] / per leg. VIIII Hi[sp].

   Note: R.C.H.M., *York*, and *RIB* restore the last line to read: [portam] per leg. VIIII Hi[sp. fecit]; but it is excessively rare for building records earlier than late second century to specify the structures to which they relate.

3. *CIL* X 1769 (Misenum): d.m. Aelius Asclepiades nati(one) [C]il(ix) mil. leg. IX vix. ann. XXXXII, mil. ann. VIII – Aelia Seleria b. m. f.
4. *Bonner Jahrbücher*, 167 (1967), 268–79 (Aachen-Burtscheid): L. Latinius L. f. Publilia Macer Ver(ona) p. p. leg. VIIII Hisp., praef. castr., pro se et suis Apollini v. s. l. m.
5. *CIL* III 87 + 14148[10] (Petra): L. [A]ninio L. f. Pap. Sextio Florentino IIIviro aur. arg. flando, trib. milit. leg. I Minerviae, quaest. prov. Achaiae, trib. pleb., leg. leg. VIIII Hisp., procos. prov. Narb., leg. Aug. pr. pr. prov. Arab., patri piiss[imo] ex testamento eius

   Note: the stone-cutter should have rendered the post in the vigintivirate as IIIviro aur. arg. aere flando feriundo, and he has left out mention of the praetorship, which should have come between trib. pleb. and leg. leg.
6. *ILS* 1077 (Rome): L. Aemilio L. f. Cam. Karo co[s.], leg. Aug. pr. pr. provinciae Cappadociae, leg. Aug. pr. pr. censitori provinciae Lugdunensis, leg. Aug. pr. pr. provinciae Arabiae, curatori viae Flaminiae, leg. leg. XXX U. V., praet., trib. pleb., quaest. Aug., trib. militum leg. VIII Aug., trib. militum leg. VIIII Hispanae, Xviro stlitib. iudic., sodali Flaviali, XVviro s. f. – C. Iulius Erucianus Crispus praef. alae primae Ulpiae Dacorum amico optimo
7. *ILS* 1062, cf. J. Fitz, *Acta Antiqua Academiae Scientiarum Hungaricae* xi (1963), 258ff. and R. Syme, *Historia* xiv (1965), 352f. (*sc.* Aquincum): [Ti. Claudio Ti. f. ——.] Maximo IIII[viro v. c.,] trib. leg. IIII Sc[yth.,] donis milit. a divo Trai. d[o]n., quaest. u[rb.,] ab acti(s) senat., tr[ib. p]leb., praet., curat[o]ri viae Aurel., leg. leg. I Ad., iuridic[o] pr. pr. utriusqu[e] Pannoniae, leg. p[r]. pr. Pannoniae infe[r.,] cos., sodali Augus[ta]li, curat. aed. sacra[r.] – canabens(es) pu[b(lice)]
8. *ILS* 1070 (Lambaesis): L. Novio Crispino Martiali Saturnino cos. desig., leg. Aug. pr. pr. provinciae Africae, procos. Galliae Narbonensis, leg. Aug. leg. I Italicae, leg. Aug. iuridico Astyriae et Gallaeciae, praetori, trib. pleb., quaestori pro praet. provinciae Macedoniae, trib. mil. leg. VIIII Hisp., IIIIviro viarum curandarum, seviro eq. Romanorum . . .

   Note: the inscription is datable to A.D. 150.

Notes

1. cf. Ritterling's detailed discussion of the evidence for this legion in *R.E.*, xii 2 (1925), 1664–70.
2. Tacitus, *Ann.* xiv, 32, implies that the whole legion was lost, apart from the mounted men, but cf. xiv, 38: Nero sent two thousand legionaries from the armies of the Rhine, *quorum adventu nonani legionario milite suppleti sunt.*
3. Tacitus, *Agr.* 26.
4. cf. Appendix, no. 1 (*ILS* 1025).
5. *RIB* 254, 255, 257 and 260.
6. cf. Appendix, no. 2 (*RIB* 665): the restoration accepted by *RIB* and by R.C.H.M., *York* makes it record the erection of a gateway (*porta*), but that is very far from certain. Military building-inscriptions of this period seldom, if ever, specify the structures in which they were set.

7. *Britannia Romana*, 1732, 79f. The inscription known to Horsley (from Gale's publication of the British section of the Antonine Itinerary) was *ILS* 1100, now known to be part of the same record as *ILS* 1094, giving the career of M. Pontius Laelianus Larcius Sabinus (suffect consul in A.D. 144) who had been, in descending order, *trib. pleb. candidato imp. divi Hadriani, ab act(is) senat(us), quaestori prov. Narb., trib. mil. leg. VI Victr., cum qua ex Germ. in Brittan. transiit.*
8. Fronto, ed. Haines, ii, 22.
9. "Es kann also mit der Möglichkeit gerechnet werden, dass ein zweiter Aufstand der Brittanier gegen Mitte oder in der zweiten Hälfte der zwanziger Jahre ausgebrochen ist, welchem die L. zum Opfer fiel."
10. R.C.H.M., *York*, xxxii.
11. Written several years earlier, but a chapter of mishaps delayed the book's passage through the press.
12. most accessibly, in German: 'Die Besatzungstruppen des Legionslagers von Nijmegen im 2. Jahrhundert nach Christus' (*Studien zu den Militärgrenzen Roms* (1967), 54–76).
13. so Ritterling, *R.E.*, xii 2, 1683.
14. cf. Appendix, no. 3 (*CIL* X 1769).
15. Observe the man's *nomen*, Aelius, and his origin in Asia Minor.
16. Kromayer-Veith, *Heerwesen und Kriegführung der Griechen und Römer* (1928), 503, n. 9: "falls es sich nicht un eine sonst nicht bekannte Neuschöpfung handelt, die ihre Aufstellung nich lange überlebte."
17. published by Herbert Nesselhauf and Harald von Petrikovits in *Bonner Jahrbücher*, 167 (1967), 268–79; for its text cf. Appendix, no. 4.
18. *ibid.*, 271ff.
19. *Roman Britain and the Roman Army*, 1953, 24.
20. for a discussion of the matter, within the context of the promotions and transfers of centurions and the significance in particular of centurions accompanying vexillations of fighting men, cf. *Carnuntum Jahrbuch* 1963/64 (1965), 21ff., especially 30.
21. evidently that in Lower Moesia, not the British cohort.
22. C. E. Stevens, *The Building of Hadrian's Wall* (1966).
23. *Britannia* (1967), 138f., taking the Nijmegen evidence into account.
24. 'Die Besatzungstruppen usw.', 68, footnote.
25. Cassius Dio, lxix, 13, 2; for the career of Julius Severus cf. *ILS* 1056, and A. R. Birley in *Epigraphische Studien*, 4 (1967), 70f.
26. cf. Appendix, no. 5 (*CIL* III 87 + 14148^{10}).
27. 'Senators in the emperors' service' (*Proceedings of the British Academy*, xxxix (1954), especially 199f.).
28. cf. Appendix, no. 6 (*ILS* 1077).
29. cf. Appendix, no. 7 (*ILS* 1062, as emended by Fitz).
30. cf. Appendix, no. 8 (*ILS* 1070).

A. R. BIRLEY

VI Victrix in Britain

VI Victrix, the last of the legions garrisoned in Britain to arrive, already had a long and glorious history. It derived, with VI Ferrata, from Caesar's Sixth, first mentioned as serving in Gaul in 52 B.C., under the command of Q. Cicero. Caesar's Sixth went on to fight at Pharsalus, in Egypt and in Pontus, then (after a temporary disbandment) in the Spanish campaign of 45 B.C. After Caesar's murder, and Philippi, it seems to have been split, one part joining Antonius's forces in the east, the other Octavian's army, forming VI Ferrata and VI Victrix respectively. The titles of the new legions point to the remarkable record of the old Sixth. Little record of the movements of VI Victrix during the next decades is preserved; but it was clearly sent to Spain by Augustus some time before 6 B.C., in which year all the centurions *leg(ionis) VI ex Hispania* jointly honoured a former tribune. It remained uninterruptedly in Spain until A.D. 68, when its support for Galba's coup gained it the credit of having toppled the Julio-Claudian dynasty. After the civil wars, Vespasian sent the Legion to serve under Q. Petillius Cerialis, then grappling with the Batavian revolt. At the end of A.D. 70 it took up new quarters at Novaesium (Neuss) in Lower Germany, remaining here until its transfer *c.* 100 to Vetera (Xanten) in the same province. While at Novaesium VI Victrix was among the legions that remained loyal to Domitian during the brief revolt of L. Antonius Saturninus in A.D. 89: it was rewarded with the titles *pia fidelis Domitiana*. The last was of course dropped after Domitian's murder and *damnatio* in A.D. 96; *pia fidelis* was retained.[1]

The transfer to Britain is directly recorded on the *cursus* inscription of one of its officers, M. Pontius M. f. Pup. Laelianus Larcius Sabinus (*cos.* by 146).[2] It adorned the base of a commemorative statue erected after his death more than

50 years later, in the Forum Ulpium at Rome. Laelianus had been *trib(uno) mil(itum) leg(ionis) VI Victr(icis), cum qua ex Germ(ania) in Brittan(iam) transivit.* His career can be dated fairly closely: almost certainly suffect consul in August 144,[3] he is securely attested as consular governor of Upper Pannonia in 146 (and again in 149).[4] His distinguished later service, also well recorded, must be omitted here.[5] The normal age at which the consulate was held was 42,[6] so he is likely to have been born *c.* 102. His tribunate, preceding the quaestorship, held at 24,[7] can hardly have ended later than 125, while if he joined his legion at 18 or 19 (like Cn. Julius Agricola and many others),[8] he would have gone to VI Victrix in Germany in 120 or 121. This evidence makes it virtually certain that the Legion was taken to Britain in 122 by A. Platorius Nepos, whose assumption of the British governorship in that year is firmly attested, on his promotion from Lower Germany to Britain.[9] Whether IX Hispana had already vacated its base at Eburacum, and, if so, whether it had now been sent elsewhere in Britain or to somewhere in Lower Germany, are questions for speculation.[10] However this may be, most of VI Victrix, if not all of it, went initially straight to the frontier zone, to assist in the construction of the new *limes.*

In comparison with II Augusta and XX Valeria Victrix, the Sixth is poorly represented in Hadrianic building inscriptions from the curtain, milecastles and turrets of the Wall. However, structural evidence has been combined with the single milecastle inscription of the Legion (MC 50 SW: *RIB* 1938) to assign to it a characteristic ground-plan, distinct from those assignable to II and XX; and with this one of the three turret-types may be associated.[11] The scarcity of epigraphic record for VI Victrix may be partly coincidental. However, it is exceptionally well represented in building inscriptions from forts on and close to the Wall, and it may well be that this work compensated for a lighter load on the curtain and structures.[12] If Mr Stevens' argument that building began in 120[13] is accepted, the scantiness of the Legion's work is still more readily explicable. It may be of interest to note here the programme which Mr Stevens has deduced for VI Victrix:

- 122: half a season's ration (16 'curtains', plus structures and foundation) – the sector T 17a – MC 22, plus a postulated special structure at Portgate
- 123: probably fort-building
- 124: fort-building, plus a small sector of foundation and structures (MC 48, T 48a and b, and a postulated Irthing bridge tower); work interrupted by a native revolt
- 125: no building
- 126: 8 stone wall 'curtains' and 8 structure and foundation sections (MC 49–52, omitting T 51a and b, already built for now obsolete part of Turf Wall)
- 127: fort-building
- 128: fort-building and filling of 'holes' in Wall.[14]

It may well be, as Mr Wright has suggested, that the Sixth built the *pons Aelius* at Newcastle-upon-Tyne also: two inscriptions of the Legion (*RIB* 1319, 1320) were found in the river, presumably fallen from the bridge.[15]

The identity of the legate in command of the Legion when it was transferred cannot be securely established, but there is a strong candidate: P. Tullius Varronis f. Stell. Varro (*cos.* 127).[16] Until firm dating evidence appears, there must remain a possibility that Varro had been replaced before 122.[17] But examination of his career and background makes it likely that he was the man. A native of Tarquinii in Etruria, he had excellent connections in high places, for his elder brother had been adopted – it would seem – by the influential Spaniard Dasumius ('the testator'), taking the names P. Dasumius Rusticus; and was the colleague of Hadrian as *consul ordinarius* in 119 (the year in which another Spaniard, known specifically as the emperor's friend, was consul suffect: A. Platorius Nepos).[18] Varro's initial career had not been particularly remarkable, but after his praetorship he had commanded the Cappadocian Legion XII Fulminata, possibly at the tail end of the Parthian war of Trajan. In that case, he would have been under the orders of Hadrian's friend L. Catilius Severus (*cos. II ord.* 120);[19] and he could have been in a position to stake out a claim to Hadrian's gratitude in the difficult time following Trajan's death.[20] At all events, it was very rare for a man to command more than one legion, and the recorded cases can virtually all be explained as the product of some unusual circumstances.[21] In the case of Tullius Varro, the pending transfer of VI Victrix to a new province would be deemed good cause for placing at its head a man with more than the usual experience. Added to this, his Spanish connections no doubt made him a particularly favoured choice to Hadrian, and welcome to Platorius Nepos. But Varro can hardly have remained long in Britain. Before his consulate, which began on 1 April 127, he had gone on to 12 months' service as proconsul of Baetica, and then the prefecture of the *aerarium Saturni* at Rome, a post sometimes held for as long as three years.[22]

Another commander of the Sixth during its first years in Britain had likewise already served as legionary legate. This was Q. Camurius Q. f. Lem. Numisius Junior, whose home was Attidium in Umbria.[23] In his case, the identity of the first legion that he commanded is unknown, but what gives his career particular interest is the fact that it had begun with a military tribunate in IX Hispana. What is more, the man assumed to be Numisius' father, the *eques* C. Camurius C. f. Clemens, whose known career ended with a minor procuratorial post during the reign of Trajan, had also served in Britain, as prefect of the milliary *ala Petriana*.[24] The details must remain a matter for speculation, but in the light of observable practice, the choice for VI Victrix of a man who had already commanded a legion, and who had, in addition, some British experience (in Brigantian territory, or further north), must be explained as the result of some emergency. It must be stressed that the dating evidence is slender – Numisius might well have been tribune of the Ninth in the 120s or later, and legate of the Sixth under Pius[25] – but one might bear in mind the clear structural evidence from the Wall of dislocation in the work and changes of plan.[26] There is too the circumstantial evidence that military action was needed in the north during or soon after the Wall's completion.[27] The appointment of Numisius Junior may have been among the measures which this provoked. Unfortunately nothing is known of his subsequent career.

The third legate to be considered can be dated with some precision: L. Minicius L. f. Gal. Natalis Quadronius Verus (*cos.* 139).[28] A native of Barcino (Barcelona) in Spain, and one of several Spanish senators with property at Tibur (Tivoli – where their imperial countryman was to build his famous Villa), Natalis was the son of one of Trajan's younger marshals. He himself began his career in remarkable fashion, serving successively in three different legions as tribune – a feat for which the career of Hadrian himself offers the only parallel. All were Danubian legions, and the third (XIV Gemina) was in the army of Upper Pannonia, undoubtedly at the time when the elder Natalis was governor of that province (117).[29] On entering the Senate as quaestor, although he would normally have stayed at Rome for the year since he was *quaestor Augusti*,[30] he was, instead, sent to Africa, of which the elder Natalis was now proconsul, where he served as legate of one of the province's *dioeceses*.[31] The year in Africa was probably summer 121–summer 122, 15 years (by now the normal interval)[32] after the elder Natalis' consulate in 106.[33] At all events, the younger Natalis' praetorship, which would normally have fallen five years after the quaestorship,[34] cannot have been held later than 128. For in 129 he competed at the Olympic Games, and the inscription which commemorates his victory in the four-horse chariot-race describes him as *στρατηγικός*, ex-praetor.[35] He had hardly had time, however, to have commanded VI Victrix, his first post after the praetorship, before his Olympic victory. It is more probable that he came to Britain in 130. In that case, he presumably served under the orders of the governor Sex. Julius Severus (*cos.* 127), whom Cassius Dio calls the outstanding general of the reign.[36] What is particularly interesting is the fact that Julius Severus had earlier commanded the Legion XIV Gemina, perhaps at the very time when Natalis was its *tribunus laticlavius*. For whereas there is clear evidence that governors could nominate officers up to the rank of *tribunus laticlavius* at their discretion,[37] they had no say in the appointment of legionary legates.[38] Only two clear cases are known where this rule was broken – and Dio comments on the anomaly, in one of them – both during the reign of Nero.[39] Here therefore there may be another case, to be explained by the exceptional *gratia* with Hadrian enjoyed by the Minicii of Barcino and by the outstanding qualities of Julius Severus. But it can hardly be coincidence that the next legate to be considered seems also to be the governor's appointee: Hadrian, one might speculate, was prepared to bend the rules in favour of his protegés. The later career of Natalis, while not spectacular, was distinguished. After two minor posts in Italy came the consulate in 139 and a consular governorship and ultimately the proconsulship of Africa.[40]

The fourth legate, P. Mummius P. f. Gal. Sisenna Rutilianus (*cos.* 146), was almost certainly another Spaniard.[41] He too had property at Tibur, and his tribe, Galeria, is predominantly Spanish in its distribution.[42] His early career was not particularly unusual. If he was consul at the normal age, 42, he would have been born *c.* 104, and have become praetor, at 30, *c.* 134.[43] Then came the command of VI Victrix. It so happens that in 135 the governor of Britain was one P. Mummius Sisenna (*cos. ord.* 133), surely a close kinsman of Rutilianus.[44] Unless the consul of 133 were an elder brother or uncle of our man, he must surely be the father. In that case, the interval of only 13 years – less than half the normal lapse of time between consulates in successive generations of one family[45] – suggests that the elder Sisenna attained the *fasces* late in life. This hypothesis is strengthened by the fact that he seems to have gone to Britain straight after the consulate, instead of governing a two-legion province first.[46] The consul of 133 seems to be the first of his family to gain the office, and as, by this time, the old practice had been firmly re-established, whereby only members of well-established families had the honour of becoming *consul ordinarius*,[47] Sisenna was, one might suggest, one of those few exceptional *homines novi* to be so rewarded, probably for distinguished military service. All this is a little conjectural, and equally it must remain an hypothesis that Sisenna Rutilianus commanded VI Victrix *c.* 135. But that would be the most likely time; and in the light of what was said earlier about Minicius Natalis, his appointment also would appear to have been somewhat irregular, another case of Hadrian showing favouritism. The later career of Rutilianus was uneventful until the end of his life, when he made a fool of himself in the eyes of the satirist Lucian (who was no doubt not the only one to mock): he fell under the influence of the charlatan miracle-worker Alexander of Abonuteichos, whose daughter he married as his second wife, and whose interests he actively promoted.[48] Ill-advised behaviour by a man in his sixties need not imply that 30 years before he had not been a competent general, though one may have leave to wonder.

VI Victrix was naturally involved, with the other two legions, in the construction of the Antonine Wall, having presumably played its part in Lollius Urbicus' successful campaign beforehand.[49] The creation of the new frontier brought with it changes further south, and, in particular, a new role for Corbridge. Part of the Legion was now stationed here.[50] More important, perhaps, and rather better recorded, is the role of the legion in the late 150s and 160s. With the abandonment of the Antonine Wall *c.* 155, and the subsequent re-commissioning of the Hadrianic frontier, VI Victrix had plenty of work. It is found 're-building' near Heddon in 158.[51] At this time the governor Julius Verus is known to have been active in a wide area, being attested at Birrens, Corbridge and Brough-on-Noe, the Sixth being responsible for the dedication mentioning Verus at the second of these places.[52] It may have been during the governorship of Verus that there were *res trans vallum prospere gestas,* commemorated by the legate of the Legion, L. Junius Victorinus Fl[avius] Caelianus, at Kirkandrews on Eden.[53] Victorinus cannot be firmly dated or identified, but it seems likely that he is identical with a governor of Upper Germany named Junius Victorinus, reckoned to have served there at some time in the years A.D. 166–208 and more probably at the beginning than the end of that period;[54] and it is possible that he is the same as the suffect consul L. Ju[. . .], whose term of office was held in either 158 or 161.[55] However this may be, the Legion certainly had further fighting to do in the 160s. In 162 Sex. Calpurnius Agricola was made governor and sent *adversus Brittannos.*[56] Inscriptions show him active in several parts of the north, on and south of Hadrian's Wall,[57] and VI Victrix is mentioned with him on two stones, at Ribchester (*RIB* 589) and Corbridge (*RIB* 1137). There may also be a numismatic record of the Legion's actions at this time. M. Aurelius and L. Verus struck a special issue of denarii to commemorate the Triumvir Antonius' Sixth Legion.[58] One might suggest that the bi-centenary of P. Ventidius' great victory at Gindarus in 38 B.C. (when he smashed an invading Parthian army), or alternatively the conquest of Armenia by P. Canidius Crassus in 37 B.C.,[59] may have been the chosen occasion. These anniversaries fell respectively in 163 and 164, when VI Ferrata, which had presumably served under Ventidius or Canidius, was again sharing in Roman victories against Parthia.[60] So much is clear enough. But G. Askew pointed out that there are two varieties of reverse. Both show legionary standards flanking an eagle, and the two spaces at the bottom are filled by: LEG VI. But on one variety one of the standards is surmounted by a figure of the goddess Victory. Askew suggested, very reasonably, that the intention was to give VI Ferrata's sister-legion its share of the glory.[61]

In the 170s, the sole event in British history of which any secure record has been preserved is the despatch here of 5,500 of the 8,000 Sarmatian cavalry demanded by Rome under the Danubian armistice of 175.[62] The motives for increasing the British garrison so markedly may have been various;[63] but part of the reason at least must have been the necessity to strengthen the province's defences – unless, indeed, the plan had now been formed to return to the line of the Antonine Wall.[64] For there can be no doubt that the policy of the Roman government was now expansionist again.[65] The giving up of a large portion of Britain by the governor Julius Verus cannot have been viewed with equanimity by M. Aurelius (however pacific that emperor may seem in the light of his *Meditations*: the true picture is rather different). An accession of strength of the order of 5,500 men would have enabled the re-occupation of southern Scotland to take place without dangerously weakening the Roman military control of the Pennines and North Wales.

M. Aurelius' necessary preoccupation with Parthia and the Danubian campaigns would have made it difficult for him to devote active attention to Britain. With his death in March 180 the situation altered. Commodus made peace on the Danube after a few months.[66] It may well be that his advisers felt the time was now ripe for a safe and easy re-assertion of Roman prestige in the far north. Roman preparations for the re-occupation of the Antonine Wall might well provide the context for what followed. Commodus' major war, Dio records, was in Britain. It began when British tribes crossed the Wall that divided them from the Roman army and created havoc, *inter alia* killing a 'general' (surely the governor).[67] Ulpius Marcellus was sent to restore the situation. Success was claimed in 184, when Commodus assumed the name Britannicus and took his seventh salutation as *imperator*.[68] It may be argued that Marcellus began the rebuilding of the Antonine Wall and its installations.[69]

The events which followed the proclaimed victory are among the most mysterious in the history of the Empire, in spite of – or perhaps because of – the existence of accounts from two writers who were alive at the time, as well as snippets in the *Historia Augusta*. But light is cast on the affair by the inscription of an officer of the Sixth, which is the justification for dwelling on it here. The version of Cassius Dio, born *c.* 164, is preserved only in extracts and in the epitome by the eleventh-century monk John Xiphilinus. Herodian, who was only a boy at the time, is in any case a writer little concerned with precise detail. Dio gives a graphic account of the character of Ulpius Marcellus. He was clearly the kind of man who may well have irritated an army not placated by a victory perhaps more apparent than real, coming after a demoralizing defeat. Besides this, the move to the Antonine Wall will have involved many of the troops in discomfort. And they are unlikely to have got any tangible reward, for the administration was in the hands of the Praetorian Prefect Sex. Tigidius Perennis, who kept a notoriously tight rein on the exchequer.[70] At any rate, the British army became mutinous.

In a passage quoted by Peter the Patrician, Dio records that a legionary legate named Priscus was offered the purple by the British army, but wisely refused.[71] Xiphilinus omits this episode, but he relates that the legionary legates (by implication all three) were "rebuked for insubordination" (surely to Marcellus, but the Priscus affair may have been the real issue), and, he goes on, "they did not calm down until Pertinax [sc. as governor] dealt with them". By "they" the legates seem to be meant, but perhaps Xiphilinus has condensed his original here, for the army as a whole is surely intended. The reaction of the legates to the "rebuke" was to select 1,500 "javelin-men" and send them to Italy to demand the head of Perennis. Commodus met them before they had reached Rome, and, on the advice of the freedman Cleander, gave way. Perennis was lynched.[72] Herodian, although he gives a graphic description of the fall of Perennis, knows nothing of the British troops being involved.[73] But the biographer in the *Historia Augusta* supplies some interesting details. Describing the career of Perennis, he says that the Prefect dismissed the legionary legates in the *bellum Brittannicum*, and replaced them with *equites*. When the legates "reported" what had happened, Perennis was handed over to the soldiers to be lynched (*lacerandus*).[74] In a later passage he mentions that "the Britons" wanted anyone rather than Commodus to be their emperor, at the time (*c.* 184) when Commodus was being called Britannicus ("by flatterers": the implication being that the British victory was in some way spurious or less real than alleged).[75]

Xiphilinus must be called on again for the aftermath. Cleander took over the power of Perennis (whose death can be assigned to summer 185), and there was a general post. Ulpius Marcellus was recalled to Rome and placed on trial, narrowly escaping conviction.[76] Pertinax, who had been in semi-exile, was brought back and went to Britain, where he suppressed the mutiny (and thereby gained great renown at Rome, as is mentioned in a flashback under the year 193).[77] The biographer records that Pertinax set about restoring discipline in Britain, but that the troops were still mutinous, wanting any emperor rather than Commodus, preferably Pertinax himself. A riot took place, and Pertinax was attacked and left for dead. He asked to be relieved of his command, asserting that his stern discipline made the troops hate him.[78] A rather different picture thus emerges from that in Dio-Xiphilinus, but the basic elements are the same.

There are still some features in this story which require explanation. Dio himself found it odd that the 1,500 British troops could make their way unchecked from Britain to near Rome.[79] There may be an answer. M. H.-G. Pflaum has pointed out that the career of the *primipilaris* L. Artorius Castus may belong to this time. He was prefect of VI Victrix, and then, with the title *dux*, took detachments from the British army to fight against the *Arm*[*oricano*]*s*. Here, M. Pflaum argues, is one of the *equites* who replaced the British legionary legates. He rightly invokes the evidence for serious trouble in the provinces at this time: the men who caused it gave the name to the *bellum desertorum*.[80] One might go further than M. Pflaum, and suggest that the men commanded by Artorius Castus were sent in pursuit of the deserter leader Maternus, whose activities are described only by Herodian. Apparently his men "roamed all over Gaul and Spain" and finally began slipping into Italy (where an attempt was made on the emperor's life).[81] It could well be that the men sent to suppress the activities of Maternus took the opportunity of presenting their demands to Commodus in summer 185 – particularly if the dismissed legionary legates combined with the intriguing freedman Cleander, and communicated with the soldiers.[82]

Whatever the truth behind this confused patchwork in the sources, it only emphasizes the mutinous behaviour of the British army during the 180s. Not long after these men had their chance. In 193 the governor Albinus received the title Caesar and in late 195, reacting to unequivocal hints from Severus that he was soon to be dropped, and to urgent pleading from his friends in the Senate, he proclaimed himself Augustus,[83] the first of many to do so from a British base. The rebellious spirit of the British legions will not have been a negligible factor in the deliberations that preceded this act.

The attempt failed. The British troops were on the point of success at Lugdunum, when a last-minute cavalry assault turned the day.[84] The legions were sent back to Britain by the victor. But they were, no doubt, chastened and seriously diminished in strength. There will not have been many troops to spare, but no doubt Severus would in any case have wanted to stiffen the ranks of recent adversaries with his own trusted men; and some possible examples can be found.[85]

According to Herodian, Severus divided the province into two after Lugdunum. He had done this to Syria after Issus in 194. Yet there is a problem, as is well known. When first certainly recorded, under Elagabalus, VI Victrix is the sole legion in Inferior, and the legate is thus also the governor, and a non-consular. Yet the three attested Severan governors, all operating in what was later Inferior, were consulars. Various solutions have been put forward. The most recent is perhaps the most satisfying: that Herodian is right, but that in A.D. 197 Inferior was consular, with XX Valeria Victrix as well as VI Victrix; and that the boundaries, and hence the status of the provinces, were altered by Caracalla, with the Twentieth and a portion of adjacent territory being transferred to Superior.[86]

During the ten years following Lugdunum VI Victrix must have been active, but few details can be supplied.[87] With the arrival of the Emperors in A.D. 208 there were new developments, on which light has recently been thrown. There had, no doubt, been several changes of policy in the previous decade. Quite what had happened to the northern frontier is now, once more, under dispute. To this writer it remains certain that there had been a large-scale irruption into the province, and widespread destruction, in which the Brigantes had participated. If, as assumed earlier, the Antonine Wall's second period began in 184, *a fortiori* that frontier and its works will have suffered in 197. There is no valid reason, on present evidence, for rejecting the hypothesis that much damage was also done then on Hadrian's Wall and at many of the forts of its hinterland.[88] What is more, from the new evidence of destruction in the late second-century *principia* at Eburacum, it looks as if the fortress of the Sixth was indeed attacked at that time.[89] It may well be that the years 197–207 were largely spent in repairing the damage all over the North. Still, some kind of military action took place, enough to excite the jealousy of Severus in Italy, and to justify the dedication to Victory by the governor Alfenus Senecio.[90]

The imperial expedition led to the building of a large new base on the Tay. VI Victrix supplied the roof-tiles, II Augusta built the *porta praetoria*. Carpow, at 29 acres, was too small for a whole legion. Perhaps it was designed for a mixed force. However this may be, the tiles of the Sixth, more than 200 of them, reveal an important fact: they bear the legend LEG VI VIC B P F. The B is new and must be B(ritannica). The title can hardly have been acquired before 209, when the emperors became Britannicus.[91] One such tile has now been found at York.[92] It would be unwise, on present evidence, to assume that the Sixth was alone of the British legions in receiving the title. It was in any case short-lived, being replaced by Antoniniana, and later, as was the fashion in an age of rapidly changing and loudly advertised loyalties, by Severiana and Gordiana.[93] The Severan expedition seems to have been the last attempt to extend the northern frontier until Rome controlled the whole island. Caracalla ordered a return to the Wall of Hadrian.

With the establishment by Caracalla of a praetorian province of Inferior, the importance of north Britain was clearly diminished, though it should be noted that reinforcements seem to have been sent to the province in his reign.[94] The legates of the Sixth, simultaneously the governors of Inferior, have been surveyed by the present writer elsewhere, and there is nothing to be gained by repeating the details now.[95] From this time onwards the history of VI Victrix is less eventful. There happens to be no record of VI Victrix on the legionary issues of either the Gallic emperors or of Carausius, but the Legion clearly remained at

Eburacum, latterly no doubt much altered in composition and organization, until the end of Roman rule.[96] Throughout the third and fourth centuries its officers and men played a large part in the administration of the north.[97] It is appropriate that the Legion's emblem, the bull, should be found together with the inscription *P(rovinciae) B(ritanniae) I(nferioris)*.[98] Lower Britain was indeed the province of the Sixth Legion.[99]

Notes

1. see for details the article by E. Ritterling in *R.E.*, xii (1925), columns 1587–8, 1599–1605.
2. *CIL* VI 1549 + 1497 =*ILS* 1094 + 1100. That these inscriptions were the two parts of one original was not always recognized, and Ritterling (*op. cit.*, col. 1605n.), who saw the possibility, was still doubtful. But see E. Birley, 'Beförderungen und Versetzungen im römischen Heere', *Carnuntum Jahrbuch* (1957), 11, and G. Alföldy, *Die Legionslegaten der römischen Rheinarmeen* = *Epigraphische Studien*, iii (1967), 28f.
3. *FC*, 41.
4. W. Reidinger, *Die Statthalter des ungeteilten Pannoniens und Oberpannoniens* (1956), 76ff.
5. Governor of Syria in A.D. 153, he was recalled to service in the 160s as *comes* of L. Verus in the Parthian war, cf. esp. Fronto, ed. Haines, ii, 148, and again as *comes* of the emperors in the Danubian wars 169–75. cf. A. Birley, *Marcus Aurelius* (1966), 173, 211f., 222, etc.
6. cf. R. Syme, *Tacitus* (1958), 652; J. Morris, '*Leges annales* under the Principate: I', *Listy Filologické*, lxxxvii (1964), 317.
7. Morris, *op. cit.*
8. Agricola, born on 13 June 40 (Tacitus, *Agr.* 44), was in Britain as tribune well before his twentieth birthday. See D. R. Dudley and G. Webster, *The Rebellion of Boudicca* (1962), 144f. for the date of the rebellion, which broke out when he was already with the army. The origin of Laelianus is customarily assumed to be Italian, but G. Alföldy (*op. cit.*, 28) makes out a good case for his suggestion that the man was a native of Baeterrae in Narbonensis.
9. *CIL* XVI 69 of 17 July 122 refers to Nepos as the incoming, Pompeius Falco as the outgoing, governor. Nepos' career is given by *ILS* 1035 (Aquileia), cf. A. R. Birley, 'The Roman Governors of Britain', *Epigraphische Studien*, iv (1967), 69f.
10. cf. E. Birley, 'The fate of the Ninth Legion' in this volume.
11. cf. esp. C. E. Stevens, *The Building of Hadrian's Wall*, Cumberland and Westmorland Ant. & Arch. Soc., Extra Series vol. xx (1966), 10f.; also J. Hooley and D. J. Breeze, 'The building of Hadrian's Wall: a reconsideration', *Arch. Ael.*, 4th ser., xlvi (1958), 98f.
12. Stevens, *op. cit.*, esp. his lists, 98f.: not many of these stones are dated, of course. See now also D. Breeze and B. Dobson, 'Fort types on Hadrian's Wall', *Arch. Ael.*, 4th ser., xlvii (1969), esp. 31f.

13. Stevens, *op. cit.*, 39f. and *passim.*
14. *ibid.*, esp. the list, 106; details, 22ff., 41ff., 56ff. Note that on p. 106 Mr Stevens assigns 10 SF sections to the Sixth under the year 126, perhaps inadvertently including T 51a and b, which he rightly excludes on p. 57.
15. Hooley and Breeze, *op. cit.*, 104, follow Wright (*RIB*, *ad loc.*). The further arguments of these authors concerning the Wall as a whole, if accepted, would not radically alter the picture given above of the share of VI Victrix; and the issues which they raise with Mr Stevens may, therefore, be passed over in silence here.
16. On this career cf. Alföldy, *op. cit.*, 26f., and *idem*, *Fasti Hispanienses: Senatorische Reichsbeamte und Offiziere in den spanischen Provinzen* (1969), 167, who has no doubts about the date. The *cursus* is supplied by *CIL* XI 3364 = *ILS* 1047 (Tarquinii).
17. If he was praetor some 12 years before his consulate (see n. 6 above), i.e. in A.D. 115, he could have commanded XII Fulminata 116–18 and VI Victrix 119–21 (for example).
18. *PIR*² D 15, cf. 13–14, 16–17, and H 5. R. Syme, *Tacitus* (1958), 794, notes the possibility that the Dasumii were kinsmen of Hadrian.
19. *PIR*² C 558.
20. cf. esp. Syme, *op. cit.*, 481ff.
21. E. Birley, *op. cit.* (see n. 2 above), 6; R. Syme, 'Governors of Pannonia Inferior', *Historia*, xiv (1965), 345; Alföldy, *op. cit.* (see n. 2 above), 77ff. and his n. 353 on p. 79. He lists 30 known cases.
22. G. Alföldy, *Fasti Hisp.* (see n. 16 above), 167; Syme, *op. cit.*, 656ff.
23. *CIL* XI 5670 (Attidium).
24. *PIR*², C 382; cf. H.-G. Pflaum, *Les carrières procuratoriennes équestres sous le Haut-Empire romain* (1960–1), no. 87. It is worth noting that father and son could well have served in Britain at the same time. Numisius had started his career as one of the highly favoured *IIIviri a.a.a.f.f.* (on which cf. E. Birley, 'Senators in the Emperors' service', *Proceedings of the British Academy*, xxxix [1953], 197ff.). The prefecture of a milliary *ala* was also a plum post (cf. E. Birley '*Alae* and *cohortes milliariae*', *Corolla Memoriae Erich Swoboda Dedicata* [1966], esp. 57ff.). The nomenclature of Numisius suggests that he had been adopted, either by Clemens or by a Numisius: practice was now flexible, cf. J. Morris, 'Changing fashions in Roman nomenclature in the early Empire', *Listy Filologické*, lxxxvi (1963), 34ff.
25. Alföldy, *op. cit.* (see n. 2 above), 65 suggests this without discussion.
26. cf. esp. Stevens, *op. cit.*, *passim.*
27. Stevens, *op. cit.*, *passim*; E. Birley, *Roman Britain and the Roman Army* (1953), 28f. argues that "there are strong chronological reasons for equating the *expeditio Britannica* mentioned in the careers of two equestrian officers . . . [*ILS* 2726, 2735] . . . with one *circa* 130, rather than with that which reached its triumphant conclusion in 119".
28. Numerous inscriptions give details of this man's career. Cf. E. Groag in *R.E.*, xv (1932) 1836ff. for detailed discussion. The consulate, formerly undated, is now known to belong to the end of A.D. 139 (*CIL* XVI 175).
29. This is revealed by *ILS* 1029, showing the elder Natalis governor of the province under both Trajan and Hadrian. Cf. Syme, *op. cit.*, 602, for 'Spanish magnates' at Tibur. On Hadrian's tribunates cf. *ILS* 308 and R. Syme, 'Hadrian in Mœsia', *Arheološki Vestnik*, xix (1968), 101ff.
30. *ILS* 1029.
31. B. E. Thomasson, *Die Statthalter der römischen Provincen Nord-Afrikas von Augustus bis Diokletian* (1960), i, 58ff.; ii, 62f.

32. B. E. Thomasson, *op. cit.*, i, 36ff.; ii, 62f.
33. *FC*, 32.
34. cf. n. 6 above.
35. *Sylloge Inscriptionum Graecarum* II^3 no. 840 (Olympia).
36. Dio 69. 13. 2.
37. cf. E. Ritterling, 'Zu zwei griechischer Inschriften römischer Verwaltungsbeamten', *Jahreshefte des österreichischen archäol. Instituts*, x (1907), 299ff. The lists in his nn. 18–19 could now be emended and lengthened.
38. E. Birley, *op. cit.* (see n. 2 above), 5f. is right in principle, but his statement that 'Es gibt keine Beweise . . . dass der Statthalter irgendeine Mitbestimmungsrecht bei der Ernennung der Legionslegaten hatte' is a little too extreme, cf. next note.
39. Annius Vinicianus, son-in-law of Corbulo, commanded V Macedonica in the latter's army (before he had even entered the Senate). Dio lxii.23.6 explains that it was because of Nero's great trust in Corbulo; cf. also Tacitus, *Ann.* xv, 28. – Titus commanded XV Apollinaris under his father, Suetonius *D. Vesp.* iv, 6. Other possible cases are: the younger Q. Blaesus under his father in Africa in 22 (Tacitus *Ann.* iii, 74); Q. Lollianus Plautius Avitus (*cos. c.* 209), probably legate of VII Gemina while his father Gentianus was governing Tarraconensis (G. Alföldy, *Fasti Hisp.* [cf. n. 16], 94f.); and – most improbably – the younger Pomponius Bassus in Moesia under his father (which depends on an unlikely interpretation of Dio lxxviii.21.3).
40. E. Groag (*loc. cit.* in n. 28) conjectured that Natalis lost Hadrian's favour since he was not *candidatus* as praetor – and the conjecture was made on the assumption that the consulate was some years earlier than 139 (n. 28): yet this is misconceived, for the man was probably praetor in A.D. 127 and hence consul at 42, *suo anno.*
41. The career is supplied by *ILS* 1101 (Tibur). Cf. *FC*, 41, for the consular date.
42. W. Kubitschek, *Imperium Romanum tributim discriptum* (1889), 270f., lists over 50 communities in the Spanish provinces enrolled in Galeria, against only 10 elsewhere.
43. cf. n. 6 above.
44. cf. A. R. Birley, *op. cit.* (see n. 9 above), 71.
45. cf. for example the Minicii Natales (p. 84f., above), consuls in 106 and 139; and the Ceionii Commodi (*PIR*^{2}, C 603–5), consuls in 78, 106, 136. Many other cases may be found in *FC*.
46. cf. A. R. Birley, *op. cit.* (see n. 9 above), 68ff.: no other second-century governor is known to have governed Britain as his first consular province.
47. E. Groag, 'Zum Konsulat in der Kaiserzeit', *Wiener Studien*, xlvii (1929), 143ff.
48. Lucian, *Alexander vel Pseudomantis*, 30ff. It should be emphasized that Lucian's remarks about Rutilianus' age are too vague to assist precise dating. E. Groag's still useful article in *R.E.*, xvi (1933), 528f. must be revised in the light of new evidence for the date of the consulate (*FC*, 41).
49. *RIB* 2101–3 (Croy Hill), 2185 (nr. Kirkintilloch), 2194 (nr. Balmuildy), 2196 (nr. Castlehill), 2200 (nr. Duntocher), 2205 (nr. Old Kilpatrick); also 2146, 2148 (on which cf. also n. 69 below) and 2151 (all from Castlecary); 2160 (Croy Hill); *JRS*, liv (1964), 178 no. 7 (Westerwood).
50. *RIB* 1120, 1122, 1125, 1130–2, 1137, 1159–62, 1175, 1190 all show the Legion at Corbridge, either in the Antonine period or undated. 1163 seems to date to A.D. 197 or later: *sub c*[*ura Viri*] *Lup*[*i v.c. cos.*].
51. *RIB* 1388–9 (the latter dated *Ter. et Sac. cos* [158]).
52. *RIB* 283, 1132, 2110 (the latter dated 158). Note also 1322 (Newcastle), recording reinforcements from the Germanies for all three legions.

53. *RIB* 2034: *Fl(avius)* rather than *Fl[avius]* might have been read here.
54. *PIR*², J 848.
55. cf. n. 54, above, and G. Alföldy, *Fasti Hisp.* (see n. 16 above), 86f. and his n. 92.
56. *S.H.A. M. Antoninus*, viii, 8.
57. *RIB* 589 (Ribchester), ?793 (Hardknott), 1137 (Corbridge), 1149 (*ibid.*, from 163), 1702 (Chesterholm), 1809 (Carvoran); cf. 1792.
58. *RIC* M. Aurelius and L. Verus no. 443; H. Mattingly, *Coins of the Roman Empire in the British Museum*, iv (1940), M. Aurelius and L. Verus nos. 500–1.
59. R. Syme, *The Roman Revolution* (1939), 223ff.
60. E. Ritterling, *R.E.*, xii (1925), 1592; cf. A. Birley, *Marcus Aurelius* (1966), 172ff.
61. G. Askew, *The Coinage of Roman Britain* (1951), 15.
62. Dio lxxi.16.2.
63. cf. A. Birley, *Marcus Aurelius* (1966), 260.
64. B. R. Hartley, 'Some problems of the Roman occupation of the Pennines', *Northern History*, i (1966), 14f.
65. cf. A. R. Birley, 'Roman frontier policy in the reign of M. Aurelius', *Proceedings of the 7th International Congress of Roman Frontier Studies 1967* (forthcoming).
66. See now F. Grosso, *La Lotta politica al tempo di Commodo* (1964), 45ff.
67. Dio lxxviii.8. 1–2. cf. A. R. Birley, *Epigr. Stud.*, iv (1967), 75, 100f.
68. H. Mattingly, *Coins of the Roman Empire in the British Museum*, iv (1940), *Commodus* no. 139, etc.
69. cf. n. 65, above. An altar at Castlecary (*RIB* 2148) could well belong to the 180s: the dedicators are *milites leg. VI Victricis pie f. . . . cives Italici et Norici*. J. C. Mann, 'The raising of new legions during the Principate', *Hermes*, xci (1963), 487f., has pointed out that although Italians to some extent, as well as Noricans, continued to serve in the legions at all times (and thus that the stone could belong to the 140s or 150s), circumstantial evidence favours a later date. The Legions II and III Italicae were formed in Italy *c.* 165 and served thereafter in M. Aurelius' Danubian wars, after which, from 180, II Italica was based permanently in Noricum. The likeliest origin of the dedicators of *RIB* 2148 is a draft from II Italica – but such a draft could hardly have been spared until after the Marcomannic wars; while the British disaster of *c.* 181 would be an obvious occasion for such reinforcements being needed.
70. On Perennis' administration cf. now F. Grosso, *op. cit.*, 164ff.
71. Dio lxxii.9.2a = *Exc. Vaticana* 122. F. Grosso, *op. cit.*, 11ff., 452ff. argues that this passage must be placed later, in the context of Pertinax' governorship; but his arguments are *a priori*. He identifies Priscus with the *cos. suff.* 192 (449f., etc.), but this is far from certain, the *cognomen* being extremely common.
72. Dio lxxii.12.2² – 4.
73. Herodian i.9.
74. *S.H.A. Commodus* vi, 2.
75. *ibid.*, viii, 4.
76. Dio lxxii.10.1–12.5 on the domination of Cleander; lxxii.8.6 refers to the trial of Marcellus. F. Grosso, *op. cit.*, 183ff. rightly emphasizes that neglected passage, but gives no valid reason for placing Marcellus' recall in late 184, as he does: better to date the fall of Marcellus after Perennis' death.
77. Dio lxxii.9.2²; 73.4.1 (the 'semi-exile' is not mentioned by Dio).
78. *S.H.A. Pertinax* iii, 3, 5–10. It would not be out of place to suggest here that the undated dedication to *Disciplina* found at Bertha might belong to this time: *J.R.S.*, xlix (1959), 136f., no. 6 (*Discipulinae Augusti* – 'second century').

79. Dio lxxii.9.3.
80. H.-G. Pflaum, *op. cit.*, no. 196. F. Grosso, *op. cit.*, 176ff. rejects Pflaum's dating, which, it must be admitted, cannot be regarded as absolutely cast-iron. However, it is an acceptable hypothesis, and Grosso's counter-arguments are hardly valid (cf. also n. 82, below). Castus was *[pr]aeff. leg. VI Victricis, duci legg. [?duaru]m Britanicimiarum (sic) adversus Arm[oricano]s*. The lettering is of excellent quality (autopsy), which would support Pflaum's dating, against the third-century date favoured by Grosso, following Ritterling in *R.E.*, xii (1925), col. 1610.
81. Herodian i, 10.
82. In other words, one may suppose that the ex-legates were by now in Italy (or Gaul) and incited the legionaries to their action from there – this weakens an argument of Grosso, *op. cit.*, 179f.
83. cf. G. Alföldy, 'Septimius Severus und der Senat', *Bonner Jahrbücher*, clxviii (1968), 118.
84. Herodian iii, 7; Dio lxxv.7.1–8; *S.H.A. Severus* xi, 6–9, etc.
85. E. Birley, 'The Roman Inscriptions of York', *Y.A.J.*, xli (1966), 728 draws attention to *RIB* 653 (York) for signs of this in VI Victrix; also in the Sixth, *J.R.S.*, lii (1962), 194, no. 21, a man from Hippo Regius. Cf. also n. 92, below.
86. J. C. Mann and M. G. Jarrett, 'The division of Britain', *J.R.S.*, lvii (1967), 61ff., differing from A. J. Graham in his article of the same title, *ibid.*, lvi (1966), 92ff. At this point mention should be made of three further legionary legates: Claudius Hieronymianus, Q. Antonius Isauricus, and Gran . . . Grattius . . . Geminius cet. None of the three can be precisely dated, but the second and third probably both belong in the period 122–*c.* 150 (cf. *PIR*², A 840–1 with *FC*, 40; G 221). But Hieronymianus might on several grounds be assignable to the Severan period, cf. E. Birley, *op. cit.* (see n. 85 above), 729f.; at any rate, he can hardly be earlier than the late 180s and early 190s (cf. also *PIR*², C 888). E. Birley also suggests, 727f. that Isauricus might be a Severan legate.
87. Note *RIB* 1163 for the Legion apparently building at Corbridge under Virius Lupus.
88. M. G. Jarrett, 'Septimius Severus and the defences of York', *Y.A.J.*, xli (1966), 516ff. rightly emphasizes the changes in policy. I cannot follow him, either here, or in his paper 'Aktuelle Probleme der Hadriansmauer', *Germania*, xlv (1967), 96ff. when he dismisses the idea that A.D. 197 marked the end of Hadrian's Wall period I (or, some might prefer to call it, Ib – or Ic). Similarly, B. R. Hartley, *op. cit.*, 18ff., questions this date. I still find it preferable to any alternative; and, from what has been already said, it will be obvious that I favour this date for the end of Antonine Wall period II also. One explanation why forts on Hadrian's Wall were (apparently) not being rebuilt until the governorship of Senecio (at earliest in 205) may surely be that Severus' intention, during the years 197–205, may have been to re-occupy the Antonine Wall (which may have seemed excessively difficult to those on the spot).
89. *J.R.S.*, lviii (1968), 182 is unequivocal.
90. Dio lxxvi.10.6; *RIB* 1337 (Benwell).
91. cf. R. E. Birley, 'Excavation of the Roman fortress at Carpow, 1961–2', *P.S.A.S.*, xcvi (1962–3), 184ff.; further work is reported in *J.R.S.*, lv (1965), 208f.; lvi (1966), 199; lvii (1967), 175; lviii (1968), 177f.
92. *J.R.S.*, liii (1963), 164, no. 29 (b). Attention should also be drawn to an inscription from Zattara in Numidia, *CIL* VIII 5180 + 17266 = *Inscriptions Latines de l' Algérie*, i (1923), 539.1: *D.M.S./T. Flavius In/genuus m(issus) h(onesta)/*[4]*m(issione) ex leg. VI Vi./B E B fidelis p/rovincie Br/itannie infer/ioris vixit a/nnos LXI/Julia Quinta/pia vix. annis LX.* Lines 3–4 have been variously restored: *VI Vi[ct]/ṛ pịạ fidelis* (*CIL* VIII 5180); *VI Vi(ctricis)/pie fidelis* (*CIL* VIII 17266); *VI Vi(ctrice)/[pia?] fideli⟨s⟩* (*ILAlg.*). It might

be better to read: *VI Vi(ctricis)/Br(itannicae) pie fidelis* (the genitive being of course a solecism). This would then be an African veteran (perhaps put into VI Victrix in A.D. 197) retiring to his native land, probably soon after 211 – before the title *Britannica* had been dropped, in favour of others (below, n. 93). One may note also the inscription published by M. Torelli, 'Contributi al supplemento del *CIL* IX', *Rendiconti dell' Accademia Nazionale dei Lincei*, 8th ser. xxiv (1969), 23f. (Luceria): *D.M. / Aur. Cupito cen. leg. VI vitri(cis)* [*sic*] */ Aur. Ursula coniux*, etc. Torelli reasonably dates this post-212 on account of the abbreviation *Aur(elius, -elia)*, and suggests that this ex-centurion of the Sixth and another man, veteran of the Second (Augusta: *ibid.*, 24f.) may have been settled in Apulia after the *expeditio Britannica*, by Caracalla. Further discussion would be inappropriate here, but is obviously called for.

93. *CIL* XIII 2616 (Cabillonum) calls the Legion *Antoniniana*; cf. R.C.H.M., *York* 114b for *Severiana* and *Gordiana*.

94. cf. A. R. Birley, 'The origins of Gordian I', *Britain and Rome*, ed. M. G. Jarrett and B. Dobson (1966), 59f.; E. Birley, 'Troops from the Two Germanies in Roman Britain', *Epigraphische Studien*, iv (1967), 103ff. discusses the implications of a dedication supervised by a centurion of II Augusta in charge of *vexil(lationum) leg. VI V. et exer. G(ermaniae) utriusque* at Piercebridge.

95. A. R. Birley, 'The Roman Governors of Britain', *Epigraphische Studien*, iv (1967), 87–92.

96. cf. *Not. Dig.* (*Occ.*) xl, 18: *praefectus legionis sextae.*

97. *RIB* 583 (Ribchester) may suffice as an example. Dr G. Alföldy kindly informs me that he reads lines 11–16 of this stone (a dedication by a centurion of the Sixth) differently, line 11 describing the man as *praep. et pr.* (not *praep. n(umeri) et r(egionis)*), and ll. 13–16 providing a consular date (1 September 241). The centurion T. Floridius Natalis, *praep. n. et regi*[*onis*] (legion not named) in *RIB* 587 (*ibid.*) shows, however, that the man in no. 583 was nonetheless a *centurio regionarius*, 'District Officer'.

98. cf. R.C.H.M., *York*, 133b–134a (no. 144) and pl. 65. The emblem marks VI Victrix as the creation of Caesar, one of whose symbols was the bull, cf. H. M. D. Parker, *The Roman Legions* (1928), 105, 263, 267.

99. Note *CIL* XIII 3162 (Vieux) = H. G. Pflaum, *Le Marbre de Thorigny* (1948). Front face, lines 14–18, reads: *Is Solemnis / amicus Tib. Claud. Paulini leg. Aug. pro pr. pro/ vinciae Lugd. et cliens, cui postea /* [*l*]*eg. Aug. p. p. in Brit. ad legionem sext*[*am*] */ adsedit* . . . It would not have been surprising if York had become known as *Legio* (as did León, garrison-town of VII Gemina).

R. M. BUTLER

The defences of the fourth-century fortress at York

During the late third or fourth century the defences of the ancient legionary fortress of Eburacum were substantially rebuilt. The fortress, at first of timber under Cerialis and Agricola, rebuilt in stone under Trajan in A.D. 107–8, and again strengthened by Septimius Severus or Caracalla in *c.* 200, was of the usual rectangular plan, 50 acres in area, and facing south-west towards the Ouse and the *colonia* on the opposite bank. The reconstruction considered here not only involved the defences, but extended to the few internal buildings so far excavated, including the impressive headquarters, the fallen columns of which were recently and unexpectedly found below the Minster in surprisingly complete condition. The fortress defences were modified on all sides but the north-east, and the alterations are known to extend around the *praetentura* from Bootham Bar, which stands on the site of the *porta principalis dextra*, to the site of the opposite gateway in King's Square.

The curtain wall was rebuilt above the foundations but remained much the same height and width as its Severan predecessor: it is estimated to have been 21ft high and 5ft thick as against 18ft and 5¾ft. One obvious difference in the external appearance of this rebuilt wall, still, as before, constructed of white magnesian limestone, was the tile cornice below the parapet and the wide band of tiles 7–8ft above the ground, which replaced the stone plinth and cornice of the earlier wall. Internally the earth rampart, incorporating the remains of earlier ramparts, was slightly higher than before, but the rampart walk appears to have been about 6ft below the wall walk.

The gates are little known. The north-west gate was of monumental character with large blocks of gritstone used in its construction. Towers 30ft square, projecting only 2ft outside the wall, flanked a central carriageway with a narrower pedestrian passage on either side, the whole being some 90ft wide. The south-west gate was probably built on the footings of the Trajanic gatehouse in which rectangular guard-rooms flanked twin passageways each 13ft wide, but with external projecting towers added to the guard-rooms. Details of the other gates are unknown, though the south-east gate probably remained standing long enough to form the nucleus of the palace of the Danish Kings of York, of which the site is recalled by the name of King's Square.

The interval towers on the north-west side, and probably also on the south-east side, although not certainly located, were, as on the north-east with its Severan wall, internal and rectangular, 15–19ft across. On the south-west side, however, six new polygonal towers were built, three on each side of the *porta praetoria*, projecting outside the curtain wall as semi-decagons 32ft in diameter, and internally with rectangular rooms 31 by 42ft. These towers were 125–130ft apart, and at the west and south angles were larger towers with ten sides outside the walls, 48½ft in diameter, and rectangular internal blocks, 44 by 35ft, sub-divided into four rooms. All but one of the interval towers have been seen in excavations, two of them when the Davygate Centre was being built between Davygate and New Street in 1967. The west angle tower, called the Multangular Tower since 1683, but known in the Middle Ages as Ellerondyng, still stands to a height of 19ft, continued upwards for a further 11ft by a wall of *c.* 1300 with an arrow-slit in each face. The remains of Roman windows with sills 11ft above the present ground level are preserved in the two faces of the tower nearest the fortress wall. It is uncertain whether these polygonal towers had open crenellated parapets or conical roofs, such as appear on coins and in illustrations to the Notitia, but, since the internal rooms must have been roofed, the latter arrangement seems more likely and would also protect artillery on the upper floors.

In the post-Roman period these defences remained substantially intact on the north-west and north-east. A gap caused by a collapse or by enemy action north-east of the Multangular Tower was filled by a rectangular, internal, vaulted, stone tower, which, together with the Roman walls, still standing 15–16ft high, was buried in the ninth-century earth rampart on which the thirteenth-century city walls were built. On the other sides the city extended beyond the fortress in the Viking period and its defences were nearer the rivers.

These new defences are usually considered, as in R.C.H.M., *York*, to have been built under Constantius I, Caesar and later Augustus in the West, and in control of Britain from A.D. 296 until his death at York in July, 306. However, some doubts have been expressed on a date for this restoration of *c.* A.D. 300.[1] An argument against the acceptance of such a date as certain is the discovery during excavations in Davygate of a coin of Delmatius issued between 335 and 337 together with pottery up to the mid-fourth century; this material was in a layer of yellow clay on top of the rampart.[2] These finds may be variously interpreted as meaning that the latest period of the rampart, and so perhaps of the stone wall and towers, is mid-fourth century; or that an addition to the rampart was made here after 335; or that this is an initial deposit of the Danish bank which eventually covered the Roman wall and, of course, includes pottery and coins of all dates in the Roman period, but especially of the later Empire, since it was scooped up from a ground surface covered with Roman rubbish.

It is the purpose of this article to consider some of the affinities of the rebuilt defences and to estimate their place in the developing science of late Roman military architecture. In particular the occurrence and date elsewhere of the most unusual feature of these defences – the polygonal towers – may indicate that one period in the fourth century is more probable for their construction than another. Comparison with other sites may help in assessing the theory that the last important reconstruction of the fortress of Eburacum was really some 40–50 years later than the date usually assigned to it.

Roman forts and fortresses until the reign of Diocletian were usually rectangular in plan, surrounded by stone walls about 5ft thick backed by broad earth ramparts, and with the towers at the gates, angles, and at regular intervals between them, projecting only internally and normally square or rectangular. During the following century, however, new forts and reconstructions of old ones were not only less regular (although rectangular or square plans were still frequently followed), but had thicker and loftier walls, built without an internal rampart, and towers, which, whether square, rectangular, round, semi-circular, or exceptionally polygonal, almost invariably projected externally. This use of projecting towers, an innovation in the architecture of the Roman army, was presumably borrowed from the fortifications around cities, which for centuries had employed projecting towers.

The new walls built to protect the former open cities of Gaul, ravaged in the third-century invasions,[3] had all the features seen in the forts of Diocletian and his successors, although the bases of their massive walls were usually constructed to a height of several feet with tombstones, column drums, friezes and blocks of stone salvaged from the destroyed buildings and desecrated cemeteries. This feature does occur to a limited extent in some forts, but on military sites such material was not usually available in quite the same profusion.[4] The walls of Rome, built by Aurelian in A.D. 271–3, show over a circuit of several miles not only the projecting towers, usually rectangular but semi-circular at the main gates, but the incorporation of earlier monuments and the absence of an internal rampart.[5] They are, however, faced with tiles, a treatment which is unusual in the West, although found at Toulouse. Later work on Rome's defences, under

Maxentius and Honorius, increased the height of the curtain and strengthened the formidable gates.

In Britain the city walls were generally added in the second or third century to broad earth ramparts which had once supported or backed a timber palisade.[6] Towers were usually internal, except at the gateways, until the addition during the fourth century of externally projecting towers, found for example at Brough, Great Casterton, Chichester and London. This modernization, ascribed by Corder to the middle of the century, may perhaps result from the reorganization under Count Theodosius 20 years later.[7] Fort design in Britain had remained conservative: few had required rebuilding since the days of Severus, since the province – or rather two provinces – had enjoyed comparative peace.

In the south of Britain, however, forts of the type soon to be the norm were built under Carausius (287–93) at Portchester and Richborough. Others were erected at the same time or later along this Saxon Shore at Burgh Castle, Walton Castle, Lympne and Pevensey. Carausius's new forts were probably erected to guard harbours and landing places, not so much against Saxon and Frisian pirates, as against the far more powerful forces of the central Empire. When in 296 Constantius and his praetorian prefect, Asclepiodotus, invaded Britain to reunite it to the rest of the Empire, Allectus moved troops from the northern frontier to this threatened coast and rebel Britons took the opportunity of attacking, severely damaging many northern forts, such as Birdoswald and Risingham. This destruction extended to Chester and is the best explanation for the widespread rebuilding required at York – if it is assigned to Constantius – although direct evidence of the burning of buildings within the fortress is still lacking.

Constantius rebuilt these damaged forts and founded new ones of the old type at Piercebridge and Newton Kyme. At Chester, although tombstones were used in considerable numbers to repair the north wall of the fortress, no projecting towers are known. The coastal fort of Cardiff, at first designed with rounded angles, but modified during its erection, as was Burgh Castle, and with projecting polygonal towers is probably to be assigned to this period.

Of the two characteristics which most distinguish the new defences at York from those which they replaced, the use of tile bonding levelling courses and the addition of projecting towers, the first feature is so common as to be of little use in dating. Many earlier city walls in Britain, such as Caister-by-Norwich, Colchester, London and Silchester, had such tile courses; on the Continent the Trajanic walls of the legionary fortress of Strasbourg were similarly decorated.[8] Virtually every city wall erected in Gaul after 270 has tile courses as a prominent feature – good examples are Périgueux and Le Mans.[9] Indeed they occur just as frequently in the walls of Salonica of *c.* 380[10] and on the great land walls of

Constantinople built soon after Britain had been abandoned by the imperial government.[11]

The projecting towers are again a common feature, being well-nigh universal on city walls built after A.D. 270 and fort defences of after 300. However, the polygonal plan of those at York is rarely used and parallels are few and far between. Earlier examples on gateways are at Turin, Avenches and Windisch.[12] A polygonal tower on the Claudian walls of Cologne probably belongs, as do the gates of Avenches and Windisch, to a rebuilding under Gallienus.[13] In Britain the Severan reconstruction of the south gateway of Habitancum (Risingham) included projecting polygonal towers of fine masonry, each with eight faces. The eastern of these was rebuilt under Constantius, when the number of sides was reduced to six, giving a plan closely resembling that of the interval towers at Eburacum.[14] At the nearby fort of Bremenium (High Rochester), however, the west gate, added during the contemporary reconstruction, had similar moulded imposts but internal rectangular towers.[15]

There are few parallels for such towers in the period around A.D. 300. On the Continent the nearest examples are in Switzerland, in the Diocletianic province of Sequania. The fort of Tasgaetium (Burg bei Stein am Rhein or Eschenz) was 296ft square and 2 acres in area with walls 9¼ft thick.[16] The angle towers were circular and solid, 25ft in diameter, but the other towers, of which there were two on each side, projected externally as pentagons and internally as rectangles, although standing on semi-circular bases. They were 30ft across and had internal rooms reached by doorways in the rear walls. The main gate was in the centre of the south-west wall and was flanked by two hollow pentagonal bastions. There were also simple arches in the centre of the north-west and south-east sides and a postern with a crooked passage west of the south angle tower. An inscription (*CIL* XIII 5256) records the erection of the fort in 294 by Diocletian and Maximian. A similar inscription (*CIL* XIII 5249) proves that the fort at Vitudurum (Oberwinterthur) about 20 miles to the south-south-west was built at the same time, yet it was polygonal in plan and the towers were semi-circular and solid.

Montagny-Chancy,[17] west of Geneva, is a little-known fort beside the Rhône guarding the road to Lyons. It consists of two enclosures, of which the earlier, to the north, is anvil-shaped 206 by 158ft, with walls 8–11ft thick. There were four solid towers, those on the north being 33ft square, but the south pair being hexagonal, 30ft across. Between these south bastions was a narrow gate, the only entrance. This fort, which seems to have been built in the reign of Diocletian on the site of a first-century villa, was extended to the south, probably under Valentinian I, when a trapezoidal fortification was added. This enclosure measured

492 by 296ft and brought the total area to 2¾ acres. Its walls were 10ft thick and there were three solid hexagonal towers, 28ft across, at the angles.

Castrum Rauracense (Kaiseraugst)[18] was built beside the Rhine below the city of Augusta Raurica, which had been ruined in the third-century invasions. Its defences enclosed a distorted rectangle, 9½ acres in area, measuring 862 by 558ft. The wall, 10–13ft thick, stands on deep foundations of re-used material, has a double plinth at the base, and included tiles with the stamp of Legio I Martia, a newly recruited regiment. The towers were solid and pentagonal, 23ft wide, projecting 10ft in front of the wall and 6in inside it. There were six on the south wall and probably four or five on each of the other known walls (the north one has been eroded by the river), apart from the slightly smaller angle towers, one of which was apparently hollow above the base. The gates were flanked by solid rectangular towers projecting equally on both sides of the curtain, and there were at least five posterns near the angles. Among the internal buildings which have been identified are a bath-house, a barrack-block, and a basilican church. A splendid hoard of late Roman silver found in the fortress is thought to have been buried in *c.* 360. Kaiseraugst is usually ascribed to Diocletian, built for the newly formed Martian Legion.[19] As at Tasgaetium this fortress guarded a crossing of the Rhine; on the opposite bank at Wyhlen[20] was a small fort with round towers, much damaged by floods, recalling by its position the bridgehead forts of Deutz opposite Cologne, built by Constantine I in 310, and Kastell opposite Mainz.

The fortlet of Turicum on the Lindenhof hill in Zurich[21] had polygonal bases to six of its ten towers, but above the bases these were semi-circular and hollow, 20ft in diameter, so that these towers are not really comparable to those of York. It was a distorted rectangle in plan, 28 by 196ft with walls 10ft thick and two gates, probably built by Valentinian I.

In Britain the only known examples of polygonal towers other than at Risingham and York occur at Cardiff and at the civil towns of Caerwent and Cirencester.[22] At these three sites the projecting towers resemble most closely in shape those of Tasgaetium and are pentagonal, or perhaps more correctly semi-octagonal. The fort at Cardiff,[23] on low ground to the west of the River Taff with the sea to the south, stood on a site occupied in the first century. Its walls enclosed a rectangle measuring 650 by 600ft and 8½ acres in extent, now the outer bailey of the medieval castle. The wall was 8–10ft thick and over 16ft high, faced with ashlar and with occasional bonding courses of flat slabs. There was a contemporary internal rampart. The fort had 18 towers, including those at the gateways and angles, all being solid at the base except for the gate towers and one other, and averaging 18ft in diameter. They projected 9ft from the curtain wall, but were not bonded into it, having semi-circular bases of varying height. The north gateway had a passage 10ft wide with double gates, and its hollow towers had doorways 3ft wide in the rear walls; the south gate, connected to it by a street, was presumably similar. The north gate and the north and east walls have been restored to their supposed full height and original appearance. There is no certain dating for this fort, other than a *terminus post quem* from coin finds of *c.* 175, but the similarities to distant Tasgaetium, a quarter of the size of Cardiff fort, suggest a similar date.

At Caerwent[24] hollow towers were added to the earlier walls; six are known on the south and two on the north. They were set on semi-circular plinths with foundations deeper than those of the curtain wall, and were carefully faced with masonry matching that of the wall. No two are the same size, but the average diameter is 17ft and the average wall thickness is 4ft. One had a postern doorway and another, still standing 12ft high, shows traces of two wooden floors, which can only have been reached from above. At a later date they were filled with earth and the south gate of the town was blocked. One tower, and so presumably the whole series, was built after a coin of A.D. 333–5 had been lost: they are assigned to a date of 330–40 as "poor copies of those of the Saxon Shore fort at Cardiff".[25]

The appearance of the gateways of Eburacum can only be guessed at, but it is possible that the *porta praetoria* as rebuilt or extended would have looked as imposing as the Porta Nigra at Trier, variously identified as the work of Severus or of Constantine, or as the less well preserved north gate at Castra Regina, the fortress of Legio III Italica, Ratisbon or Regensburg on the Danube. The best parallel in the neighbouring provinces of the Empire for the modernization of a legionary fortress is at Strasbourg.[26] There the Trajanic wall of Argentoratum, the headquarters since A.D. 70 of Legio VIII Augusta and set between branches of the River Ill, was thickened by 9ft under Valentinian I or Julian, and projecting towers were added. The new wall, built on foundations of re-used material and with a plinth of ashlar blocks at the base, was of rubble concrete, laced with timber and faced with small masonry in which patterning occurred. The towers were solid and semi-circular, 22½ft in diameter, and projecting 11½ft. Beams one foot square ran through the concrete core to bond the towers with the curtain wall. There were probably 19 of these towers on the north, 12 on both the east and west and six on the south, where nine of the internal rectangular towers of the earlier walls were still used. The towers were spaced about 80ft apart. The angle towers were circular, 65ft in diameter. The north-west gate had a twin-arched passage, 32ft wide, flanked by solid rectangular towers projecting on both sides of the wall, each one being 20ft wide and 21ft deep; the other three gates appear to have been similar. A ditch 22¼ft wide and 6½ft deep surrounded the fortress 13¼ft from the walls. The use of timber in the core of the towers is parallelled in Britain at Pevensey and Richborough, where, as on the city walls of Le Mans and Sens, patterns made from different coloured stones also occur.

The polygonal-shaped tower has some advantages over other types as an artillery platform, and may have first been designed for that purpose in *c.* 280 B.C.[27] However, this plan seldom seems to have been preferred by Greek and Roman engineers to the rounded or semi-circular plan. When the great inner land walls of Constantinople were built in the early fifth century, 40ft high and 15½ft thick, they were provided with rectangular towers, but among these are 19 polygonal examples. Most of these are octagonal with one side attached to the curtain: they are probably the latest parts of the original work on the wall, or were rebuilt after the earthquake of 447. At Spalato Diocletian's palace, built when Constantius was ruling Britain, and much the same size as the fort at Cardiff, had square towers at the angles, six rectangular interval towers, but octagonal bastions flanking the three landward gates. Its massive scale, with walls 50–70ft high and lofty internal temples, halls and courts, make any comparison with York misleading; the northern fortress, although six times the size, must have looked squat when compared with the Dalmatian palace. Another contemporary example of polygonal towers flanking a gateway is at Barcelona.[28] There all but one of the four gates had this type of tower and the interval towers, over 70 in number and very closely spaced, were rectangular. The walls of this city, surrounding a polygonal area of about 30 acres, otherwise resembled in thickness and construction, including the footings of re-used blocks, the city walls of Gaul.

This brief survey of late Roman parallels for the polygonal towers of York shows that this type of tower is unusual anywhere. The rarity of the type must make the student suspect that a single designer or unit with a preference for this plan was responsible not only for the rebuilt defences of Eburacum, but also for the forts of Tasgaetium, Castrum Rauracense, Montagny-Chancy and Cardiff. The added bastions at Caerwent were presumably copied from those of Cardiff when British cities generally were being encouraged or ordered to bring their walls up to date by the addition of projecting towers for artillery. Although this shape of tower was first devised by Hellenistic architects in the third century B.C. and used at Paestum and Asine, it was never popular. In the late third century A.D. a military architect working for Constantius designed Tasgaetium and nearby forts with such towers. It seems likely that he, his pupils, or his unit was brought to Britain by Constantius and employed at York, Cardiff and Risingham. A later date for the use of this feature seems unlikely, since the forts

1a. Cowlam, 1969. Barrow C, showing the square-plan ditch (2-metre scale).

1b. Aerial photograph of the south part of the Burton Fleming cemetery, showing square barrow ditches, some of the central graves, and the boundary ditch. Looking north-west (cf. fig. 1).
(Photo: J. K. S. St Joseph. Copyright reserved, Cambridge University)

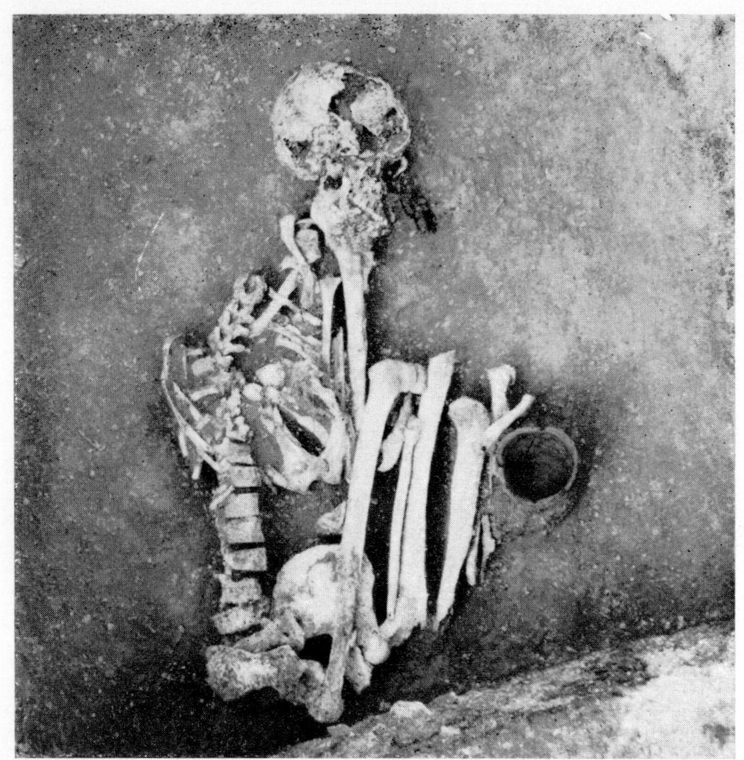

2a. Burton Fleming. A contracted inhumation, with iron brooch (in front of the face), pot, and pig bone (by the legs).

2b. Burton Fleming. A partly excavated grave (skull visible), showing the outline of a rectangular coffin (30-cm scale).

3a. Burton Fleming, 1969. Graves surrounded by square barrow ditches (crossed by medieval ridge-and-furrow) (2-metre scales).

3b. Burton Fleming, 1969. Graves and barrow ditches (crossed by medieval ridge-and-furrow) (2-metre scale).

4a. Garton Slack. Chalk figurine, 4in. high.

4b. Garton Slack. Detail of sword on figure in 4a.

4c. Garton Slack. Chalk figurine, 5in. high. (The head has been attached for display purposes: it does not belong to this body.)

4d. Garton Slack. Chalk model of shield, 5½in. high.

5. Fremington Hagg Hoard. Objects in the British Museum. (From top left: nos. 5, 4, 3, 1 and 2.)
(By courtesy of the Trustees of the British Museum)

6. Aerial photograph of the main part of the walled enclosure at Catterick. (*Photo: J. K. S. St Joseph. Crown copyright*)

7. Aerial photograph of the west part of the walled enclosure at Catterick, showing the re-entrant angle. (*Photo: J. K. S. St Joseph. Crown copyright*)

8. York. Crouched and extended burials in Trentholme Drive cemetery, looking west. (*Photo: L. P. Wenham*)

built by Constantine I at Deutz and Haus Bürgel, and his fortlets along main roads around Trier, have circular towers. The numerous forts erected by Valentinian I along the Rhine frontier, especially in Switzerland, generally have semicircular towers, though square ones also occur.[29]

Like the use of the fan-shaped tower, found on such Danubian frontier forts as Campona and Transaquincum at the same period,[30] but with the only British examples at Ancaster and, less closely parallel, at Aldborough, the occurrence of this unusual tower plan is no doubt due to the movement across Europe of an expert or a military unit. So in the same period Jerome could move from Dalmatia to Trier and eventually settle at Bethlehem, a unit once stationed in Gaul or Spain may appear in the Notitia as part of the field army of the East, an emperor reared in Asia Minor might campaign in Gaul but die in Mesopotamia. Such mobility in the Roman army, administration and upper classes was as usual during the fourth century as it had been in the days of Hadrian or Caesar.

The reason for the strengthening in this way of the river front at York, a side less exposed to attack than the north-east, is not explained by any military need. It could hardly have been expected that raiders would sail up the Ouse to assault the main centre of Roman power in north Britain, still less that a rebellion of citizens in the *colonia* would make that side more vulnerable. The purpose of the new wall and most modern embellishments on the south-west front must surely have been to impress visitors and citizens approaching from London or Gaul with the strength, authority, and enduring nature of Roman military power, even in the most distant province. Similarly the most splendid gates of Constantinople and Salonica were on the route by which most visitors approached those cities. The Golden Gate of the capital was resplendent with marble gates and gilt inscriptions, statues of Victories, Fortunes and of the emperor. The more functional main gates of Rome were similarly stronger on the most frequented approaches and decorated with statues of the emperors.

The evidence of comparative fortifications, although inconclusive, supports the ascription of the latest defences of Roman York to Constantius I. His son might have built here a fortress more like Deutz, his grandson something more like Strasbourg, while Alzey and Boppard show the sort of work Valentinian I's architects designed. At none of these are there remains as impressive as York's Multangular Tower, still erect 16 centuries after its construction.

Notes

1. *Y.A.J.*, xli (1966), 52; xlii (1968), 162–4; M. G. Jarrett and B. Dobson (eds.), *Britain and Rome* (1965), 6.
2. *Y.A.J.*, xl (1962), 525–8.
3. *Arch. J.*, cxvi (1959), 25–50.
4. At Alzey an internal building, at Neumagen the fortlet wall, were founded on re-used altars and tombstones: *Mainzer Zeitschrift* (1933), 4ff.; W. von Massow, *Die Grabmaler von Neumagen* ii (1932), 1ff.
5. I. A. Richmond, *The City Wall of Imperial Rome* (1930).
6. *Arch. J.*, cxix (1962), 103–13.
7. *Arch. J.*, cxii (1955), 20–42; J. S. Wacher (ed.), *The Civitas Capitals of Roman Britain* (1966), 52–3.
8. R. Forrer, *Strasbourg-Argentorate*, i (1927), pls. vii, xix, figs. 50–2.
9. *Révue Historique et Archéologique du Maine*, ix (1881), 252–3; *Congrès Archéologique de France* (1927), 9ff.
10. O. Tafrali, *Topographie de Salonique* (1913).
11. F. Krischen, *Die Landmauer von Konstantinopel*, i (1938); B. Meyer-Plath and H. M. Schneider, *Die Landmauer . . .* ii (1943).
12. R. Laur-Belart, *Vindonissa, Lager und Vicus* (1935), 28–36; F. Staehelin, *Die Schweiz in römischer Zeit* (1948), 604ff.
13. *Bonner Jahrbuch*, cxxxix (1934), 64ff.; W. Zimmermann (ed.) *Kölner Untersuchungen* (1950), 4–28; *CIL* XIII, 8261.
14. *Northumberland County History*, xv (1940), 82–8; *Arch. Ael.*, 4th ser., xiii (1935), 191.
15. *ibid.* (1940), 108.
16. Staehelin, *op. cit.*, 272ff., 622.
17. *ibid.*, 307f., 612.
18. *ibid.*, 279ff., 603ff.; *J.R.S.*, lix (1969), 179n. However, all the towers may have been rectangular.
19. Römische-germanische Kommission, *Bericht*, xxxiii (1943–50), 172.
20. *Badische Fundberichte*, iii (1933–6), 150ff.
21. E. Vogt, *Der Lindenhof in Zürich* (1948), 8ff.
22. Examples are now known at Cirencester: *Britannia*, i (1970), 238–9.
23. *Arch.*, lvii (1901), 5ff.
24. *ibid.*, lxxx (1930), 25–88.
25. O. E. Craster, *Caerwent Roman City* (M.P.B.W. Guide, 1951), 7.
26. Forrer, *op. cit.*, 39–265, pl. xviiik for use of timber.
27. E. W. Marsden, *Greek and Roman Artillery* (1969), 147–50.
28. M. A. Basch, J. de C. S. Rafolo and J. C. Roca, *Carta Arqueologica de España, Barcelona* (1945), 54ff., pls. iii–vi; *Archaeology*, xiv (1961), 188–97.
29. See bibliography in *J.R.S.*, lix (1969), 182–6.
30. *Acta Archaeologica* (*Hung.*) (1952), 189–220; cf. Capidava in Roumania: G. Florescu, R. Florescu and P. Diaconu, *Capidava* (1948).

G. A. WEBSTER

A hoard of Roman military equipment from Fremington Hagg

The circumstances of this discovery are apparently not known. The hoard was found some time prior to 1833, when objects from it are first mentioned as the "ancient caparison of a horse, from the moors near Reeth", and were presented by Mr Daniel Tuke to the Yorkshire Museum.[1] Before 1852 other items were given to the Yorkshire Museum by Captain Harland. They are described in the Museum handbook of 1852 as "several specimens of silvered bronze horse-furniture, ornamented with slightly-engraved patterns. Found on Fremington Hagg, near Reeth, in Swaledale", a description repeated in subsequent editions.[2] Soon afterwards Professor Phillips wrote "at Fremington, near Reeth, many ornaments of brass inlaid with silver (the work of ingenious Gaul), apparently trappings of a horse, and belonging to Roman times, have been dug up: they are now in the Yorkshire Museum".[3] In the eighth edition of the museum handbook (1891) the exhibit is described as "a large collection of bronze articles . . . probably . . . the stock in trade of some travelling artisan".[4] Either the original bequest was augmented or the first description was too modest.

There was, however, a separation of the finds, since in 1880 some of the finer items were presented to the British Museum by A. E. W. Franks. Exactly how these came into the possession of Franks is a matter for conjecture. It is not certain that these are the only objects which may have been in the Yorkshire Museum during this period and are now to be seen elsewhere. The find-spot is also unknown. There are two hamlets, High and Low Fremington, east of Reeth, and Hagg Wood and Hagg Cottage are situated one mile east of High Fremington, some 600 yards north of the Swale. The Hagg presumably refers to the limestone scar, now known as Fremington Edge, which rises north of these places.

The composition of the hoard

The hoard consists mainly of decorated pieces of Roman cavalry horse harness, but other fragments have become associated with it. In view of the history of the collections in the Yorkshire Museum it is impossible to be certain that these other items were ever part of the original hoard. They are therefore described below, but placed in a separate section.

The main, and probably the only elements of the hoard, are pieces of cavalry harness, consisting of pendants, roundels, flat strips and studs. The most complete collection of similar items is the Doorwerth hoard,[5] now in the Rijksmuseum van Oudheden at Leiden. The pieces in that hoard, all tinned and decorated with niello, can be grouped into four categories:

1. Pendants, mostly of trifid form with the central terminal somewhat longer than the other two and slightly raised in relief. There is, however, one of oval form with a single terminal (Afb. 6).
2. Roundels, of three different sizes, generally saucer-shaped.
3. Thin flat strips with a moulded outline, some having attached domes or conical studs. Their function was to attach the pendants to the thinner traces.
4. Moulded and fretted plates from the saddle cloth (Afb. 7).

The conclusion drawn by Holwerda is that the Doorwerth hoard was lost in the Rhine during the rebellion of Civilis, *c.* A.D. 69. Pendants having a very similar relief pattern occurred at Newstead in a destruction deposit of Flavian date.[6] It is also significant that another pendant of similar design was found at Brecon in a late-first–early-second-century deposit.[7] Since pendants with raised relief do not seem to occur in pre-Flavian contexts, it seems likely that this particular pattern was not introduced until *c.* A.D. 60–70. Other examples occur at Mainz,[8] Xanten,[9] and Aislingen.[10]

The Fremington Hagg hoard is therefore most likely to be pre-Flavian and cannot be associated with the conquest of Brigantia in A.D. 71. There were, however, earlier incursions of Roman troops into this area. Tacitus records the events following the divorce of Venutius, when Cartimandua was kept on her throne by force of Roman arms, and fighting may have continued until the end of the governorship of Gallus (*Annals*, xii, 40). The circumstances of the find, although our total knowledge is at present confined to the name of the find-spot, would nevertheless seem to indicate a cache of loot taken after an engagement and hidden by a follower of Venutius, never to be recovered. It is even possible to imagine that the warrior may have been deceived by the sparkling, tinned sheen of the trappings into thinking of them as solid silver. It is difficult to conceive of this hoard being buried under Roman auspices.

Catalogue of the Hoard

Pieces in the British Museum (1–5, plate 5; figs. 9–10)

1. (B.M. Acc. no. 80, 8–2, 150) A pendant decorated with niello leaves and berries, unusual for its trifid terminals and scalloped edging round the central terminal.
2. (80, 8–2, 151) Small pendant attached to a roundel (see also no. 37 below), with niello decoration.
3. (80, 8–2, 152) A large roundel with an elaborate scheme of decoration of panels and stylized leaves.
4. (80, 8–2, 153) A small roundel, with central boss, decorated with niello leaves and berries.
5. (80, 8–2, 154) A bowl-shaped roundel with a central petal design.
6. (80, 8–2, 155) A round chape-shaped pendant (or an actual chape), pierced with two pelta openings.
7. A roundel identical to nos. 8 and 9, except that the leaves are slightly less well formed and there are four symmetrically placed loops on the back. This piece has no accession number and its provenance is not known but it is so like the others that it almost certainly belongs to this hoard (not illustrated).

Pieces in the Yorkshire Museum (figs. 11–17)

Those most probably from the original hoard

8. (Acc. no. H. 141, 17) A large saucer-shaped roundel with stylized leaf decoration and four loops on the back, two to take a strap about an inch wide, and the other two a strap of a narrow width. This is almost identical to no. 7.
9. (H. 141, 15) A large roundel of identical shape and decoration to no. 8 but with three loops for a narrow strap and an attachment for a pendant on the back (not illustrated).
10. (H. 141, 10) A roundel with leaf decoration, some of which have feathered edges with three loops and an attachment for a pendant on the back.
11. (H. 141, 11) Identical to no. 10 (not illustrated).
12. (H. 141, 19) Identical to no. 10 (not illustrated).
13. (H. 141, 9) A saucer-shaped roundel with leaves and berries in a formal cruciform pattern with two loops on the back.
14. (H. 141, 12) Identical to no. 13, except that it has four loops on the back (not illustrated).
15. (H. 141, 13) Identical to no. 13 (not illustrated).
16. (H. 141, 16) A large roundel identical to no. 3, except that the York example has four loops at the back (not illustrated).
17. (H. 141, 18) Identical to no. 16 (not illustrated).
18. (H. 141, 4) A small pendant with a central acorn terminal and a simple leaf decoration.
19. (H. 141, ?) A large oval-shaped pendant with trifid terminal and decorated with stylized niello leaves and berries.
20. (H. 141, 20) A small pendant of similar shape to no. 19, with a formal leaf pattern of decoration and with the terminal broken away.

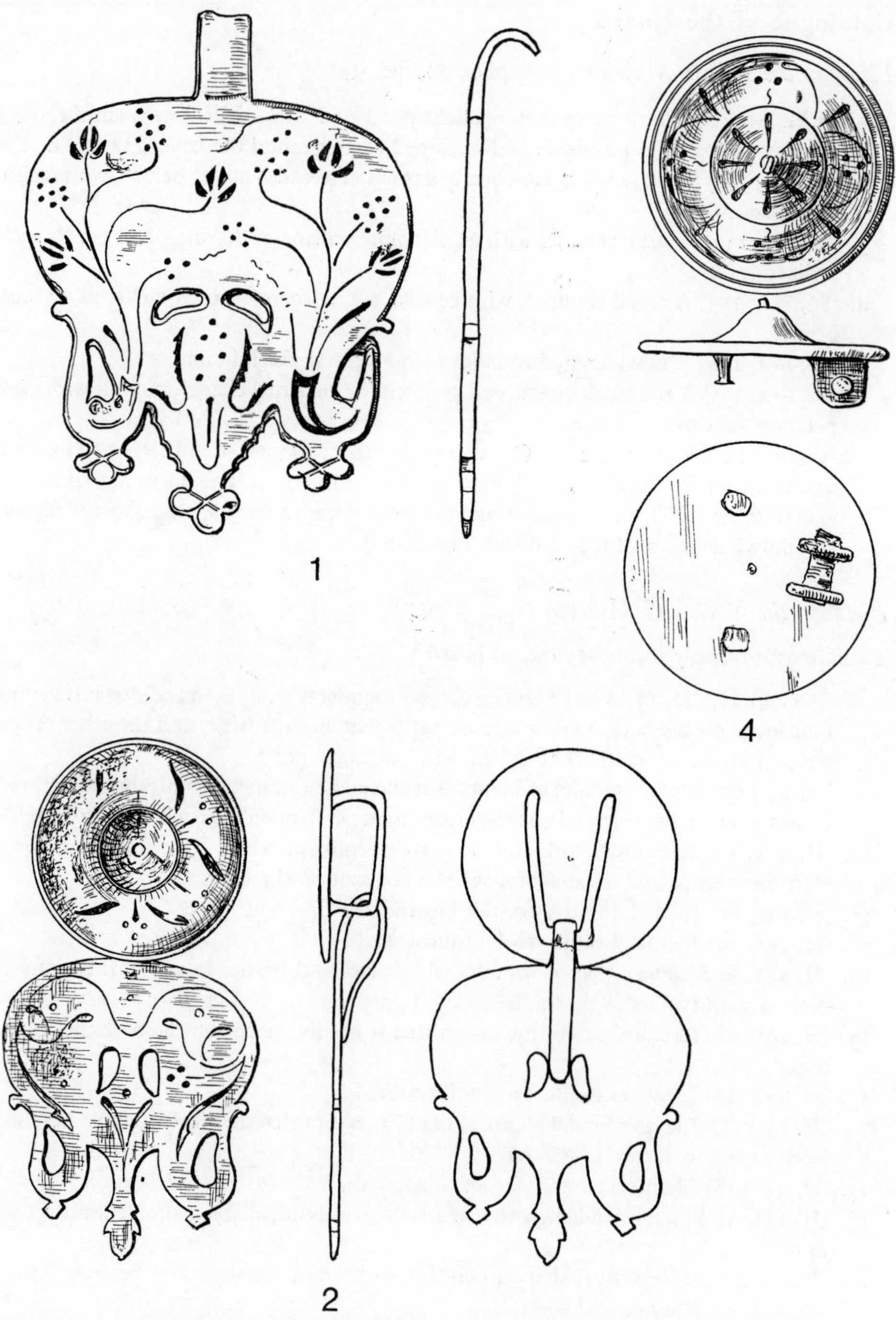

Figure 9. Fremington Hagg Hoard: objects in the British Museum ($\frac{1}{2}$).

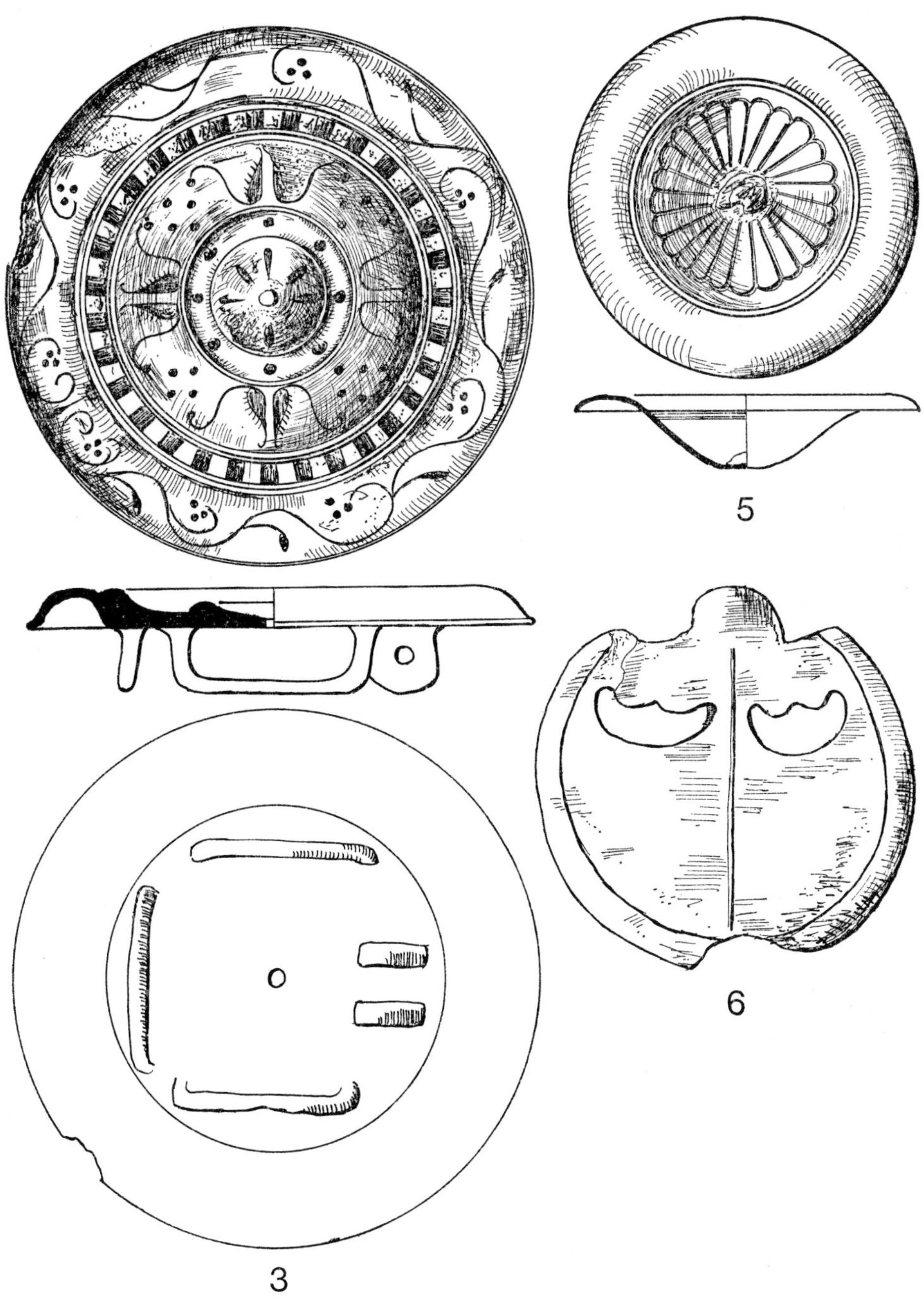

Figure 10. Objects in the British Museum ($\frac{1}{2}$).

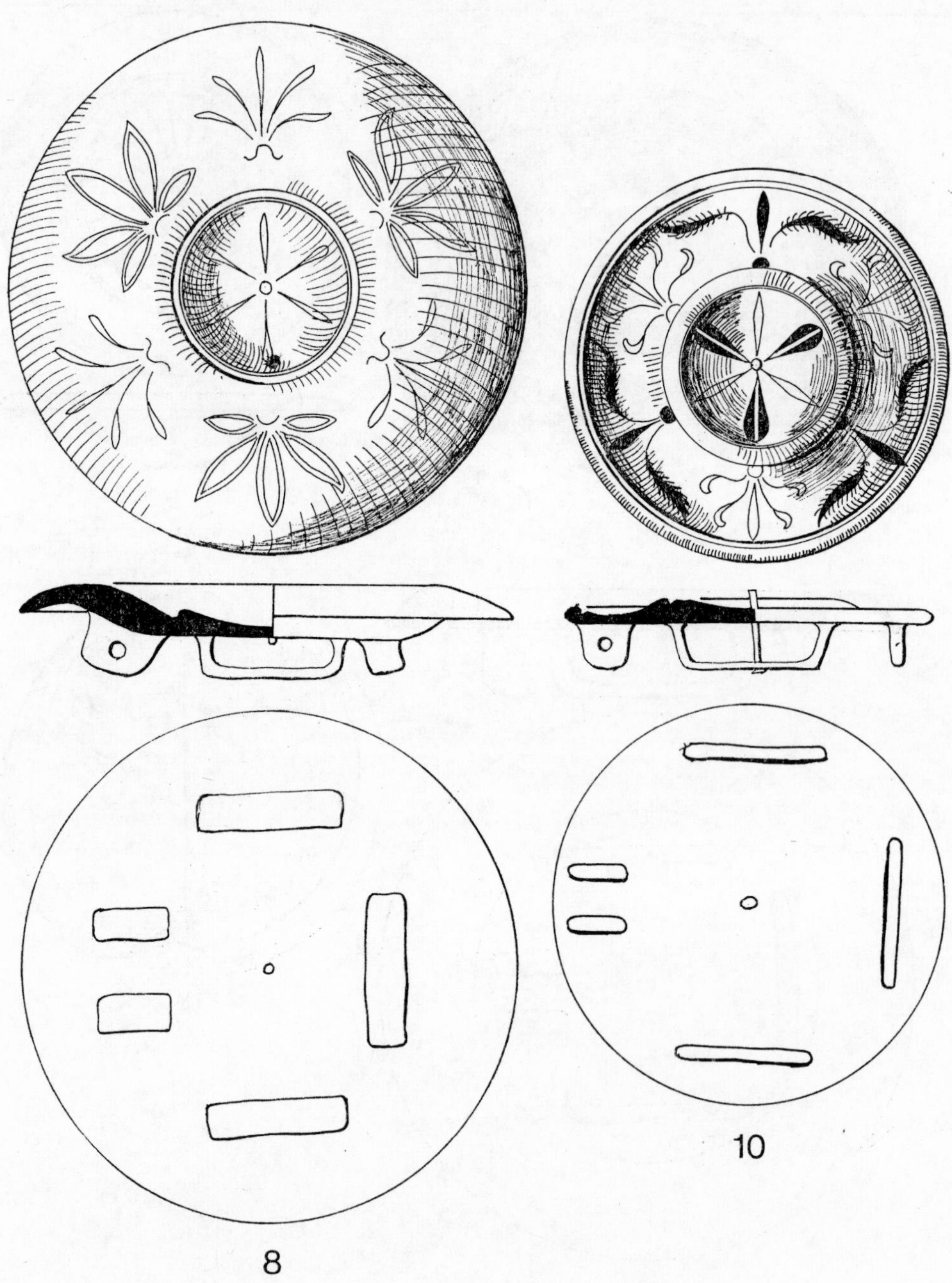

Figure 11. Objects in the Yorkshire Museum (½).

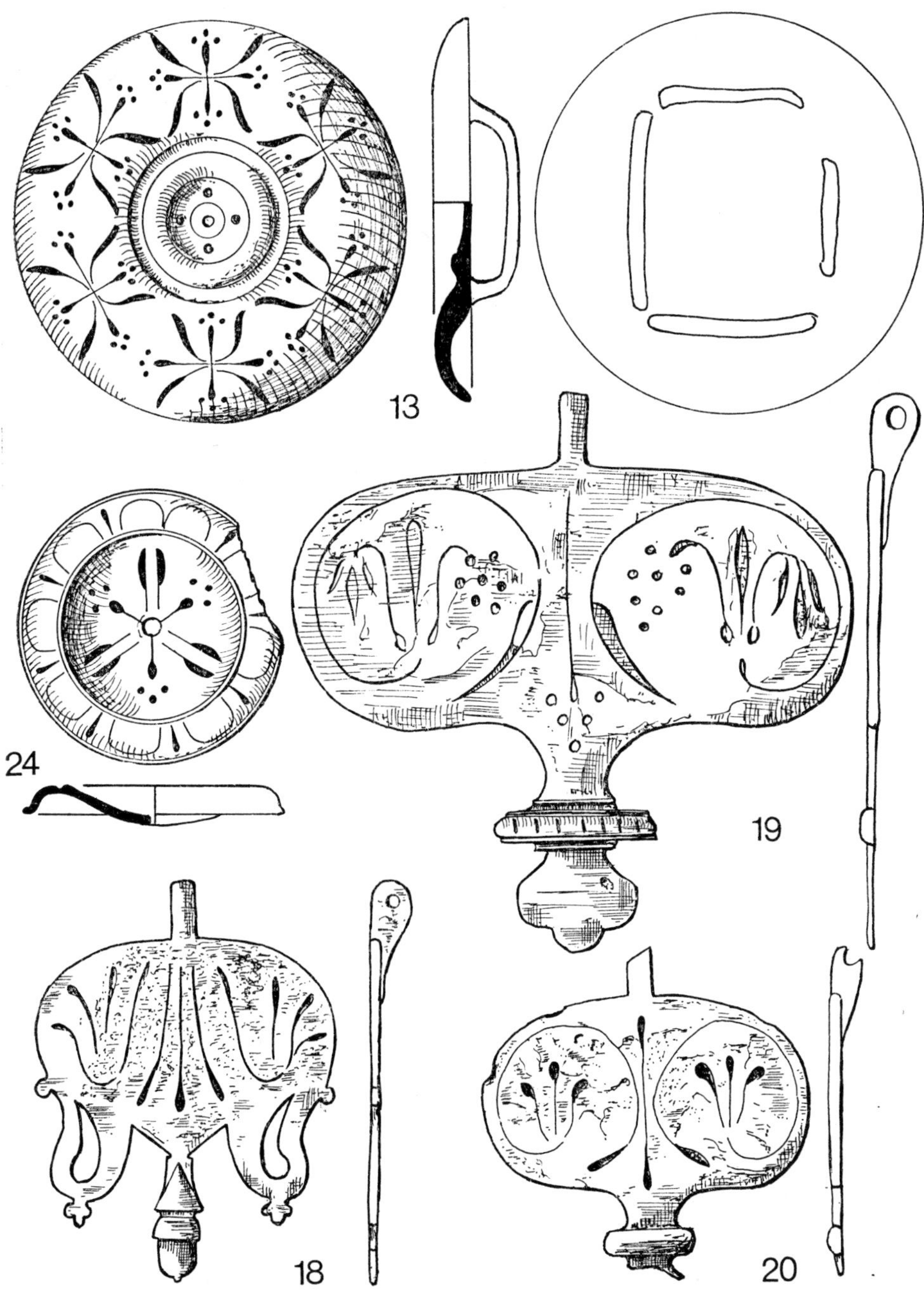

Figure 12. Objects in the Yorkshire Museum ($\frac{1}{2}$).

21. (H. 141, 2) A small pendant identical to no. 2 (not illustrated).
22. (H. 141, 3) Identical to no. 21 (not illustrated).
23. (No Acc. Number) A small roundel with stylized decoration and with attachment for a pendant on the back, as in the case of no. 2 above, and two rivets for attachment to a leather trace.
24. (No Acc. Number) A small saucer-shaped roundel with formalized leaf decoration and hole for rivet attachment at the centre.
25. (H. 141, 54, K. 4) A dome-shaped stud with cruciform leaf and berry pattern.
26. (H. 141, 55, K. 35) Identical to no. 25 (not illustrated).
27. (H. 141, 56, K. 11) Identical to no. 25 (not illustrated).
28. (H. 141, 57, K. 2) A dome-shaped stud with a cruciform leaf pattern.
29. (H. 141, 58, K. 3) Identical to no. 28 (not illustrated).
30. (H. 141, 60, K. 15) Identical to no. 28 (not illustrated).
31. (H. 141, 69, K. 6) Identical to no. 28 (not illustrated).
32. (H. 141, ?, K. 39) Identical to no. 28 (not illustrated).
33. (H. 141, 61, K. 51) A dome-shaped stud with cruciform leaf and berry pattern.
34. (H. 141, 63, K. 47) Identical to no. 33 (not illustrated).
35. (H. 141, 64, K. 43) Identical to no. 33 (not illustrated).
36. (H. 141, ?, K. 50) Identical to no. 33 (not illustrated).
37. (No Acc. Number) A decorated roundel almost identical to no. 2 and with two loops arranged in a V-shaped pattern at the back.
38. (H. 141, 43, K. 36) A small decorated stud.
39. (H. 141, 45) Identical to no. 38 (not illustrated).
40. (H. 141, 36, K. 10) A dome-shaped stud with simple leaf pattern in the form of a cross.
41. (K. 49) A small, decorated dome-shaped stud.
42. (H. 141, 67, K. 1) A plain tinned, dome-shaped stud.
43. (H. 141, 69, K. 14) Identical to no. 42 (not illustrated).
44. (H. 141, 70, K. 7) Identical to no. 42 (not illustrated).
45. (K. 12) Identical to no. 42 (not illustrated).
46. (K. 13) Identical to no. 42 (not illustrated).
47. (K. 45) Identical to no. 42 (not illustrated).
48. (H. 141, 73, K. 38) A small plain, tinned, dome-shaped stud.
49. (H. 141, 75, K. 42) Identical to no. 48 (not illustrated).
50. (H. 141, 76, K. 44) Identical to no. 48 (not illustrated).
51. (H. 141, 77, K. 48) Identical to no. 48 (not illustrated).
52. (H. 141, 78, K. 52) A dome-shaped stud attached to a plain strip, having a tang with a toggle end.
53. (H. 141, 79, K. 53) An example similar to no. 52 but in poorer condition (not illustrated).
54. (H. 141, 86, K. 54) An example similar to no. 52, but in poorer condition (not illustrated). There are four other examples of the studs only (K. 38, K. 42, K. 44 and K. 48).
55. (H. 141, 74, K. 41) A dome-shaped stud rather thicker than the above examples and having a thick tang with a washer.

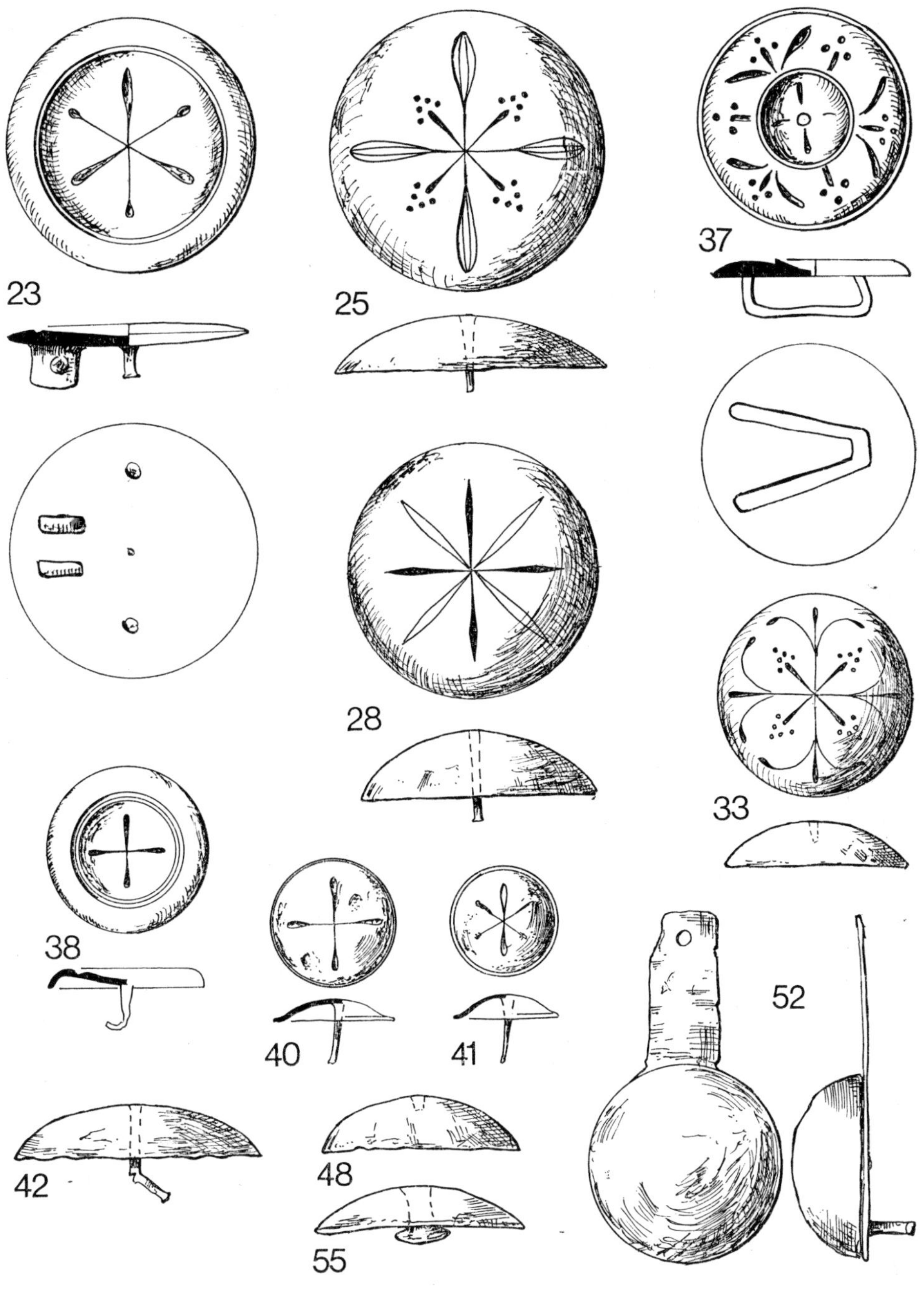

Figure 13. Objects in the Yorkshire Museum ($\frac{1}{2}$).

56. (H. 141, 59, K. 64) A tinned strip with niello decoration and moulded in the centre with two tangs for attachment to leather. One of the tangs still has a washer attached.
57. (K. 61) A flat, tinned strip with niello decoration with evidence of a centre piece which has become detached.
58. (K. 62) Identical to no. 54 (not illustrated).
59. (H. 141, 40, K. 68) A similar, but somewhat larger, but incomplete, strip to the above with a saucer-shaped roundel still attached. It is probable that the latter had a dome-shaped stud attached.
60. (H. 141, 41, K. 59) Identical to no. 59 but without the roundel (not illustrated).
61. (H. 141, 42, K. 60) Identical to no. 59 but without the roundel (not illustrated).
62. (K. 69) A similar strip with indications of a roundel having been attached at the centre as with no. 59.
63. (H. 141, 33, K. 55) A similar strip with indications of a roundel having been attached at the centre as with no. 59.
64. (H. 141, 34, K. 57) Identical to no. 63 (not illustrated).
65. (H. 141, 36, K. 58) Identical to no. 63 (not illustrated).
66. (H. 141, 46, K. 55) A smaller thin, tinned strip than the above and without a centre attachment.
67. (K. 63) Almost identical to no. 66 (not illustrated).
68. (K. 65) A similar strip to nos. 66 and 67.
69. (H. 141, 50, K. 56) A similar but wider strip, incomplete.
70. (H. ?, K. 67) A similar strip to the above, but incomplete. One of the tangs still has a washer attached.
71. (H. 141, 70, K. 26) A moulded, tinned strip with niello decoration with a tang at one end and an attachment for a hinge at the other. Similar to *Hod Hill,*[11] (fig. 3/A. 37).
72. (K. 27) Upper part (i.e. as drawn), of a piece similar to no. 68 (not illustrated).
73. (H. 141, 29, K. 124) A plain, dome-shaped stud with a saucer-shaped surround.
74. (H. 141, 28, K. 127) A slightly larger but similar example to no. 73 (not illustrated).
75. (H. 141, 53 (?), K. 66) A tinned and nielloed strip with a heavy, rounded terminal at one end. Although there is nothing like it in the Doorwerth hoard, a Newstead pit produced two (Curle, *The Roman Fort at Newstead*, pl. lxxii, nos. 8 and 10), in association (no. lv) with pieces of harness mounts, and other examples have been published from Aislingen (Taf. 18) and Risstissen[12] (Taf. 62), also with harness, so that it is likely to have belonged to the hoard.

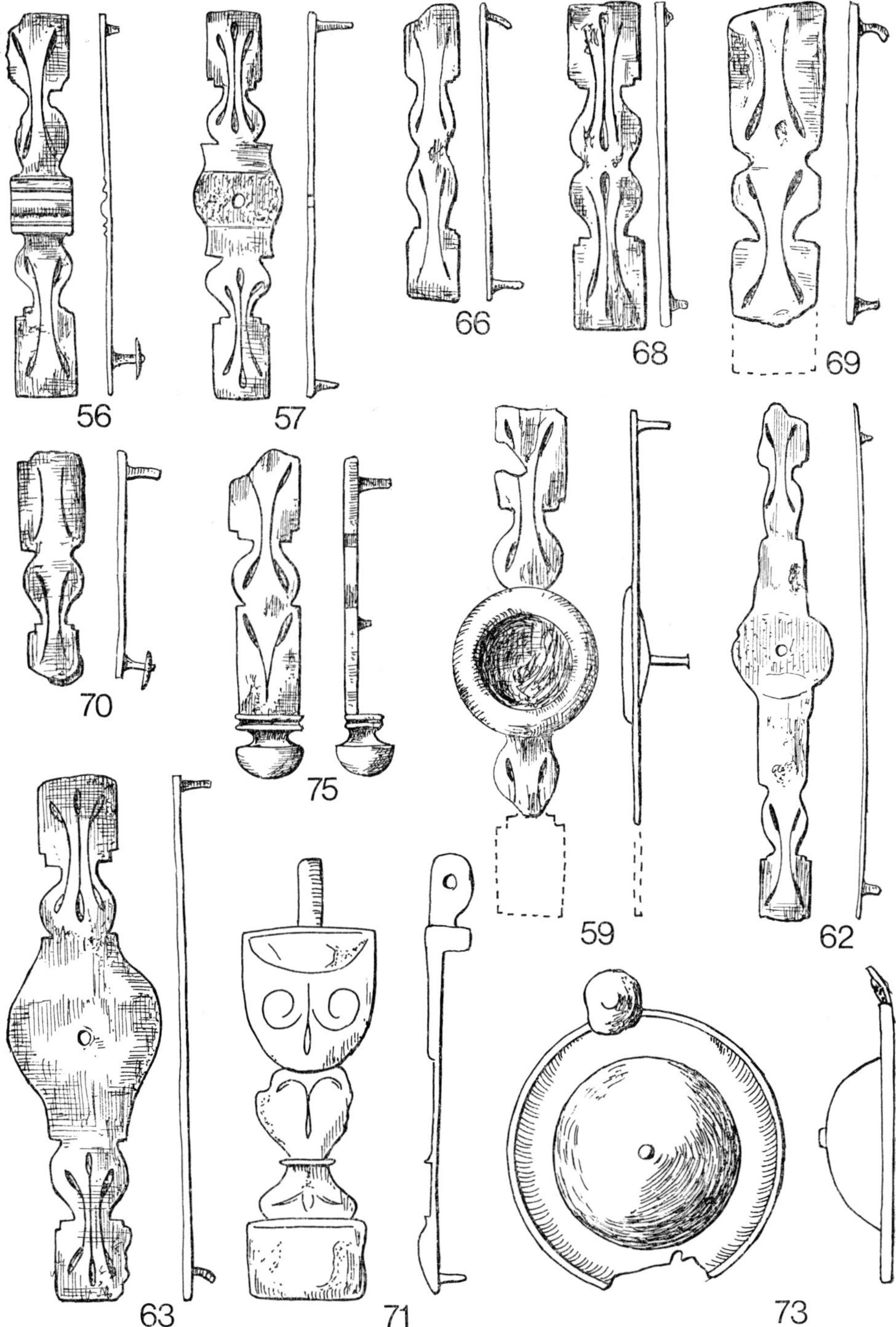

Figure 14. Objects in the Yorkshire Museum (½).

Objects which may not belong to the original hoard

76. (Acc. No. H. 141, 114, K. 29) A strap-end with a projecting button at the front for attachment to leather or cloth and a small hook at the back. The nearest parallel to this object is one from Risstissen (report forthcoming, I am grateful to Dr G. Ulbert for drawing my attention to this parallel). Most belt or strap fasteners of this type (*Richborough V*,[13] no. 102, and Hod Hill, unpublished) are hinged rather than fixed into a slotted terminal, as in this case.

77. (K. 13) A plain circular dress-fastener. Although assigned by Mr J. P. Gillam to the second century (*Roman and Native in North Britain* (1958), 81), examples of this kind of equipment from Hod Hill (fig. 5/A. 127–130)[14] and Wroxeter (*Arch. J.*, cxv (1958), fig. 8, no. 255), clearly indicate a continuity from Claudian times. It would be impossible to give a firm date to this particular piece in the absence of decoration (cf. Prysg Field, Caerleon,[15] fig. 38, no. 11, where it is dated to the second century).

78. (H. 141, 104, K. 18) A pair of harness rings joined together with a projecting ring at the back for attachment to a trace. In general decorative treatment it is similar to one from Newstead (Curle, *op. cit.*, pl. lxxv, no. 1).

79. (H. 141, 107 (?), K. 118) A roundel with a female mask. These decorative features have often been described as *phalerae*, and they were commonly used on horse harness (cf. Curle, *op. cit.*, pl. lxxvii, no. 11).

80. (H. 141, 113, K. 25) A strap-end with a large terminal knob and loop at the back for a strap about 20 mm wide, in general pattern resembling no. 76. The decoration on the front panel appears to be in the form of lettering but this interpretation seems unlikely.

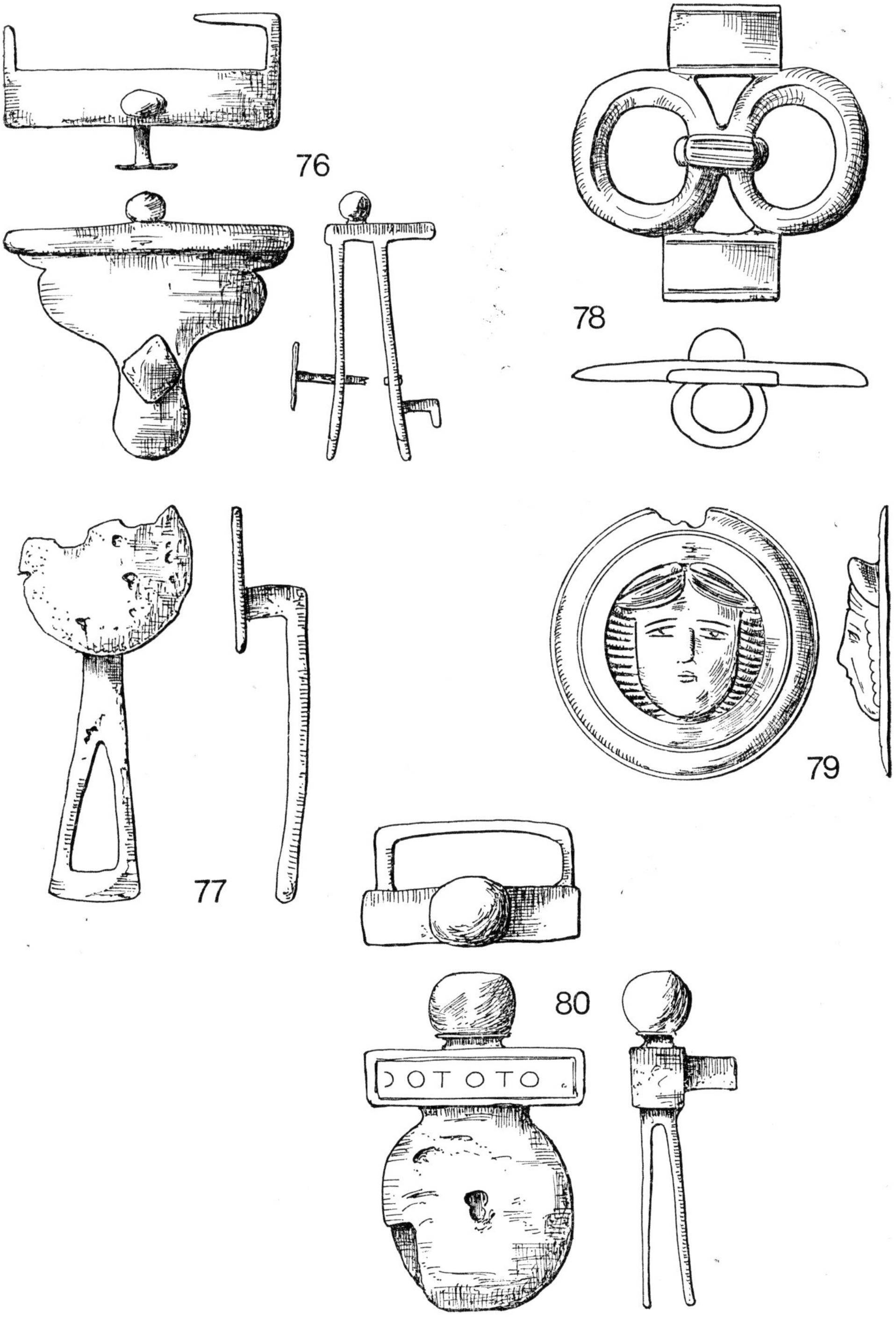

Figure 15. Objects in the Yorkshire Museum which may not belong to the Hoard ($\frac{1}{2}$).

81. (H. 141, 130, K. 30) A belt mount in poor condition and with part of one side missing. The decoration at the centre consists of a ring and central circle of blue enamel. The presence of a loop at the back, probably matched by one on the other side, indicates the function of this piece as a belt or strap mount.
82. (H. 141, 87, K. 83) A scabbard-mount which was attached to the back of the scabbard, the sword belt passing through the slot where the mount is raised from the scabbard surface (cf. Zugmantel,[16] Taf. xi, nos. 24–6; Prysg Field, Caerleon, fig. 36, nos. 2–9; Eastern Corner, Caerleon,[17] fig. 32, no. 9).
83. (H. 141, 88, K. 84) A scabbard-mount similar but smaller than no. 82, with part of the top ring and terminal missing.
84. (H. 141, 139, K. 129) A heavy, decorated bronze knob with tang for inserting into wood, with a small hole for fastening at the end. These knobs are fairly common and used mainly for decorating vehicles. They could also have held two thin wooden members together.
85. (H. 141, 95, K. 20) A small pelta-shaped bronze mount with two thick studs at the back (cf. Zugmantel, Taf. xii, no. 11).
86. (H. 141, 101, K. 91) An incomplete terret-ring, decorated with three raised mouldings.
87. (H. 141, 102, K. 88) An incomplete terret-ring decorated with three flat panels each quartered into four segments with alternating red and blue enamel, although these are so decayed that it is not possible to be certain of this scheme. There is a similar, but more elaborate, example in the Downing Street Museum, Cambridge, from the Braybrooke Collection, and of unknown provenance (Acc. No. 48, 1172).

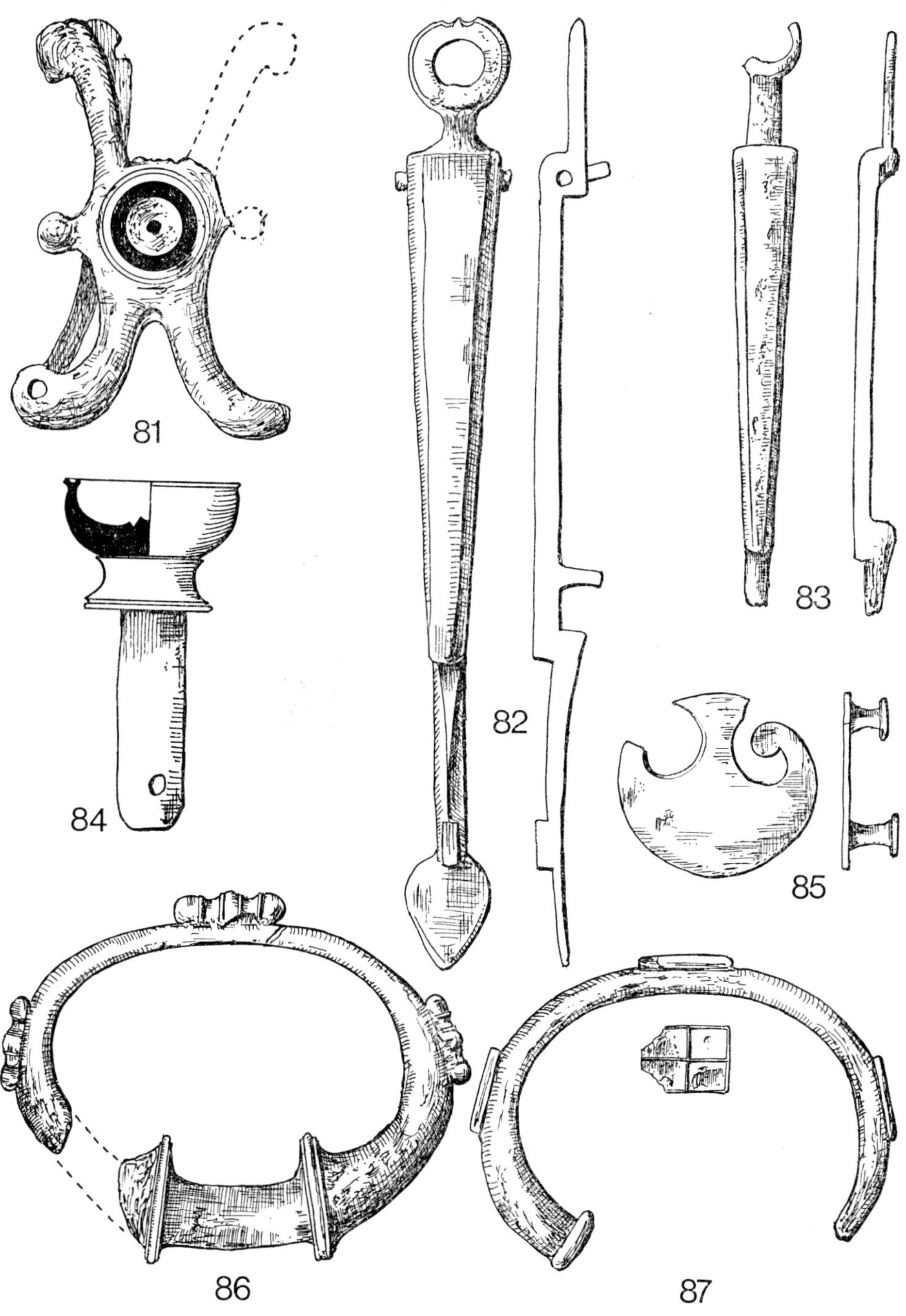

Figure 16. Objects in the Yorkshire Museum which may not belong to the Hoard ($\frac{1}{2}$).

88. (H. 141, 91) A bronze scabbard chape, too damaged to be classified (cf. Prysg Field, Caerleon, fig. 34, no. 41; fig. 36, nos. 17–20; Zugmantel, Taf. xi, nos. 2 and 5 etc.).
89. (H. 141, 131, K. 92) A thin bronze stud decorated with a goddess with a snake (?). This is probably a mount for a seal-box lid (cf. *Wroxeter, 1914*,[18] pl. xviii, no. 26).
90. (H. 141, 93, K. 24) A bronze mount with a flat face on the back and consisting of two arms meeting at a narrow angle at a rounded terminal, probably for decorating a box.
91. (H. 141, 6) An oval harness mount with a lunate terminal at one end, the other is broken. At the back there is a rivet and a loop to hold a trace passing at right-angles to the main axis of the object. It is similar to one from Mainz (*Mainzer Zeitschrift*, xii, xiii (1917–18), Abb. 8, no. 29).
92. (H. 141, 170, K. 128) A leaf pendant with no visible surface decoration. This appears to be a degenerate copy of a form which is widespread in the first century (cf. *Richborough V*, no. 147).
93. (H. 141, 110) A small stud with a stylized human face with radial marks on the rim. The hair style is similar to a mask published in *Richborough I*,[19] (no. 29).
94. (H. 141, 109) A small decorated stud with a face mask similar to no. 93 (not illustrated).
95. (H. 141, 32 (?) K. 19) A stylized leaf-shaped pendant. This object is most unlikely to have belonged to the hoard since it is common on second-century sites, but not in earlier contexts (cf. Zugmantel, Taf. xii, nos. 61 and 62; Wiesbaden,[20] Taf. x, no. 35; Novaesium,[21] Taf. xxxiv, no. 56; Mainz, *Mainzer Zeitschrift*, xii, xiii (1917–18), no. 18).
96. (H. 141, 92) The rounded end of a bronze mount for a long box lid, although Jacobi identified it as a form of scabbard mount (*Das Römerkastell Saalburg* (1897), 486 and Taf. lvi, nos. 3–5). The fretted type of decoration and the contexts of the finds of these objects place their use in the second century, and it seems unlikely that this object belongs to the original hoard. (Other examples, from *O.R.L.*, are: Kapersburg, Taf. vii, no. 7; Faimingen, Taf. viii, no. 29; Feldburg, Taf. vi, no. 53; Rückingen, Taf. ii, no. 2 etc.
97. (H. 141, 66, K. 49) A large, plain circular, convex stud for decorating woodwork.
98. (H. 141, 82, K. 10) A plain circular stud with long pointed tang for driving into wood.
99. (H. 141, 81, K. 102) A plain, dome-shaped bronze stud for decorating woodwork.
100. (H. 141, 83, K. 104) A plain, hollow stud, with heavy tang curved as if having been drawn from wood.
101. (H. 141, 84) A stud similar to no. 100 (not illustrated).
102. (H. 141, 89, K. 123) A belt-mount with fret decoration of second-century date, and therefore not belonging to the hoard (similar to Novaesium,[22] Taf. xxx, no. 66) (not illustrated).
103. (H. 141, 100, K. 23) A masked harness ring with decorated attachment of second-century date and therefore not of the original hoard (cf. Lauriacum,[23] fig. 8) (not illustrated).

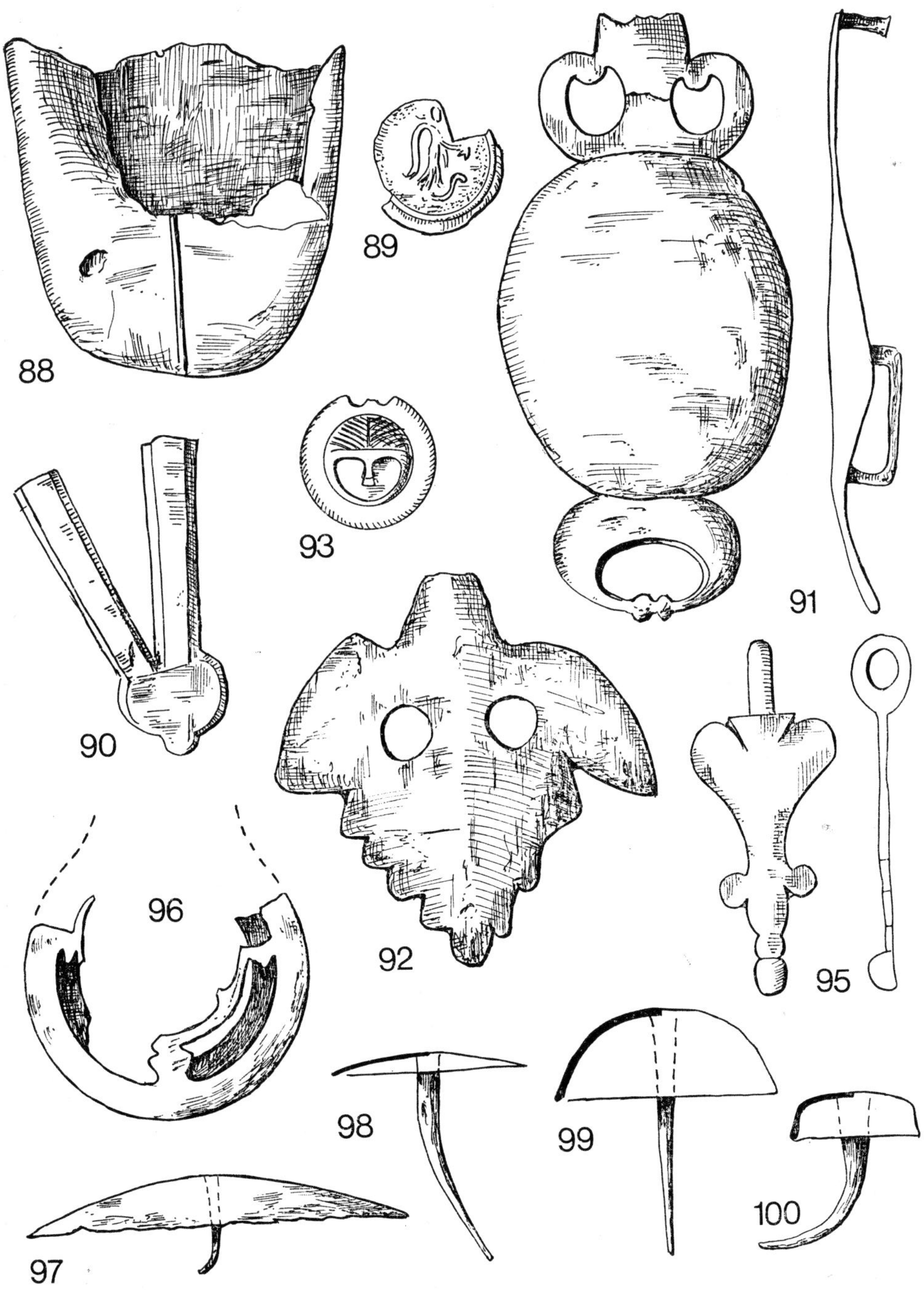

Figure 17. Objects in the Yorkshire Museum which may not belong to the Hoard ($\frac{1}{2}$).

There are also other bronzes which clearly do not belong to the hoard and have therefore been excluded from the list. They include:
(1) five locks, (2) a cloak fastener, (3) a decorated knife handle, (4) a jug handle, (5) a small bronze stand, (6) two probes, (7) a mount in the form of a dolphin, (8) a clasp knife case, the blade missing, (9) two brooches, and (10) a plain stud with a button loop (H. 141, 32, K. 40) which is probably modern.

Acknowledgements
I am most grateful to Mr G. F. Willmot, Keeper of the Yorkshire Museum, for allowing me free access to all the material in that museum, and also to Mr J. Brailsford and Mr K. Painter of the British Museum. Various people have tried to help me with references to the discovery and I am grateful for all their efforts, in particular Mrs Mary Chitty, Miss Dorothy Greene and Mr B. R. Hartley.

Notes

1. *Y.P.S.R.* (1833), 27.
2. *Y.M.H.* (1852), 59.
3. J. Phillips, *The Rivers, Mountains and Sea-coast of Yorkshire* (1855), 52. Edmund Bogg suggested that the discovery dated back as far as "the forepart of the eighteenth century" (*Regal Richmond and the Land of the Swale*, n.d., but *c.* 1906, 208), but failed to substantiate this statement.
4. *Y.M.H.* (1891), 132. In 1891 a large collection of antiquities, including curiosities collected by Edward Wood of Richmond, was given to the museum by George Alderson Robins of Reeth. It is possible that some of the items came in this bequest.
5. J. H. Holwerda, 'Een vondst uit den Rijn bij Doorwerth', *Oudheidkundige Mededeelingen*, supplement bij nieuwe reeks xii (1931,) 1–26.
6. J. Curle, *The Roman Fort at Newstead* (1911), pl. lxxiii. There are two samian stamps of CRISPVS and SEVERVS from the same pit. These are more likely to be early Flavian rather than later, and this would appear to date the pit to the Agricolan phase rather than to the destruction of *c.* A.D. 105. (I am most grateful to Mr B. R. Hartley for this comment on these stamps.)
7. *Y Cymmrodor*, xxxvii (1926), fig. 57, No. 2.
8. *Mainzer Zeitschrift*, vii (1912), Abb. 4, No. 18.
9. Curle, *op. cit.*, fig. 44.
10. G. Ulbert, *Die Römischen Donau-Kastelle Aislingen und Burghöfe*, in *Limesforschungen*, Band 1 (1959), Taf. 20, Nos. 1 and 2. This fort has some Flavian occupation.
11. J. W. Brailsford, *Hod Hill I* (1962).
12. *Limesforschungen*, i (1969).
13. B. W. Cunliffe (ed.), *Fifth Report on the Excavations of the Roman Fort at Richborough, Kent* (1969), Research Report of the Society of Antiquaries.
14. Brailsford, *op. cit.*
15. *Arch. Camb.*, lxxxvii (1932).
16. *O.R.L.*
17. *Arch. Camb.*, lxxxv (1930).
18. J. P. Bushe-Fox, *Excavations on the Site of the Roman Town of Wroxeter, 1914* (1916),

Research Report of the Society of Antiquaries.

19. J. P. Bushe-Fox, *Excavations of the Roman Fort at Richborough, Kent* (1926), Research Report of the Society of Antiquaries.
20. *O.R.L.*
21. *Bonner Jahrbuch*, cxi–cxii (1904).
22. *ibid.*
23. *Der Römische Limes in Österreich*, xiv.

B. M. DICKINSON AND K. F. HARTLEY

The evidence of potters' stamps on samian ware and on mortaria for the trading connections of Roman York

Few of the objects of trade in the Roman period can be so easily assigned to their origins as pottery bearing makers' stamps. The collections of the Yorkshire Museum at York are particularly rich in such material. As its evidence was not considered in the recent volume on Roman York by the Royal Commission on Historical Monuments,[1] it may be worthwhile here to attempt a summary of the sources of the samian ware and mortaria at York,[2] the former involving trade with the Continent, the latter trade primarily within Britain. For this purpose, material from York in other museums has been included.[3]

It should be mentioned at this point that a lot of the older finds in the Yorkshire Museum carry no indication of provenance.[4] Nevertheless, it seems reasonable to assume that the bulk of the collection is from York or its immediate vicinity.

Pottery known definitely not to be from York is, of course, excluded. Dr F. Oswald's *Index of Potters' Stamps on Terra Sigillata* sometimes gives York as the provenance of pieces in the Yorkshire Museum known to be from other sites.[5] All stamps on samian ware or mortaria for which there are no certain provenances are distinguished by an asterisk in the text. It should also be remembered that there is often no distinction for the provenanced pieces between material from the fortress and other sites in York.

Although the primary purpose of this note is to deal with the sources of supply of pottery to York, it may perhaps be worth discussing briefly the bearing of the samian ware on the date of the foundation of the site (p. 131 below), and on the subsequent fluctuations in the density of its occupation.

Potters' stamps on samian ware

It is unfortunate that of the 1,155 identified, literate potters' stamps in the Yorkshire Museum and elsewhere, only 321 can be said with certainty to have come from York. However, histograms showing the range of distribution in date, based both on the whole collection and on the pieces with a definite York provenance (p. 129, below) are so alike as to suggest that the bulk of the collection is indeed from York. In assessing the proportion of stamps from all sources, distinction is made as far as possible between the true and the probable number of York stamps.[6] In order to illuminate the York situation, comparison has been made with the records for the samian stamps from Colchester, Leicester, Corbridge, Caerleon, Chester and Carlisle.

Little need be said about the first-century pottery from York, of which almost all, as at most sites in Britain, was manufactured at La Graufesenque, and falls within the range of *c.* A.D. 30–110.[7] The five stamps from the South Gaulish factory at Montans are second-century, and have been classed with the early second-century samian. There are no first-century stamps from Montans. The York stamps of Acutus and Bilicatus* seem by their fabric and distribution to be from La Graufesenque rather than Montans, where both potters also worked. There is little or no evidence for the presence of Banassac ware at York, though the situation is a difficult one to assess, since little is known in detail yet about the dies of Banassac potters with homonyms at La Graufesenque. Allowance must be made too for the possibility of migration of potters from the one to the other. Similarly, there is no first-century Central Gaulish ware from the Lezoux kilns. This is never very common in Britain, but occasional sherds have been found at sites as far north as Staffordshire and North Wales, mainly in Neronian and early-Flavian contexts.

The situation at York in the second century and later is much more complicated and rather different from that at most other sites in Britain. From about A.D. 125 to the end of the century, samian was supplied to York mainly by the large Central Gaulish factories at Lezoux (Puy-de-Dôme). This is quite normal, but the proportion of Lezoux samian at York, 66.1 per cent, is rather low, considering the average of 80 to 85 per cent at the sites used for comparison here.[8] The stamp of Venermidus* of Toulon-sur-Allier is the only one from this source in the Yorkshire Museum. Pottery from Toulon is not at all common in Britain and it is possible that this piece was brought to York as a personal possession rather than in regular trade.[9]

The period *c.* A.D. 110–25 and the proportion of second- and third-century pottery from East Gaulish factories are worth more detailed discussion. Most striking is the very low proportion of early second-century potters' stamps from the kilns at Les Martres-de-Veyre, on the west bank of the Allier near Clermont-Ferrand.[10] Of the 18 Les Martres potters whose stamps have been found at York, only Paterclus and Vitalis are represented by more than one sherd. The lowest point in the histogram (fig. 18) occurs at the period A.D. 110–20, at a time when Les Martres was the main source of samian ware for Britain. Only 1.2 (3.1) per cent of the second-century and later stamps at York are from Les Martres, compared with 8.3 per cent at Colchester, 9 per cent at Carlisle, 10.9 per cent at Chester, 11.2 per cent at Leicester and 11.6 per cent at Caerleon. The normal range at northern and Midland sites is thus approximately 10 per cent. Corbridge admittedly has only produced 2.9 per cent of stamped pieces from Les Martres, but it should be remembered that the lower levels of occupation there have been less completely explored, and that the total is heavily weighted by the large deposits associated with the end of the second Antonine fort.[11] There seems to be no reason to suppose that samian ware was reaching York from potteries other than Les Martres in the early second century, apart from Flavian-Trajanic ware from La Graufesenque and five second-century pieces from Montans, three of Chresimus (two definitely from York), one of Felicio* and one of Q.V.C.*[12]

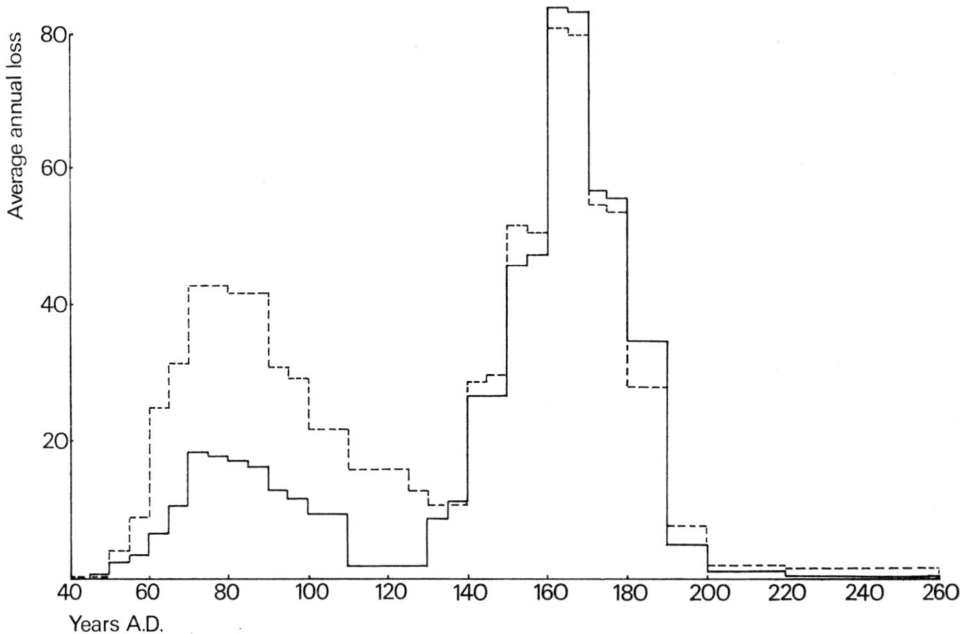

Figure 18. Histogram of samian potters' stamps from York (solid), and probably from York (broken).

It is just conceivable that a few of the very earliest East Gaulish sherds might have reached York by A.D. 125, but not enough is yet known of the dating of the potteries at Chémery-Faulquemont, Blickweiler and La Madeleine to be certain.[13] The results of a comparable survey of the pottery from Verulamium suggest that no systematic error in dating is involved at this period.[14] The obvious sharp drop in the annual breakage rate at York is therefore probably indicative of a reduction in the density of occupation of the site in the period A.D. 110–25.

In Britain, the proportion of East Gaulish stamps to others of the second century and later, particularly to those of the Central Gaulish factories at Lezoux, is normally rather low, and most of the East Gaulish ware is from Rheinzabern (see table, p. 132). It is also noticeable that there is, in general, much less East Gaulish samian ware found at sites inland or in the west than at those in the eastern half of the country. Comparison of a few selected areas illustrates this point well, with one marked exception. Of the inland or western sites, Chester with 1.6 per cent of East Gaulish stamps, Leicester with 2.5 per cent and Caerleon with 3.6 per cent contrast with 8.5 per cent at Corbridge, 12.3 per cent at Colchester and 13.1 per cent at York. Carlisle has the extraordinarily high proportion of 20 per cent of East Gaulish stamps of the second century or later, and it is likely that this was carried overland from the Tyne, perhaps as part of the normal supply system to Hadrian's Wall. However, Carlisle and, to some extent, Birrens, depart from the normal pattern and cannot be considered in detail here. From Hadrian's Wall in general, 16.5 per cent of the stamps of the second and third centuries are East Gaulish, and this high proportion can be explained by the ease of access for consignments of samian shipped up the Tyne. York, with almost the same proportion, was evidently equally accessible.

It is noticeable that of the East Gaulish stamps at York, 50 (47.2) per cent are on Rheinzabern ware. Pottery from Chémery-Faulquemont, Sinzig, La Madeleine, Blickweiler, the Argonne[15] and, possibly, Heiligenberg also occurs there, though in much smaller quantities (see table, p. 132). So it is in the late second and third centuries, when Rheinzabern was active, that York was receiving the bulk of its East Gaulish ware. During the period A.D. 160–200, Rheinzabern pottery must have overlapped with imports from Lezoux, but from about A.D. 200 until the final disappearance of true samian ware in the middle of the third century, Rheinzabern ware and a very small quantity of Trier ware alone reached York.

The high proportion of East Gaulish samian at York is clearly to be explained by the position of the site. Merchants shipping from the Rhineland to Britain would naturally tend to seek harbours on the east coast and clearly the Tyne and

Humber both received direct shipments from the Rhine. For trade connections between Britain and the Rhineland we have both epigraphic evidence[16] and the probable trading of objects in Whitby jet made at York.[17] The presence of Rhineland glass in some quantity at York is also well attested.[18] One might note, too, the relative abundance at York of motto-beakers from the Moselle or the Rhineland.[19]

The evidence may now be summarized. In the first century York received its supplies of samian ware virtually entirely from La Graufesenque, on the Tarn at Millau. Shipping down the Tarn and Garonne may be assumed, with transference to sea-going ships at Bordeaux. What we do not know is how the pottery was distributed once it reached Britain. The likely guess would be landing at a south-eastern port, such as London or Richborough, with distribution to York by coasters, rather than overland, in view of the relative costs.

Such pottery as reached York from Les Martres-de-Veyre and the much greater volume from Lezoux would presumably have been shipped (or rafted?) down the Allier to Nantes, again with transference there to sea-going vessels. Again, however, it is difficult to be sure of the distribution method in Britain.

With the East Gaulish wares, however, the situation is clearly quite different, and the relatively high proportion at York is certainly due to direct shipping from the Rhineland to the Humber. It is particularly interesting that the one East Gaulish centre not in close contact with the Rhine, namely the Argonne, is much more poorly represented at York.

The evidence of potters' stamps on samian ware for the history of the site

As is well-known, there are some stamps of pre-Flavian, or partly pre-Flavian, potters at York: 1.6 (4.5) per cent of the first-century stamps can be said to be definitely pre-Flavian and a further 8.1 (7.7) per cent belong to potters whose activity is partly pre-Flavian. This is comparable with the situation at Caerleon, where 16 per cent of the first-century stamps are of pre-Flavian or partly pre-Flavian potters. The stamped samian alone cannot be taken either to confirm or deny the possibility of pre-Flavian occupation at York, since even bowls of Acutus or Bilicatus for instance could have been in use in A.D. 71.[20] However, it clearly does not give any very strong support for the idea of occupation before A.D. 71, let alone showing that any that there might have been was Roman and military.[21] Comparison with the situation at the native site of Stanwick is instructive.

The potters' stamps at York show the greatest densities of occupation in the Flavian and Antonine periods, as might be expected. They also strongly suggest a drop in occupation about A.D. 100–25. Civilian settlement may be assumed to have been increasing gradually from the foundation of the fortress, and it is unlikely to have decreased seriously in the early second century. The drop in the total of stamps is, therefore, more likely to reflect changes in the military situation.

The latest inscription of Legio IX Hispana from York is dated Dec. 107–Dec. 108.[22] Professor Sheppard Frere suggests that the Sixth Legion, which replaced the Ninth at York, arrived in Britain about A.D. 122,[23] but it must almost immediately have been engaged primarily in work on Hadrian's Wall. On the York evidence it is at least conceivable now that Legio IX might have disappeared from York before the arrival of Legio VI in Britain. A tile stamp of the Legio IX from the Nijmegen fortress and a mortarium from the Nijmegen legion's tilery at de Holdeurn, in local fabric and stamped ⅃GVIIIIHIS, suggest the presence of Legio IX (rather than a vexillation of it) at Nijmegen.[24] Professor J. E. Bogaers believes this to have been between *c.* A.D. 121 and its final disappearance, but presumably because he envisages immediate replacement by Legio VI at York. It also seems possible on the evidence of tile stamps from Carlisle and Scalesceugh that the Legion might have been stationed in that area, presumably at Carlisle, for a time after it left York.[25] The low density of samian stamps of the period A.D. 110–25 at York might be relevant to either situation.

As for the vast rise in the histogram for the Antonine period, this is something which York has in common with almost every site of Roman Britain. And certainly the material used by the civilian community must now swamp that connected with the Legion. No conclusions may, then, be made about the latter. That the town of York, whether already a *municipium* or not, was flourishing is evident.

	York	Colchester	Leicester	Corbridge	Caerleon	Chester	Carlisle
Chémery	2.0	1.2	—	6.1	—	—	—
La Madeleine	10.4	16.8	11.1	6.1	10.0	—	—
Blickweiler	2.6	12.0	—	0.9	—	—	—
Heiligenberg	3.3	—	—	5.2	—	—	—
Ittenweiler	—	1.2	—	—	—	—	—
Sinzig	0.6	14.5[26]	—	—	—	—	—
Argonne	5.9	12.0	—	0.9	10.0	25.0	20.0
Rheinzabern	47.2	24.3	77.8	60.9	70.0	75.0	55.0
Trier	2.6	6.0	—	1.7	10.0	—	5.0
E.G. unassigned	25.4	12.0	11.1	18.2	—	—	20.0

Table 1: comparative percentages of East Gaulish potters' stamps.

The mortaria from York

Forty-two mortarium stamps are recorded from York, a further 37 in the Yorkshire Museum, and two in the Bateman Collection (University Museum of Archaeology and Ethnology, Cambridge) are likely to be from York, though they are without provenance. There is nothing among the unprovenanced pieces unlikely to be found at York and, even if one or two were from nearby sites in Yorkshire, they would not cloud the issue as far as sources of supply are concerned.

The 81 stamps necessarily belong to the period *c.* A.D. 65–200, when stamping of mortaria was widely, though not invariably, practised. They are from at least nine, possibly ten different sources, all but one probably in Britain. The stamps are listed under workshops or areas of production, together with the dates they indicate for the workshops' sales of mortaria to York. In order to fill out the picture and to extend it to the end of the Roman period, 102 unstamped fragments known to have been found in York are listed separately according to date and origin. Even in the first two centuries these can be useful because, as has been noted above, not all mortaria were stamped. The unstamped mortaria are referred to where they help to clarify the picture.

In the Flavian period two large civilian mortarium potteries supplied most of Britain's needs: one either in south-eastern England (Kent?) or, less probably, Gallia Belgica, was making primarily *Gillam* 238,[26] (Pottery 1).[27] The other pottery, south of Verulamium and near Watling Street, included the kilns at Radlett and Brockley Hill (Pottery 2).[28] The proportions of stamps from these two potteries at York (52.2 per cent and 42.2 per cent respectively) appear at first sight to suggest almost equal supplies from both of them; but the mortaria from Pottery 1 never carried more than one stamp, while all other potteries mentioned as stamping mortaria used at least two impressions, one on each side of the spout, thereby giving more probability of finding the stamps in excavation. This fact partly accounts for the large number of unstamped pieces from Pottery 1, but entirely unstamped rims of this class are also known. Thus it emerges that Pottery 1 was decidedly a larger factor than Pottery 2 in supply to York, especially as the latter's mortaria were always stamped.

The general distribution pattern for products of Pottery 1 indicates the special importance of coastal traffic in dispersal, and the easy access to York from the Humber must have been decisive. Pottery 2, in the Verulamium region, was for the Province as a whole, at least as important as Pottery 1. It evidently sold mortaria to York, presumably mainly by overland distribution as for much of its market, but at York it was clearly of lesser importance.

The unstamped mortaria are useful for correcting the balance for the Flavian period, since unlike most sites in Britain York was using a large proportion (in total perhaps equivalent to Pottery 1) of mortaria which were not stamped. Mortaria of type *Gillam* 237, while widely dispersed on military sites, are not usually found in large numbers; the York total of seven is the largest so far recorded for one site. This type shows some similarity in form to the work of A. Terentius Ripanus, who probably worked at or near Gloucester, but there is increasing evidence to show that this likeness is due to mutual links with army production. The five other undoubted Flavian mortaria in red-brown fabric are highly unusual; there is no evidence to suggest that civilian potters were making mortaria in the North at this time, and even in the Midlands and South there was as yet virtually no competition for Potteries 1 and 2. It is, therefore, suggested that they and, perhaps, the mortaria of type *Gillam* 237 may be from military potteries at or near York.

Wide distribution from Pottery 1 virtually ceased and the distribution from Pottery 2 gradually contracted after the end of the first century, so that in the second century the 'outside' suppliers are entirely different. The stamps leave no doubt that the largest proportion (39.7 per cent) was provided by the potters at Hartshill and Mancetter in Warwickshire (Pottery 5),[29] though most of the total of 28 date from the period A.D. 135–90.

In the second century, local potters were staking their claims in the mortarium trade wherever raw materials and demand permitted, and some were certainly trying to extend their markets, so that, despite the importance of the Warwickshire potters, more than six other sources for mortaria are evident.

The only mortarium certainly an import is that of Verecundus, whose kiln has recently been found at Soller (Kreis Düren) in Lower Germany.[30] He is the only Continental potter believed to have been exporting mortaria to Britain in the second half of the second century. His work, however, is very specialized, for he concentrated almost entirely on outsize mortaria (diameters of the order of 30in.), perhaps for use in commercial bakeries. His work is dispersed throughout Britain in much the same proportion as at York.

The Colchester workshops of the second half of the second century enjoyed a brief burgeoning of markets in the North, especially in Antonine Scotland but to a lesser degree in north-eastern England (with two stamps at York).[31] This brief flowering must have been at least as largely due to the favourable position for traffic up to the east coast as to business acumen.

Contemporary potters working near Lincoln also developed markets in the North, Crico largely in Scotland, but Aesico (and others) only in north-eastern England.[32] Vitalis I of Lincoln had succeeded in selling mortaria at York and in north-eastern England generally in the Flavian-Trajanic period, but this trade was largely confined to him and dwindled thereafter. Lincoln was even better placed than Colchester for finding a market at York.

Their relative position and the possibility of using water transport might well lead one to expect the Colchester and Lincoln potters to have supplied a far higher proportion of the York mortaria than they did (2.8 per cent and 9.2 per cent respectively). By contrast, the success of the Mancetter and Hartshill potters is brought out not only by the high proportion of their products, 39.7 per cent, but also by the undeniable fact that they possessed no outstanding advantage for serving York, other than that of good roads, unless the Anker-Trent system was used. Yet there is no occupied site in north Britain where the Warwickshire potters are not well represented from the second to the fourth centuries. This argues not only large-scale production, now clearly attested at the production end, but also an extensive, well-organized and continuing commercial nexus extending over the whole of north Britain and the Midlands. Finally, if hardness, and therefore durability, were the factors to seek, their mortaria usually surpassed Lincoln, Colchester and all the northern products, even those from the Crambeck kilns.

As might be expected at York, the products of known northern kilns are represented. One mortarium stamped by Doccius(?) or Docilis III, is certainly from kilns in the north-west and almost certainly from Wilderspool.[33]

One or, possibly, two semi-literate potters working at or close to Aldborough were able to sell mortaria (4.3 per cent) at York, no doubt on account of its proximity.[34]

However, 18 other York stamps by 10 different potters (Agripp–; Divict–; Mercator; Mittius?; Muco; Sarus; Vitalis V; A.T–, and a man of uncertain name (fig. 19, no. 26)) are all certainly from the North and have some factors in common, notably distribution and fabric.[35]

When four mortarium potters like Divict–, Mercator, Vitalis V and even Agripp–, who are otherwise unknown, have so many mortaria (three, five, three and two respectively) in so limited an area, the possibility of local manufacture is raised. It is not possible to argue with the same force for the others, but they fit with the four above so remarkably well that local manufacture is probable for these also. If all ten worked locally, then local kilns supplied 25.5 per cent of the second-century total of stamped mortaria.

The lack of known kilns at or close to York certainly should not be taken to disprove local production; if suitable clay could be found, potters would certainly not have neglected the potential market of a fortress and its attendant civil settlement. In view of York's military status it is perhaps worth noting that both dies of Agripp–, as well as those of Muco, A.T– and the potter of fig. 19, no. 26, had ansate panels, a convention sometimes used on military tile-stamps and inscriptions, and very uncommon among mortarium potters in a normal civilian background.

Seventeen unstamped mortaria in red-brown fabrics, many of them perhaps never stamped, and attributable to the second century should be mentioned here. They are all of northern origin and all could fit with the above group.

Eleven second-century stamps cannot be strictly assigned to their sources, though they are all from kilns in the North and Midlands (15.6 per cent of the second-century total). The unstamped fragments indicate that the Oxfordshire potteries sold a little to York,[36] but it has to be admitted that the number for the Warwickshire potters is inexplicably low in the unstamped group, even allowing for the fact that they seem to have stamped all their mortaria for as long as the practice survived. The presence of the so-called Raetian mortaria in small numbers is to be expected on a military site; these mortaria were made in Britain at Wroxeter and Wilderspool,[37] and possibly elsewhere, although some of the early ones may well have been imported. The two York ones are probably British.

During the third century, and in the fourth century down to A.D. 370, the Hartshill and Mancetter potters had control of the market, supplying 20 out of a possible total of 31, or 64.5 per cent. The Nene Valley potteries,[38] which became prominent for mortarium production only in the third century, provide only a relatively small proportion, 25.8 per cent, during the third and fourth centuries together. Indeed the number of mortaria at York from the Nene Valley (8) is small and all could be earlier than A.D. 370. However, some might be later, since the Nene Valley potteries supplied colour-coated ware to the north after the Picts' War and were still making mortaria then.

It is, however, at this particular time, *c.* A.D. 370, that radical changes in sources of supply occur both at York and in the North generally. The fact that these developments seem to follow the Picts' War (A.D. 367) directly, strongly suggests that they are either a result of it or of some contemporary disturbances affecting manufacturing centres in the Midlands or damaging the marketing communications. Whatever the reason, Mancetter and Hartshill mortaria do not occur in the North later than A.D. 370. The Crambeck potteries in east Yorkshire began work about the middle of the fourth century[39] and had only a moderate market until A.D. 370; after this date they had a stranglehold on the northern market, supplying all the mortaria which can be dated with certainty to this period. There are some hints that the Warwickshire potteries may have produced mortaria after A.D. 370, and it is not safe to assume that the reason for the change is to be sought there. It is interesting that the black-burnished wares disappear from the North at the same time as the Warwickshire mortaria, while the floruit of the late 'Huntcliff' cooking-pot coincides exactly with that of Crambeck;[40] it raises the possibility of a deliberate policy of buying pottery as far as possible within the limits of Flavia Caesariensis or, at least as locally as possible.

The mortaria from York thus present a fairly clear and straightforward picture. York would certainly be an attractive market for potteries outside the area; and following the general rules which hold elsewhere some local production would be expected at least in the second century. Of local potters, or even northern potters, there is little sign after the second century until Crambeck emerged, working on a much more ambitious scale and supplying the whole of the North. The existence of military potteries in the Flavian period, if not later, must also be regarded as a possibility.

Potteries and potters

1. South-east England, perhaps Kent, or less probably Gallia Belgica. Total 5.
   C. Julius Pri(vatus?); Lossa; Q. Valerius Veranius (1,1*). A.D. 70–100. Q. Valerius Se(cundus?).* A.D. 55–80. (Q. Valerius Se-, may have worked at Colchester, in Kent, or, less probably, in Gaul.)
2. Potteries south of Verulamium, near Watling Street (including the kilns at Radlett and Brockley Hill).
   Total 4.
   Albinus (1,1*); Marinus I*; Sollus. A.D. 70–100.
3. Near Lincoln (a. Technical College kiln; b. probably all South Carlton).
   Total 7.
   a. Vitalis I. *c.* A.D. 90–115.
   b. Aesico (3,1*); Crico*; unidentified (1). A.D. 150–90.
4. Colchester.
   Total 2.
   Martinus II; Herringbone I.* A.D. 150–200.
5. Hartshill-Mancetter potteries, Warwickshire.
   Total 28.
   G. Attius Marinus. A.D. 100–30; Vitalis IV (3*). A.D. 120–45; Illiterate A. A.D. 100–140; Bonoxus;* Bruscius;* Gratinus (1,1*); Icotasgus (3,2*); Junius (1,1)*; Loccius Vibius (2,1*); Minomelus; RBIVS*; Sarrius (1,1*); Similis I (3*); Illiterate B; Fragmentary (1). All A.D. 135–90.
6. Soller (Kreis Düren), in Lower Germany.
   Total 1.
   Verecundus. Probably A.D. 150–200.
7. Aldborough, Yorks.
   Total 3.
   One, or possibly, two semi-literate potters whose stamps can be read as Nator, Nacol, etc. (2,1*). A.D. 95/100–40.

8. Probably Wilderspool.
   Total 1.
   Doccius or Docilis. *c.* A.D. 120–50.
9. Uncertain Midland sources.
   Total 3.
   Mar-;* -artetumus; Marcelinus? A.D. 130–90.
10. North Midlands or Yorkshire.
    Total 2.
    Genialis (2).* Most of his products were made in the Midlands, but all nine mortaria stamped with this die are in a fabric which is more probably northern, and all nine are from sites in Yorkshire. A.D. 100–40.
11. North or Midlands.
    Total 6.
    Baro.* This potter has trituration grit very like that used at Rossington Bridge and his mortaria could perhaps have been made there. A potter of this name worked at Colchester in the second century; if it is the same man he must have migrated to the North. A.D. 160–200. Unidentified fragmentary stamps (3,2*).

Potters probably working in the vicinity of York

The distribution of their known stamps is given in full.

Divict(us)	York (3, from different vessels). Second-century, probably earlier than A.D. 150 (fig. 19: 1, 2, and 17).
Mercator	York (3,2,* all from different vessels). A.D. 130–80 (fig. 19: 3–6, and 18).
Vitalis V	York (3,* from different vessels). *c.* A.D. 120–80 (fig. 19: 7–9, and 19).
Agripp(a?)	Malton, York.* Agrippinus or Agrippianus are possible expansions, but are less likely than Agrippa, since the York stamp is complete. The two stamps are from different dies, each showing horizontal striations suggestive of wood graining. Second-century (fig. 19: 10 and 20).
Metilius	York.* Second-century (fig. 19: 11 and 21).
Mittius?	York. Second-century (fig. 19: 12 and 22).
Muco	Bar Hill[41]; York.* *c.* A.D. 130–70 (fig. 19: 13 and 23).
Sarus	Doncaster; York. Perhaps A.D. 100–40. It has not been possible to locate the York example, but a rubbing and sketch show it to be identical with the Doncaster one, which is reproduced here (fig. 19: 14 and 24).
A. T-	York. Probably mid-second-century (fig. 19: 15 and 25).
]LV?LI	York.* Only further examples will permit a complete reading. Second-century (fig. 19: 16 and 26).

The mortaria of these potters are all in red- to orange-brown fabric, occasionally with grey core and mostly with a cream slip, though a few are self-coloured. When the trituration grit is preserved, it is largely white, though some have a few grey grits also, and Mercator used some brown grit too.

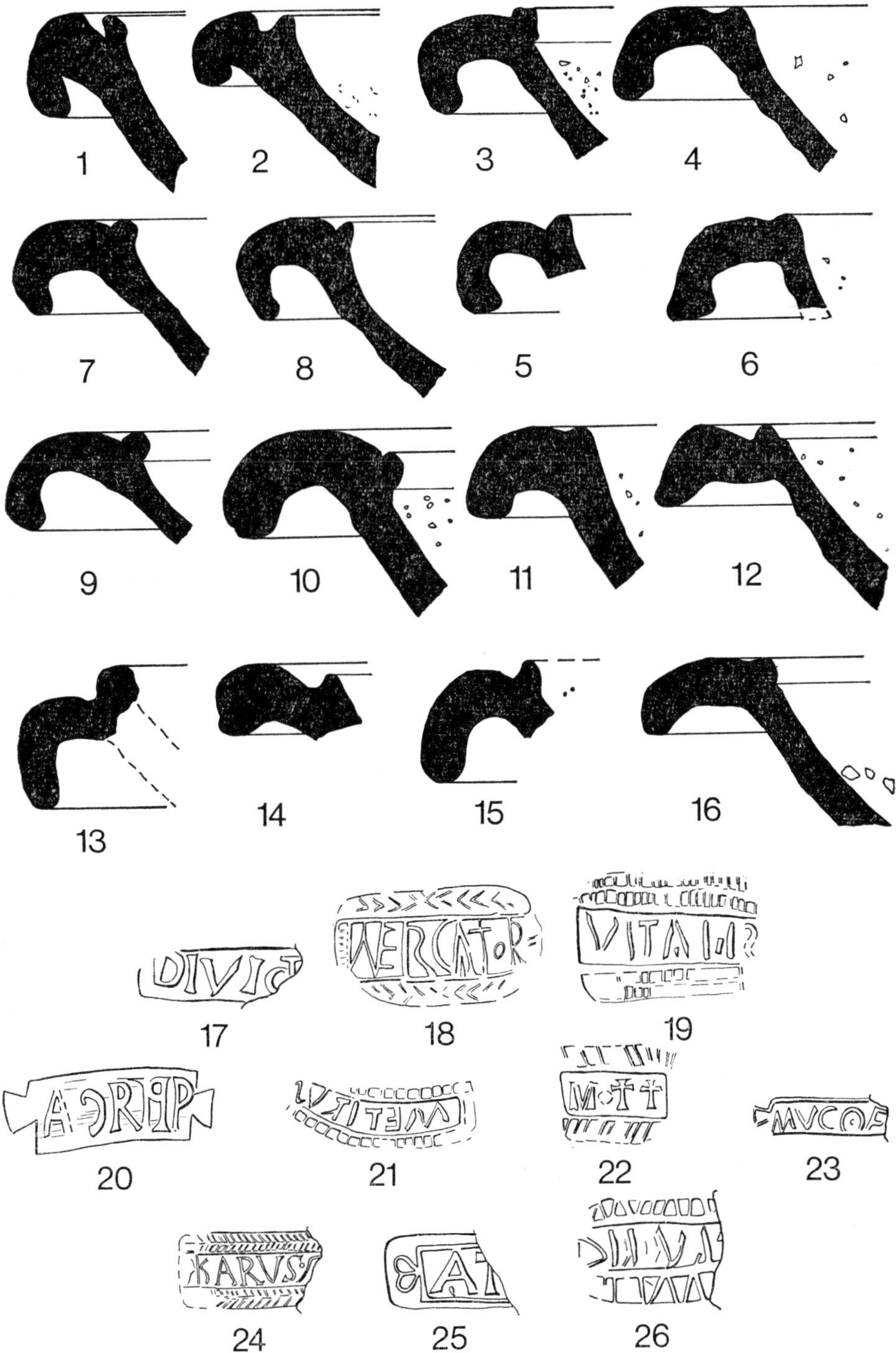

Figure 19. Rim-sections of mortaria probably made at or near York, with the corresponding potters' stamps ($\frac{1}{2}$).

Unstamped mortaria from York (102 in the sample)

† indicates that these products were never stamped.

To A.D. 125

† *Gillam* 237. A.D. 60–90. Total 7.
† Other Flavian mortaria in red-brown fabrics, probably made locally. *c.* A.D. 70–100. Total 5.
Gillam 238 (Pottery 1). A.D. 70–100. Total 12.
† A variant product, perhaps from Pottery 1. *c.* A.D. 95–125. Total 1.
Pottery 2. A.D. 90–125. Total 1.
Made in Italy. Probably within the period A.D. 80–125. Total 1. Italian mortaria are very rare in Britain and it is unlikely that any of those in Britain date later than A.D. 125.

Second century to early third century

Potteries near Oxford, where mortaria made after *c.* A.D. 160 were never stamped. Total 2.
Red-brown fabrics probably mostly made locally and not always stamped (including one mortarium with 'Raetian' type slip, which could perhaps be local though Wilderspool would provide a ready source). Total 17.
Pottery 5. Total 4.
Pottery 4. Total 3.
† 'Raetian' type mortaria. Total 2.

†*Third and fourth centuries down to A.D. 370*

Pottery 5. Total 20.
Potteries near Oxford. Total 1.
Near *Gillam* 272. Probably made in the south of England in the third century. Total 1.
Wall-sided mortarium possibly made in the North-East (close parallels from Malton and Aldborough). Total 1.

†*Third and fourth centuries*

Stibbington-Castor potteries in the Nene Valley. Total 8.

†*c. A.D. 350–400*

Crambeck potteries, east Yorkshire. Total 16. Although these potteries began in the second half of the fourth century their major production was confined to the period after A.D. 370.

Notes

1. R.C.H.M., *York*.
2. A study of the stamped amphorae of York is also desirable.
3. The other collections having stamped samian ware from York are: the British Museum, the University Museum of Archaeology and Ethnology, Cambridge, Kingston-upon-Hull Museums, Sheffield City Museum, Bootham School, York and St John's College, York.
4. *CIL* VII quotes catalogue numbers and provenances for most of the York stamps it records, though the numbers were apparently not marked on the sherds and referred to their arrangement in the cases.
5. *CIL* VII notes some stamps from Lincoln in the Yorkshire Museum. They were inadvertantly included by Dr Oswald as coming from York. The same is probably true of some London stamps at York, and it is unknown how many of the early unprovenanced pieces are from these sources.
6. Percentages without brackets refer to definite York finds. Those in brackets are based on the total stamps in the Yorkshire Museum and elsewhere.
7. The most common potters, in order of frequency, are: Secundus, Patricius, Calvus, Crestus, Cosius Virilis, Primus, Frontinus, Cotto, Coelus and Rufinus. Curiously enough, Vitalis of La Graufesenque, normally the most prolific of the Flavian potters, only has four stamps at York. This may be connected with the drop of material in the later Flavian period.
8. This percentage is based on the stamps of potters definitely known to have worked at Lezoux. A further 17 (15.6) per cent of the stamps are Central Gaulish and probably almost all from that centre.
9. Compare the situation at Richborough (B. W. Cunliffe (ed.), *Fifth Report on the Excavations of the Roman fort at Richborough, Kent* (1969), 147).
10. See now J. R. Terrisse, *Les céramiques sigillées gallo-romaines des Martres-de-Veyre* (*Gallia* Supplément xix, 1969).
11. For an impression of the quantities of material involved see J. P. Gillam's interesting study in *Arch. Ael.* 4th ser., xxviii (1950), 177ff. It may be noted, however, that neither the suggested date (*c.* A.D. 200), nor the significance of the deposit, is as secure as was then thought.
12. That Chresimus and Felicio worked at Montans is certain, as many of their stamps have been found there. The third potter Q(uintus) V(alerius?) C( ) is assigned to Montans on grounds of fabric and distribution. Seven burnt cups of his, all stamped with the same die, were found at St Katherine Coleman, London, with identical burnt cups stamped by Felicio (Guildhall Museum 1926.105). As all have unworn footrings, they were probably from a shop involved in the Second Fire of London (*Ant. J.*, xxv (1945), 52ff).
13. Stamps from all three occur in the Saalburg Erdkastell (Schönberger and Hartley, *Saalburg Jahrbuch*, xxvii (1970), 21, where a date of A.D. 135–9 is suggested for the end of the fort).
14. Cunliffe, *op. cit.*, 146.
15. Argonne ware is not uncommon in Britain (Table 1). York's percentage is rather low in comparison, and it may be noted that the Argonne potters were in an unfavourable position for direct shipping to York.
16. *ILS* 4751 (Domburg) attests a *negotiator cretarius Britannicianus* appropriately at the mouth of the Rhine.

17. R.C.H.M., *York*, 141f.
18. *ibid.*, 137–41.
19. *ibid.*, 135.
20. Potters whose work is entirely or largely pre-Flavian are: Abitus*, Acutus, Aquitanus*, Bilicatus*, Castus*, Felix, Gallicanus*, Masc(u)lus (three, one*), Modestus (three, two*), Niger (two, both*), Passenus (three*), Sabinus and Scotnus.
21. Sir Mortimer Wheeler, *The Stanwick Fortifications* (1954), 30–1.
22. *RIB* 665.
23. Sheppard Frere, *Britannia* (1967), 138.
24. *Studien zu den Militärgrenzen Roms* (Vorträge des 6. internationalen Limeskongresses, 1967), 74.
25. Frere, *op. cit.*, 134–40 discusses all the factors involved; see above pp. 76–7.
26. for *Gillam* forms see J. P. Gillam, *Types of Roman Coarse Pottery Vessels in Northern Britain*, 2nd edition (1968), Oriel Press.
27. Cunliffe, *op. cit.*, 179, note on Q. Valerius Veranius.
28. E. E. Richards and K. F. Hartley, 'Spectrographic Analysis of some Romano-British Mortaria', *Bulletin of the London Institute of Archaeology*, no. 5 (1965), 34.
29. *J.R.S.*, li (1961), 173; lii, 168; lv, 208; lvi, 206.
30. information about this has kindly been supplied by Frau Dr D. Haupt of the Rheinisches Landesmuseum, Bonn.
31. M. R. Hull, *The Roman Potters' Kilns of Colchester* (1963), 114–16.
32. *Bull. London Inst. Arch.*, no. 5 (1965), 32–3.
33. *ibid.*, 27.
34. Attributed largely on the distribution of stamps: (i) Aldborough (6); Bainbridge; York*. (ii) Aldborough (12); York (2). They may all be the work of one potter, but it is impossible to be certain that two are not involved.
35. Mortaria in orange- or red-brown fabrics differing only slightly from each other, are common in the North and West of England. The potters producing these fabrics might be local, as at Aldborough. Alternatively, potters like those at Rossington Bridge, near Doncaster, and at Wilderspool might make a bid for a more extensive regional market. Distinction between these fabrics is not always a simple matter, but differences in the trituration grit, rim-forms and the distribution of known potters' work can all provide useful additional criteria. York was clearly in or near an area where such a fabric could be produced (one of the two fabrics used at Aldborough, and that used at Rossington Bridge are both in this range); the rim-forms involved at York seem to include earlier types than were made at Rossington Bridge, which started production in the Antonine period. The grit of the York mortaria is not remotely like that used at Rossington Bridge. Moreover, the lack of mortaria, stamped or unstamped, which can be confidently assigned to Rossington Bridge or Wilderspool suggests that there were nearer sources for these mortaria.
36. *Bull. London Inst. Arch.*, no. 5 (1965), 37.
37. *ibid.*, 27 and 31.
38. B. R. Hartley, *Notes on the Roman Pottery Industry in the Nene Valley* (1960), 17.
39. *Ant. J.*, xvii (1937), 392–413.
40. *Carnuntina*, iii (1956), 73–6.
41. Perhaps carried by a soldier of Legio VI, though the presence of this Legion is not attested epigraphically at Bar Hill.

A. F. NORMAN

Religion in Roman York

By the mere accident of survival, religious attitudes in Eburacum in the period immediately following its foundation are revealed with remarkable clarity. The monuments and inscriptions which may be assigned with certainty to the period of the Ninth Legion indicate the patterns of religion with a vividness of expression which, however conventional and formalized it may appear, confirms and supplements the accounts of the contemporary literary authorities. The great leap forward under the Flavians which brought about the harrying and occupation of the North under Cerialis and its settlement and consolidation thereafter, may be signified, in physical terms, by the foundation of the legionary fortress, which was to remain the key to the North. The literary tradition, represented by Tacitus, puts into the mouths of both Agricola and the native chieftain, Calgacus, at Mons Graupius, the sentiments of the executors and opponents of this policy. The devotion of the army, which has led them to the very edge of the world, is translated into eagerness to secure the prizes of victory – prizes which are exemplified by the exploitation of Pateley Bridge lead mining under army control, in the governorship of Agricola himself. Simultaneously, the Greek tradition of scholarship, with its more intellectual and cosmopolitan approach, sheds light upon the religious superstitions and beliefs current in Britain. In Plutarch's treatise on 'The Cessation of Oracles', with the Pythian festival of A.D. 83–4 as its chronological setting, Demetrius of Tarsus entertains a casual gathering of Greek intellectuals with information on the subject, gained during an official reconnaissance of the outer islands of Britain, from which he had but lately returned.[1] Indeed, it would appear that this mission, completed in Agricola's governorship, is the source of some of the information vaguely outlined in Tacitus. The discovery in York of the two bronze votive tablets written in Greek,[2] "To the deities of the governor's headquarters, the scribe Demetrius", and "To Ocean and Tethys, Demetrius", rounds off the converging literary traditions, confirms what they have to say concerning the religious attitudes then current in Roman Britain, and focuses them upon life in Eburacum, for the identification of the scribe Demetrius with the grammarian Demetrius of Tarsus is rendered all the more probable by the nuances of dedication. In this cosmopolitan society of the military headquarters, the religious standpoint and terminology of the administrative class are revealed most fully. A temporary civil servant, imbued with the literary culture of Hellenism, marks, in his private capacity, his official conformity and individual loyalty to the traditions and aspirations of imperial Rome. "The deities of the governor's headquarters" combine the concepts of the *genius loci*, or ruler worship, since the governor's headquarters are *ex hypothesi* so maintained under imperial auspices, and of service discipline. In his first dedication, then, Demetrius follows the true Roman tradition. That to "Ocean and Tethys", however, betrays his personal background and his interpretation of the mission of Rome. The phrase deliberately transfers to the conquerors of the furthest province of the West the religious terminology which Alexander the Great had employed to mark his own point of furthest penetration in the East. The classical Greek allusion betrays the scholar; his combination of formulae reveals his confidence in Rome's destiny in the West and his individual conception of her as the heir and successor to the greatest conqueror and civilizer of the ancient world.

The orderly-room clerk of the Ninth Legion, Vitalis, in his dedication of an altar to the holy god Silvanus,[3] is no less revealing in his religious motivation. If Demetrius' language indicated confidence in Rome's mission, the straightforward expressions of the Roman N.C.O. are, perhaps, more indicative of awe at his new surroundings. Silvanus, god of the countryside, as a '*deus sanctus*', is to be propitiated by, and identified with the aspirations of the soldiery serving in his domain, and in the process he has become militarized. The formula of dedication is conventional, but there is a significant addition of a more personal character, presumably by Vitalis ("Let the gift, this gift, form part. I must not touch."). Here is a note of personal piety and more urgent veneration, whether of Vitalis himself or of some other, reflecting one man's reaction to his new environment. For all that the military seek to mould him in their own image, Silvanus has evidently not yet been completely assimilated, and is treated with more than casual regard.

The successful implantation of the Roman way of life under the shadow of the fortress is exemplified, in this pioneering period, by the memorial of the unnamed soldier of the Ninth from Novaria.[4] The concentration of ancillary services of every description for the benefit of the Legion promoted and maintained a romanized social order with its own civilian and religious attitudes, however military its inspiration. This funerary stone marks the first extension into the North of the system of family piety which bound together, in dutiful service and acts of religious observance, the members of the family, whether free-born or freedmen. The freedmen of the dead legionary perform their last obligations to their master in the manner that the Romans will make the standard to be accepted here, as throughout the Empire. The army had indeed brought with it the traditions and structure of the civil society, which it would maintain and protect with an emphasis equally expressed by the Emperor Trajan, in his building of the fortress defences in stone, and by his legionary Duccius in his epitaph.

For all units of the army, great or small, a standard calendar of religious occasions was to be observed, whereby the pattern of ritual, as laid down by Augustus himself, was duly maintained in unbroken tradition. The *Feriale Duranum*, dating from the third century A.D. and originating from the other end of the Empire, indicates the strength of this unit tradition, preserving all the virtues of the Roman inheritance. Loyalty to the imperial house (and how could it be otherwise when even Caracalla officially counted among his ancestors Marcus Aurelius, Trajan and Nerva?), worship of the pantheon upon which was based the welfare of the Roman people, and observance of time-honoured Roman holidays, all formed part of this pattern, and were combined with specifically military celebrations, such as the festivals of the *Rosalia* or *armilustrum*, in a formalized tradition which was to become universal. The tradition and sense of duty inculcated in both citizen legionaries and provincial auxilia inevitably spilled over into the civilian community fostered by the fortress. The forms of ritual practised in the chapel and hall of the headquarters building quickly find their counterpart in a civilian context in the adjacent *canabae* and civil settlement, as is evident from the offering to Juppiter Optimus Maximus by the resident villagers of Carriden (Velunia) on the Antonine Wall.

If, in the more anonymous period that follows its foundation, the religious life of the legion based in York becomes more obscure, legitimate inferences concerning it may be drawn from the record of dedications made by detachments and individuals, while absent on active service. In the field, as in the headquarters' garrison, the military, whether as unit formations or individuals, reveal their eagerness to conciliate the presiding deities of their new station by dedications which fall outside the official calendar of religious events. Thus, unit dedications by vexillations of the Sixth Legion are to be found at Carrawburgh[5] and at Croy Hill[6] to the Nymphs, or at Howgill on Hadrian's Wall, to Cocidius.[7] Of such vexillationary offerings the most informative is perhaps that dedicated at Corbridge to Sol Invictus under Calpurnius Agricola,[8] with its later erasure of the title of the deity. This would seem to indicate the state of flux in which pagan ritual was to find itself in the late second century, whereby an offering to the military version of Sol, who was to become equated with Mithra, was within a generation erased, presumably because of the divine pretensions of Commodus who was so hated by the British legions. Vexillations, as well as less official groups, offer their thanksgivings to deities which are either members of the pantheon or inseparable from the destiny of Rome. At Chesterholm,[9] a centurion of the Sixth pays due honour to the Fortune of the Roman People. Fortune herself is honoured by joint vexillations of the Sixth and Twentieth at Castlecary,[10] while a group of soldiers of the Sixth, "citizens of Italy and Noricum", erected there a shrine and statuette to Mercury, in their private capacity.[11] In view of these private dedications, it is no surprise to find the great festivals of the military calendar also celebrated in the forward stations. Soldiers of the garrison at Corbridge pay their vows to Juppiter Optimus Maximus, for the safety of detachments of the Sixth and Twentieth, perhaps with more insistence than would have been the case had they remained snugly at base headquarters,[12] while in the dedication to Mars Ultor[13] under Julius Verus, the ritual devotion of the detachment of the Sixth at the festival of their chief war-god, was no doubt sharpened on this occasion by the recollection of the crisis so recently past. The most comprehensive dedication from the legion while on active service is, however, the private offering at Corbridge, made in Severan times by the centurion Apolinaris.[14] Here the cults of the military, the locality and of the traditional Roman are fused, under imperial inspiration, in the significant combination of Juppiter Dolichenus, Caelestis Brigantia and Salus. The British army and the northern province, so lately in arms against him, were directed by Severus, through religious propaganda and allegory and the deliberate identification of Brigantia with the person of the empress, to identify their aspirations and future welfare with his new imperial dynasty.

It was in the imperial palace established in Eburacum for his British campaign that Severus died. The temple of Bellona, for the existence of which no other evidence survives, is connected with this event. The location of palace and temple is unknown, but judging from parallels in second-century Carnuntum and fourth-century Antioch, it lay outside the area both of fortress and of colony, easy of access to both. From the surviving remains, it may be hazarded that the most likely area for such a complex is that of High Ousegate, with its record of temples to Hercules and to the divinities of the emperor and the goddess Ioug[. . .][15] and observed temple enclaves and extensive bath and building remains. The monumental work embodied in the old Ouse Bridge may well have been associated with it also.[16]

It is, indeed, with Severus that Eburacum reaches maturity. As a colony and capital of a province, the place is no longer exclusively military, and civilian deities, both native and foreign, come to be of more account in this growing and more cosmopolitan community. The links with the military and with officialdom, naturally, remain as strong as ever. Of the military religions of the out-stations, Juppiter Optimus Maximus appears in a dedication from the *colonia* by P. Aelius Marcianus, prefect of a cohort,[17] but in conjunction with the gods and goddesses of hospitality and the penates – a private form of thanksgiving. The presence of the locally executed York Gorgon[18] may indicate the worship of Minerva, which certainly would be part of the community's religious life, as is Neptune,[19] and the Dioscuri.[20] Mars appears in three manifestations, of which two[21] are bald inscriptions, and the third the impressive life-size cult statue.[22] Mercury receives some of the veneration that is his due, with a crudely executed relief and altar[23] while Fortune presides over the baths in the civil settlement and the fortress, just as she does in the out-stations,[24] and allows a glimpse into the life of the ladies of the garrison. When Sosia Juncina, wife of the legionary legate, sets up her altar in the settlement baths, we may assume that here was a polite meeting place for the ladies also, though segregation from the males would of course be the social rule. The role of the military officer in promoting the worship of oriental religion is to be observed in the building of the temple to Serapis by Claudius Hieronymianus, commander of the Sixth. This devoted pagan follows the lead given by Severus to the spread of Eastern religions in promoting such a cult and incidentally stressing the more soldierly interpretation of it by his emphasis upon Serapis as a '*deus sanctus*' and his representation of the standards, with their careful confusion of cult and military emblems.[25] A similar conformity in expressing the combined religious and political aspirations of the emperors, though perhaps more to be expected from one of his station, is revealed by the imperial freedman Nikomedes, with his dedication of a statue of Britannia Sancta.[26] This links with the dedications to Dea Brigantia made by the units serving on the Wall or by the communities in Wharfedale and Airedale, and is to be interpreted as an expression by a member of the imperial household of those policies, religious and political, which were to secure the loyalty of the civilian communities by this identification of interests, visually represented. If in Adel or Slack, the dedication is to Dea Brigantia or Deus Bregans, or in Greetland and Castleford to Dea Victoria Brigantia[27] as the personification of the local area and its place in the imperial scheme of things, it is appropriate that in the new colony and provincial capital an imperial servant should give expression to a wider view of the role of the community more appropriate to its new station.

The tie between the divinity of the reigning emperor and the deities of the locality had long been accepted and expressed in conventional terminology. This does not necessarily imply, however, that such belief was not sincerely held, for the form of religious expression was held to be no less important than the content. Indeed, with the promotion of Eburacum to colonial status, the bond between the community and the emperor became more closely-knit, with the performance of religious obligations towards the imperial house based on a more formal and regular ritual. The institution of the sevirate in particular, which allowed the socially inferior mercantile and freedman classes to demonstrate their loyal devotion to the colony and the Augustus, at considerable financial cost, encouraged the fullest possible social integration, and a more personal participation in the ritual of emperor worship. Clearly, the sevir M. Verecundius Diogenes and his wife Julia Fortunata[28] are persons of property and pride in their station, with some pretensions to literary culture, if the poetic tag (*fida coniuncta marito*) which ends Fortunata's memorial means anything. M. Aurelius Lunaris, "sevir Augustalis of the colonies of Eboracum and Lindum in the province of Lower Britain", is filled with loyal sentiments towards his "Protecting Goddess, Boudig" and to Salus, one of the potent deities that preserve the welfare of the empire, upon the successful completion of his journey to Bordeaux in A.D. 237.[29] The nuances of the combination of the British deity Boudig, the Celtic equivalent of Victoria, and of Salus, in the imperial context of that year, show the genuine patriotism of this British businessman as expressed in religious terms.

The colony's own deities were recognized as closely conjoined with the imperial destiny, both by members of the garrison and by those of the civilian community. It may be merely accidental that the two local deities that are peculiar to Eburacum, Arciacon[30] and the goddess Ioug[. . .][31] are both linked with the divinity of the emperor(s). What is not accidental is the dedication to the conjoined divinity of Augustus and the genius of Eburacum on the site of what must certainly have been the administrative centre of the *colonia* in Railway Street.[32] The head of Constantine,[33] probably from the headquarters in the fortress, points to the retention of this cult of imperial loyalty in the post-pagan period. Old habits died hard, and the expression of loyalty through worship of the emperor was transmuted into a religious cult of which the emperor was the sponsor. The political result was the same: religion and loyalty to the régime remained synonymous.

Religious life inevitably became more cosmopolitan, and with immigrant population came immigrant deities. From the German provinces came the gods Veteris[34] and Sucelus,[35] to be worshipped by the civilian population. From the Celtic provinces came the worship of the Mother Goddesses, the triad of nature deities who provide the inspiration and means of civilized life. Both military and civilian treat them with deep and personal veneration: they are "the mother Goddesses of the home"[36] to Julius Crescens, "his own mother goddesses" to the veteran Rustius,[37] while from the legionary river-pilot, Minucius Mudenus, probably from the nature of his calling, the "mother goddesses of Africa, Italy and Gaul" receive their due honours.[38] An altar[39] depicts the pattern of ritual and offering which these protecting and all-pervasive deities might normally receive.

The strength of oriental cults, already observed in the case of Serapis, may be further assessed by the Mithraic remains from the colony. It would be natural that in the religious experience of the high ranking military officers and civilians of the third-century provincial capital, that such cults, with their insistence on duty, self-discipline and endurance, would have the greatest appeal, especially when they enjoyed the increasing support of the emperors. Thus, the discovery of the Mithraic relief of the bull-slaying near the centre of the colony comes as no surprise,[40] but the representation of the various grades of initiation and the ritual of ordeal which it contains is a significant addition to the corpus of Mithraic art. So is the statue dedicated to Ariman, from the edge of the colony near Station Road.[41] This, the only dedication in the province, represents the Mithraic god of evil and death, and is full of Mithraic allegory. The sceptre of his rule, the keys of heaven, the wings of the wind, and the snake course of the sun's progress are the powers of destiny which the initiate must be trained by ordeal to meet, and overcome. Mithraism in fact remained a religion almost exclusively practised by the higher officers of the army and the local community, ascetic and masculine in its appeal. In the funerary monuments, also, the influence of the Orient may be seen in the representation of the mourning Atys,[42] with which the worship of Cybele, the Magna Mater, is to be associated. The manner in which such oriental religions could diverge into magic is shown by the gold amulet found in the Old Railway Station site, inside the colony. Of its two lines, the first consists of a number of magical symbols, the second of Coptic Greek letters, which may be interpreted as a Coptic invocation, or as a Hebraic magical formula, analogous to that from Caernarvon.[43] For the organization of worship of the various cults, comparatively little evidence survives. It has been suggested that the persons who dedicated the temple to Hercules, Titus Perpet[. . .] and Aeternus, were members of a priestly college or magistrates of the colony, and the existence of a craft-guild is attested by the scratched greeting on a roof-tile, "Pollio to the guild; good luck",[44] but otherwise arguments are those of inference from elsewhere.

It is, however, in the ceremonial of burial that the religious piety and family duty of the inhabitants, whether military or civilian, are most intimately expressed, and changes of custom most clearly observed. Here the well-to-do, whose articulate professions on tombstones and sarcophagi reproduce sentiments common throughout the province and Empire, have confirmation of their attitudes in the silent witness of more anonymous burials by the common folk. The funerary banquet scenes on the memorial stones of Julia Velva,[45] of Mantinia and Candida,[46] or of Aelia Aeliana,[47] conventional though they may appear, are certainly not to be divorced from current faith and practice. In the cemeteries of the Railway Station area, the Mount and Trentholme Drive, the banquet in which the deceased were held to share is actually provided for them. Animal bones, dishes and cups are the tangible and surviving remains of the grave offerings with which dutiful relatives supplied their deceased kinsfolk. Similarly the hexameter verses which mark Corellia Optata's cremation,[48] though conventional in form and indicative of more than usual pretensions to culture in a military community, are not to be dismissed as merely formal expressions of loss and empty words. The sentiments, however high-flown, are as genuinely pathetic and religious in tone as the description of Simplicia Florentina as "a most innocent soul",[49] while the tenderness of the family portraiture, such as that of Julia Brica[50] or the woman's head from Fishergate, finds its counterpart in the adornments and grave goods which accompany the burials of the poorer classes. It is clear that, inside the family, the *Di Manes* consistently received their due and more, and that preoccupations with the after-life were never far distant from the ceremonial of pagan ritual.

Thus, the practice of cremation, current through the first to third centuries A.D., proceeded with due piety on the part of the family, and in accordance with the laws and customs of a Roman community. From the second century, however, the simultaneous practice of inhumation comes into operation, and variations of the ritual of burial become more immediately obvious. Here there may be seen the survival of the age-old native custom of crouched burial in examples from the Station area, the Mount and Trentholme Drive, indicative, perhaps, of some influx of the native population of the countryside into a Roman urban community. More appropriate to the military class, and perhaps an imported practice, are the recorded upright burials, and for a rather higher social class, provision is made for the pursuits practised in life to be continued after death, by burying the deceased in company with his dog, horse and drinking cup.[51] The link with the hunting scenes so often depicted on mosaics is here most obvious, as is the care and consideration for the welfare of the deceased in his after-life. Whether he was of high or low degree, the primary object of his family was to surround him with the objects with which he had been familiar on earth, for his solace and comfort thereafter. The belief in the after-life among the common folk of Roman paganism was not one of remote philosophic speculation nor yet an empty parade of pessimistic ritual. That there was life after death, and a two-way relationship between the deceased and his kin is proclaimed in optimistic terms and with reference to a continuing physical existence both by monuments and grave goods.

The information gained from the crematorium and cemetery of Trentholme

Drive[52] is necessarily of the greatest value in the assessment of this aspect of pagan religious beliefs and practice during its period of use, which was from Antonine to Constantinian times at least. The status of the deceased was almost entirely that of civilians of the lower class; the overlapping of inhumation and cremation is confirmed with certainty, and the cemetery was without formal layout or organization. In the case of cremations, which lasted into the third quarter of the third century, various rituals are to be observed. Fragments of fused glass represent the lachrymatories which accompanied them to the pyre: the remains of coins and gifts – food, pottery, gaming counters – are also found, while in some cases the ritualistic use of the urn which contained the ashes was emphasized by the deliberate boring of holes, which would prevent any intruding grave-robber from using them.

Inhumation, as practised from the later-second century onwards, also shows some remarkable features. The relatively restricted area of the burial ground contains a heavy concentration of interments over a long period and a continued re-use of the site, with drastic disturbance of existing burials (plate 8). Nothing is more indicative of the determined, almost ruthless, piety of the family to secure a decent funeral for their own dead, than the mangled remains which have survived from the earlier burials following the intrusion of later funerals. Skeletons are dug through and skulls detached, and the bits and pieces of disarticulated bones hurriedly jumbled together in the filling of these later graves. Clearly, the major preoccupation of the mourners was with the decent disposal of their own dead, and this act of piety extended no further than the family. The influence of the *Di Manes* was thus confined to a restricted circle, and there is no question of it applying to other members of the community, nor, in the burial of the dead, was there any question of sacrilege or pollution in the disturbance of the remains of those outside the immediate family group. It also follows that, in this stratum of the population at least, the overriding necessity is for the ceremony actually to take place. The survival of the interment intact, however desirable in itself for the well-being of the family, was in the nature of things impossible to guarantee, although they did their best, by the provision of coffins, cairns, or in a higher income group, of burial cists, to secure this. In only too many instances, however, such efforts were to be in vain.

A further feature of this cemetery is the probability of a further change of burial customs associated with inhumation itself. The grave-goods run from Antoninus to Constantine, according to the evidence of the associated pottery, and then cease; but evidence of coinage contradicts this, for over one fifth of the coins found on the cemetery site are issued in the period 330–75 A.D. – a proportion which appears too high to be explained as merely casual losses. The inference must be that burials proceeded through that period, but that the custom of burying pots with the dead had ceased. Although there is no explicit evidence for Christianity here, the possibility remains that this is a change of burial custom inspired by Christian influence.

The only explicit evidence for Christianity in York, in fact, consists of the records of the Council of Arles, convened by Constantine in A.D. 314,[53] and one burial. At Arles, in company with other bishops, a presbyter and a deacon, Eborius, bishop of the city of Eburacum, attends. Evidently at this early period the bishop has assumed a name homonymous with that of his see. The burial contains a valediction which is undoubtedly Christian ("Farewell, sister. Live in God"), but the whole collection of finery and grave goods associated with it indicates the survival of pagan practices.[54] Clearly at this time there had been no complete break in burial customs caused by the spread of Christianity.

Such a break is, in fact, observable in a different context. Pagan tombs and sarcophagi, both military and civilian, are found re-used. Thus, the coffin of Aelia Severa, "*honeste femine*" (and so possibly connected with the decurionate), is re-used for a gypsum burial of an adult male, the tombstone of Flavia Augustina, wife of a legionary veteran, being used as lid.[55] The remains found in the coffin of Julia Fortunata, wife of a sevir of the colony,[56] appear to be masculine and indicate re-use while the coffin of the decurion, Flavius Bellator,[57] who died at 29, contained the remains of one much younger. In particular, the memorials of relatives of the centurionate, which were severely elegant as befitted their station, suffered by such re-use. In Castle Yard, Julia Victorina, wife of a centurion,[58] is replaced by a male gypsum burial, and the coffin deliberately buried to hide the inscription, as was that of the centurion Aurelius Super.[59] Elsewhere, the coffin of Simplicia Florentina, a centurion's daughter who died at 10 months, contained the bones of a much older child. Such a breach of the traditions shared by both colony and legion could only have occurred at a time when the machinery of civilian and military administration in its classical form had lapsed – that is from the end of the fourth century, when presumably Christianity would more commonly provide the ritual of burial. Most significant in such a context is the actual burial of the sarcophagi in the secondary interments of Super and Victorina, along with the complete absence of grave-goods in all these burials.

Yet another clue to the growth of Christian influence in Eburacum may perhaps be found in the use of lead recorded in numerous burials. This may have had its origin as a pagan custom, as the rich female burial in Walmgate, with its coin of Septimius Severus, would indicate.[60] There are records of more than a score of burials in which lead was used as coffins or linings, several being accompanied by gypsum. Grave-goods are recorded in only half a dozen instances, the probability thus being that the majority of lead burials are Christian. This would square with the known use of lead in some quantity for Christian baptismal tanks and coffins in Lincolnshire in the fourth century. While the presence or absence of grave-goods may not of itself indicate religious change – there is, for instance, record of a gypsum burial in lead coffin accompanied by a cremation in a lead container and grave-goods consisting of four glass flasks, which survive – the cumulative effect of their absence in so many leaden coffins is impressive; and one example, at least, the child's burial in Castle Yard, is to be regarded as closely related with the re-used coffin of Julia Victorina, both in level and alignment. If this secondary burial is Christian, then the use of a lead coffin should be also.

Eburacum, indeed, provides a striking example of the continuity of religious development in the province, and its cultural legacy to the post-Roman period. The religious life of Roman paganism is often described and dismissed as merely empty and formal ritualism, ripe for the take-over by the more universal teachings of Christianity. But the evidence here shows that its effects can be traced in the life of all sections of the population. Its identification with the régime – an identification which Christianity was to inherit – sets the pattern for future survival, and encourages the growth of the combined notions of *patria*, *civis* and Christian religion which Gildas in the sixth century sees as the criteria of the British people.

Notes

1. Plutarch, *Moralia*, 410 A, 419 F.
2. R.C.H.M., *York*, no. 142; *RIB* 662–3.
3. *ibid.*, no. 32; *RIB* 659.
4. *ibid.*, no. 91; *RIB* 680.
5. *RIB* 1547.
6. *RIB* 2160.
7. *RIB* 1961.
8. *RIB* 1137.
9. *RIB* 1684.
10. *RIB* 2146.
11. *RIB* 2148.
12. *RIB* 1130.
13. *RIB* 1132.
14. *RIB* 1131.
15. R.C.H.M., *York*, nos. 53, 52; *RIB* 648, 656.
16. R.C.H.M., *York*, nos. 13–14.
17. *ibid.*, no. 29; *RIB* 649.
18. R.C.H.M., *York*, no. 70.
19. *ibid.*, no. 127.

20. *ibid.*, no. 69.
21. *ibid.*, nos. 30–1; *RIB* 650–1.
22. R.C.H.M., *York*, no. 59; and jacket of the present volume.
23. *RIB* 655.
24. R.C.H.M., *York*, no. 33; *RIB* 644–5.
25. R.C.H.M., *York*, no. 54; *RIB* 658.
26. R.C.H.M., *York*, no. 57; *RIB* 643.
27. *RIB* 620, 623; 627–8.
28. R.C.H.M., *York*, nos. 110, 106; *RIB* 678, 687.
29. *J.R.S.*, xi (1921), 102ff.
30. *RIB* 640; R.C.H.M., *York*, no. 40.
31. *ibid.*, no. 52.
32. *ibid.*, no. 35.
33. *ibid.*, no. 8.
34. *RIB* 660; R.C.H.M., *York*, no. 39.
35. *ibid.*, no. 140.
36. *ibid.*, no. 38.
37. *ibid.*, no. 37.
38. *ibid.*, no. 36; *RIB* 652–4.
39. R.C.H.M., *York*, no. 45.
40. *ibid.*, no. 67.
41. *ibid.*, no. 56.
42. *ibid.*, no. 124.
43. *RIB* 436.
44. R.C.H.M., *York*, no. 24.
45. *ibid.*, no. 82; *RIB* 688.
46. R.C.H.M., *York*, no. 84; *RIB* 689.
47. R.C.H.M., *York*, no. 71; *RIB* 682.
48. R.C.H.M., *York*, no. 73; *RIB* 684.
49. R.C.H.M., *York*, no. 108; *RIB* 690.
50. R.C.H.M., *York*, no. 80; *RIB* 686.
51. R.C.H.M., *York*, p. 85 (b) v.
52. Wenham *et al.*, *The Romano-British Cemetery at Trentholme Drive, York* (1968).
53. Mansi, *Concilia* ii, 476.
54. R.C.H.M., *York*, no. 150.
55. *ibid.*, nos. 103, 77; *RIB* 683, 685.
56. R.C.H.M., *York*, no. 106.
57. *ibid.*, no. 106.
58. *ibid.*, no. 107.
59. *ibid.*, no. 104.
60. *ibid.*, p. 703(i).

D. CHARLESWORTH

The defences of Isurium Brigantum

Ten years ago a study of the defences of Isurium,[1] based on excavation in 1924 and 1934–8, established beyond doubt their circuit and suggested the construction of a sandstone wall with internal towers, backed by a bank and with a single ditch in front, not earlier than A.D. 150 but not much later. Bastions were added in the mid-fourth century and a new ditch dug. More recent work[2] has shown that the defences developed during the later second and third centuries and that the town wall was built more than half a century later than the first encircling bank and ditch.

The defences enclose an almost rectangular area of 74 acres (fig. 20) comparable with Ratae Coritanorum (Leicester) 100 acres, Venta Silurum (Caerwent) 44 acres and Venta Icenorum (Caistor) 34 acres.[3] There is no obvious physical reason for the chamfering of the north-east and south-west corners and no indication that the line of the defences was ever altered. The regular outline with four gates, all slightly off-centre, looks as though it were planned by army surveyors to take in an existing area of settlement which had already had a regular layout imposed upon it, to the extent at least of its main streets and forum. This is still reflected in the present village plan. The road from York still enters the village at the site of the south gate and the Boroughbridge road leaves it at the site of the west gate, at the Manor House, where one of the massive blocks with a pivot-hole was found.[4] The present road leading east to Lower Dunsforth is an eighteenth-century line, moved south from its earlier course to enlarge the grounds of Aldborough Hall.[5] The road to the north to the crossing of the River Ure went out of use with the building of the bridge at Boroughbridge. There is occupation to the north of the defended town[6] and there seems no reason to doubt that the area within the defences was fully occupied. The interest of the Lawson, later Lawson-Tancred, family concentrated research on the land they owned. Fine houses are known in the south-west quarter and traces of buildings were recorded near the defences in 1924 and 1938 near the north gate, in 1934 inside the north-west angle and in 1965 on the east side of the town.

There is no evidence of military occupation at Isurium. One stamped tile of the Ninth Legion, illustrated by Eckroyd Smith (*Reliquiae Isurianae*, pl. xxviii, 10) but its finding unrecorded, and one incomplete, inscribed military bronze badge are not adequate evidence. No structural remains of a fort have been found and indeed, although an early fort may be expected here, it might be expected either at the river crossing, or immediately south of the later town where high ground would give a better outlook. Isurium is overlooked on the south by higher ground. Eckroyd Smith's 'barracks' near the west wall are part of a later town house.[7]

The first defences of Isurium were a bank and ditch. This is not immediately obvious because of the unstable nature of the bank material, largely dirty sand derived from the ditch. This sand was encountered in the earlier excavations[8] and again in 1960 on the west side and in 1965 on the east. It was only after the 1965 excavations when both sections showed tip-lines indicating a bank centred behind the wall, not piled up against it, and one section (fig. 21) had patches of grey clay identical with that of the wall foundation clay on the bank slope that this became clear. The section shows the dirty sand and crushed sandstone slipped forward from the bank filling the trench dug for the wall foundation, as well as occupation debris at the level of the base of the footings. It could be argued that the presence of sandstone indicates that the bank is contemporary with or even later than the wall, but this is not necessarily the case. The ditch could not provide all the material required for the bank. Some of it was brought from within the town. The presence of domestic refuse, mainly pottery and bone, shows this. At one point a whole sack- or basket-load of bones was tipped in at a low level of the bank. The sandstone, a very friable, easily eroded stone, could come from building works in the town. The two sections in 1965 were the only ones where it has been recorded, so it is evidently only an occasional feature in the building up of the bank. In the section through the west bank (fig. 22)[9] the situation was obscure. The first stage of the bank was thought to be contemporary with the building of the wall. Here the foundations themselves were in natural sand with no trace of a foundation trench and a robber trench had removed the whole of the wall. The earliest levels are not piled against the wall, however, and have probably slipped forward. They could represent the eroded remains of an original free-standing bank. Both turf lines represent stages in the post-wall bank. Section IV (1935)[10] shows the wall foundation cut into a layer of dirty sand and it was noted at the time that "a diminishing trail of sandstone chips . . . under the clay bank, served

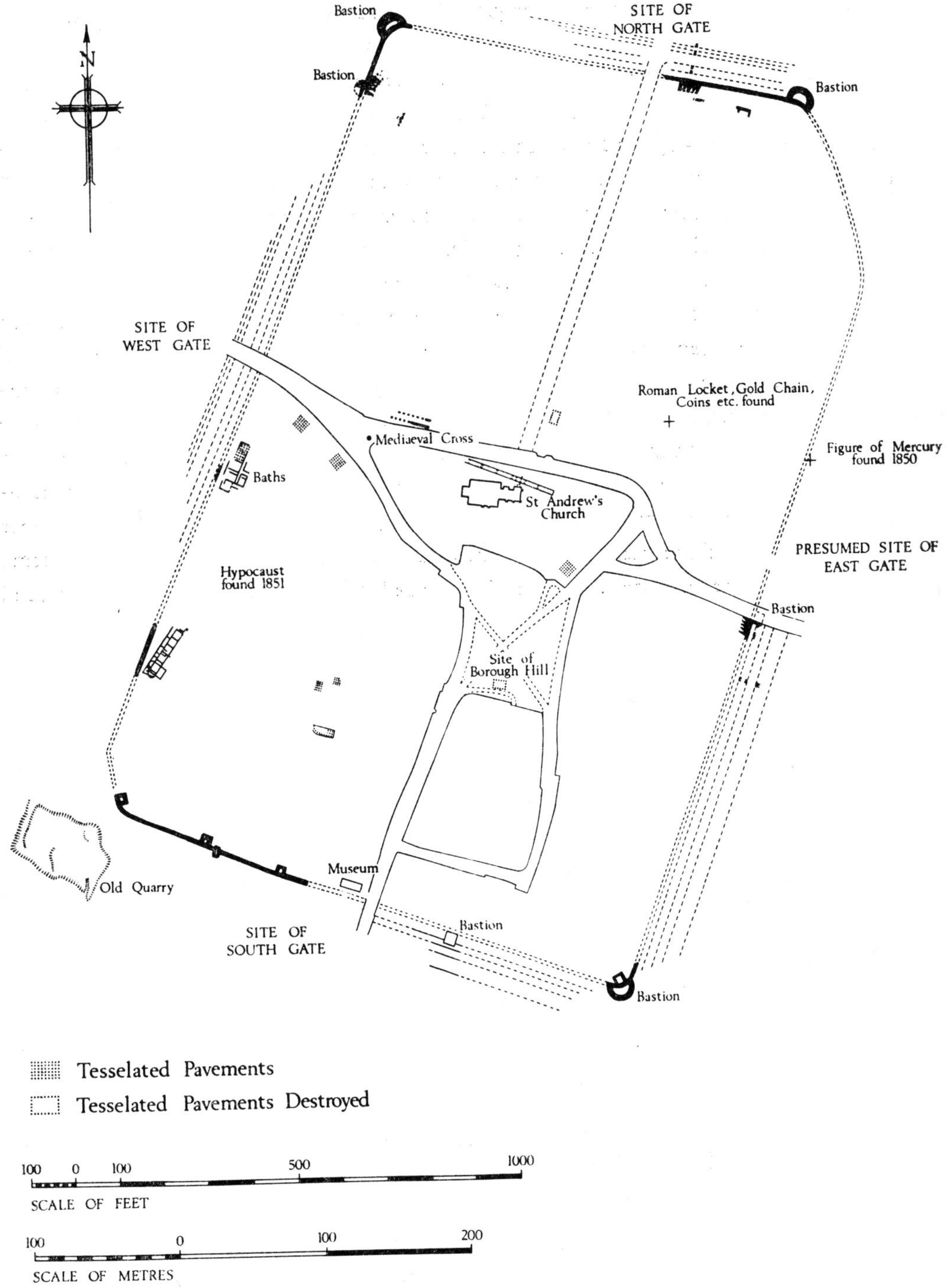

N
Bastion
Bastion
SITE OF
NORTH GATE
Bastion
SITE OF
WEST GATE
Roman Locket, Gold Chain, Coins etc. found
Figure of Mercury found 1850
Mediaeval Cross
Baths
St Andrew's Church
PRESUMED SITE OF EAST GATE
Hypocaust found 1851
Bastion
Site of Borough Hill
Old Quarry
Museum
SITE OF
SOUTH GATE
Bastion
Bastion
Tesselated Pavements
Tesselated Pavements Destroyed
100 0 100 500 1000
SCALE OF FEET
100 0 100 200
SCALE OF METRES

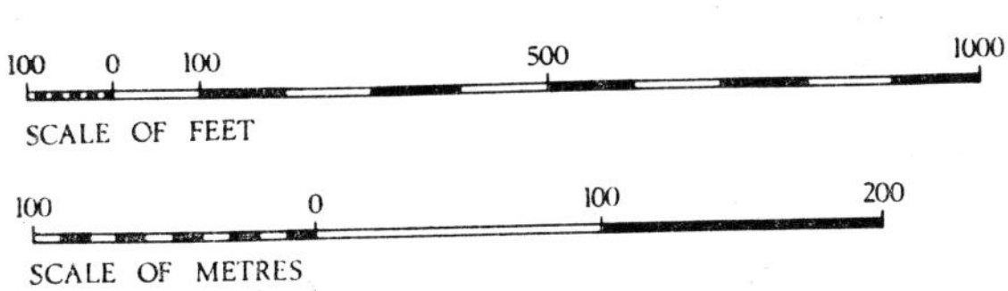

Figure 20. Plan of Roman Aldborough. (*Crown copyright*)

to demarcate it from the underlying dirty sand, which rose steadily behind the wall". This seems to be a pre-wall sand bank underlying a post-wall clay bank. Section V shows the same features but the situation is less clear as the sand is sinking, not rising, behind the wall. Section III shows both the occupation layer and the heaped-up sand and sand-and-turf cut away for the wall.[11] The clay bank is the only part obviously contemporary with the wall.

In no case does the evidence run counter to an interpretation of a bank preceding the wall and such dating evidence as there is definitely supports it. Dateable material from the bank is mainly of the mid- and later-second century. For example, the cooking pot with the wavy line on the neck mentioned as a frequent find in the "deposits just preceding the building of the wall"[12] is the latest of Gillam's three types with this decoration, type 129, *c.* 140–80. There is a considerable amount of earlier material, including rustic ware, but this is only to be expected in a bank made up partly of debris from the town site. In the 1965 sections the coarse pottery was similar to that published from the earlier excavations. There was not much of it but two fragments of samian[13] in a deposit near the bottom of the bank are by Cinnamus (A.D. 150–80). They probably came from the site of a collapsed or demolished building for the deposit included

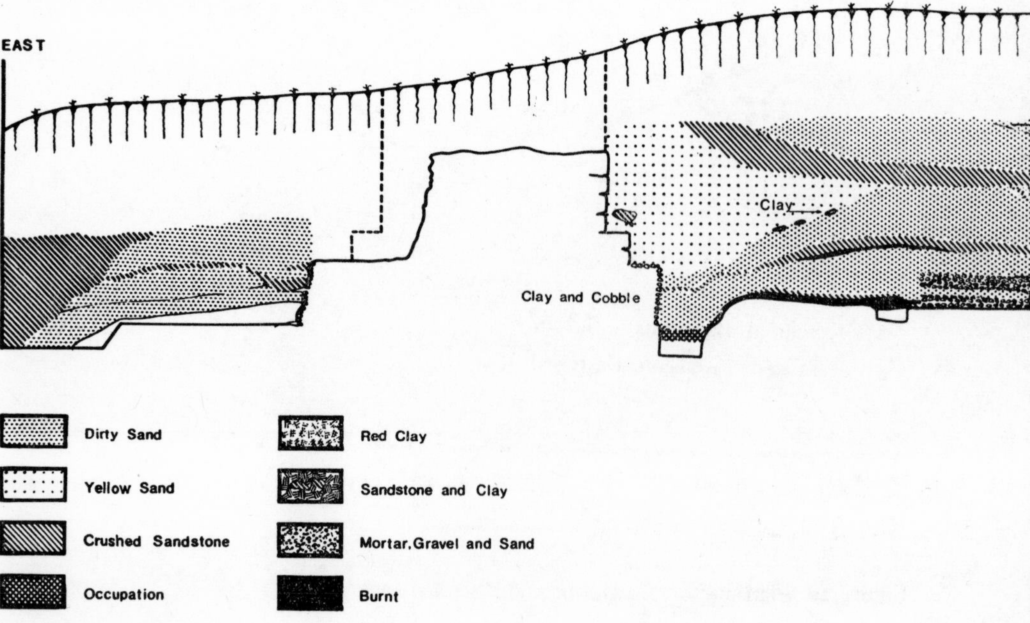

pieces of daub with wattle marks, bones and shells. From the layer of dirty sand on the berm, through which the wall foundations were dug, came part of a thick, clumsy form 33, stamped PATRVITVS, "almost certainly later than 160 and could be considerably later" (B. R. Hartley). This is the latest piece associated with the first defences. Most of the material is of Hadrianic-Antonine date and the only coin found in the bank in 1965 was Hadrianic. On the other hand a hunt cup (*Gillam* type 85, A.D. 170–220) was associated with a hearth and occupation layer probably contemporary with rather than earlier than this bank and certainly earlier than the wall and renewed bank. The loose fill made excavation at this depth difficult, both to dig and to interpret. There is not enough stratified material to give precision. All that emerges is a date definitely later than the Brigantian revolt of A.D. 155 and earlier than 200. The troubles of 169 or 180 provide an obvious context. If, as has been argued, all town defences are the immediate result of an imperial decree then it must, on the evidence from Dorchester (Oxon.) and Chichester, be the later date.[14]

The town must have been provided with gates at the time the first defences were built. These could have been either of timber, as at Brough-on-Humber,[15] or of stone. There is no evidence. The north gate has been dug only in part and

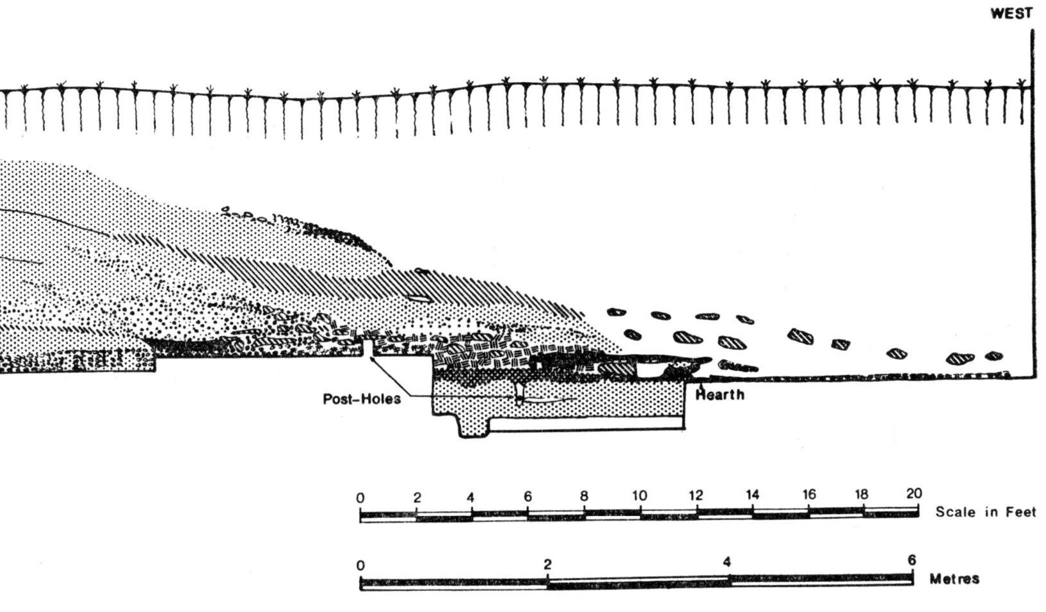

Figure 21. Aldborough: section of east defences.

at two different times, with puzzling result.[16] The character of the gate associated with the early road surface, road IV which ante-dates footings of a stone gate, is not known. Road VI which is contemporary with the footings can now be seen to have been dated too early. The revised dating of the samian, particularly of Cinnamus, whose pottery also occurs in the first bank, makes this road at least contemporary with the first defences. The other gate free of modern roads, the east gate, has never been dug, but may be seriously damaged. A large pivot-stone from it is recorded by Eckroyd Smith (*Reliquiae Isurianae*, p. xxii). In 1964 only the east corner of the south gate was uncovered and its relation to the defences is not known.[17]

The town wall has been examined at intervals since 1794, when its foundation was found to be 15ft thick and the wall itself 10ft.[18] In later sections the wall is recorded as between 8 and 9ft wide. The longest stretch exposed was that west of the south gate, now in the care of the Ministry of Public Building and Works. The visible part is almost entirely nineteenth-century restoration. An attempt to re-examine certain features in 1967 produced no useful result: the earlier work had been too thorough. The bank had been removed or cut back to a steep slope to expose the back of the wall and the internal towers. The easternmost tower, its back wall entirely nineteenth-century work, is so damaged at its junction with the curtain wall that their relationship could not be determined. The tower to the west of it was reduced neatly to foundation level, possibly because stone was required to improve the curtain wall, and it is not clear how Smith's draughtsman missed the back wall in his plan. The internal tower in the south-west angle was not examined as its condition gave no hope of new evidence. These towers will have been a regular feature of the defences on all sides. The angle-tower in the south-east corner, excavated in 1937, was contemporary with the wall and it may be assumed that the whole system of towers belongs to that phase. Towers within an earth bank are, in any case, exceptional on the present evidence, being known only at Cirencester.[19] The building of the stone defences may have been a lengthy process. In the 1965 sections there was evidence of a pause in the making of the clay and cobble foundation. A layer of mud covered the lower part of it as though it had lain open for a winter, or similar short period of time.

The date of the stone defences cannot be earlier than the third century. The vital piece of evidence is the very worn coin, a *denarius*, which Wade thought could be of Julia Domna.[20] Whether or not this is so, it is a third-century coin and its presence stratified in the foundations in section 1 (1938) implies a date in the mid-third century and makes impossible a second-century date. There is, unfortunately, little supporting material. The two rim sherds of cooking pots, stratified in the yellow sand of the second bank, contemporary with the wall, in 1965, are of

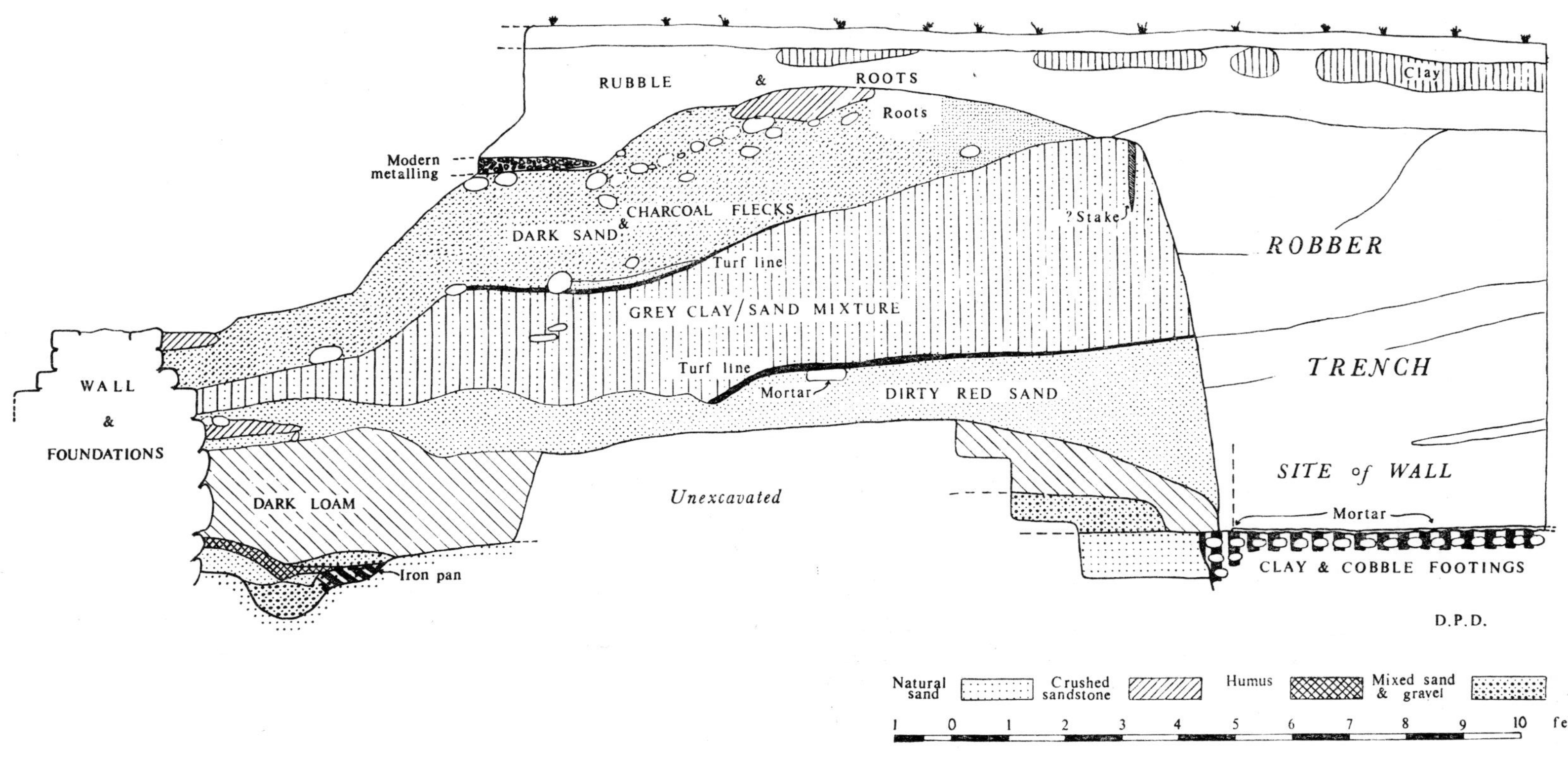

Figure 22. Aldborough: section of west defences. (*Drawn by D. P. Dymond*)

Gillam type 142, but with acute cross-hatching. This type is most recently dated A.D. 190–280.[21] These rims are similar to one found in the angle-tower in 1937, but which was thought, at the time of publication, to be earlier than this.[22] The acute-angled cross-hatching is not necessarily an indication of earlier date. Recently it has been noted on cooking pots of third/fourth-century shape, at Brougham (Brocavum) cemetery. Another piece of evidence which could be relevant is the re-making of the road at the north gate, road VIII, in which was a coin of Antoninus Pius and on which was a coin of Severus Alexander.[23] The building of the stone defences could well be linked with a re-building of the gates, but in a more durable stone than the wall, millstone grit. The evidence is too slight to provide a date for the wall, but the middle of the third century is clearly indicated. As Frere[24] has pointed out, the style, with internal towers, is that of the second-century forts. Moreover internal artillery-platforms were built as late as the reign of Elagabalus (A.D. 220) at High Rochester (Bremenium) and one restored from ground level in the reign of Severus Alexander, *c.* 225–35.[25]

The bastions at Isurium, as elsewhere, were added not earlier than the mid-fourth century[26] and probably in the time of Count Theodosius.[27] At the same time a new ditch was dug further out from the town wall. The original ditch was only filled where it was necessary to carry the bastion foundations across it. This was clear from the 1965 excavations where the section south of the bastion showed only silting. The section under and near the bastion had a fill of almost solid crushed red sandstone. Of all the bastions now dug only the foundation and an occasional block of ashlar facing has been found, except for that recorded by Eckroyd Smith. This bastion which he describes as "semi-circular" is shown on his plan as straight sided and curved only at the front. The ghost of one of the corners of the bastion east of the south gate showed that it had been rectangular[28] and it is probable that all but the angle-bastions were that shape. They were not made of red sandstone but of more durable material, millstone grit, limestone and yellow sandstone. But they were allowed to fall into disrepair before the wall. A length of wall near the south-east corner was found to have been rebuilt for at least 50 feet, partly from the foundations, and its masonry included five large, re-used blocks of millstone grit, almost certainly from the near-by bastion. The repair could not be dated.[29] A burial on the offset was a later insertion, a skeleton with an iron knife, late Roman or even Anglian. The knife is not distinctive.[30] Another bastion was thought to have been completely demolished "at a fairly early date" (Eckroyd Smith, p. 25). An undated and disturbed burial was found immediately over the footings. Eckroyd Smith (p. 22) recorded a piece of the south wall "which had been forced out of its original position and retains traces of fire. Here several skeletons were discovered". But there is no mention of any grave-goods and he goes straight on to refer to the burials in the cemetery outside the south gate, so it is not certain that he intended any real connection between the defences and the skeletons. Isurium is not in a position subject to attack in the late Roman period. The defences may never have been put to the test. The coin series, Theodosius 4 + 1?, House of Theodosius 3, Arcadius 7 and Honorius 1, indicates a town still trading peacefully into the fifth century. There is no evidence of late military occupation, as at Catterick.[31] There are some post-Roman objects, an Anglian burial with girdle-hangers and a small thread-box of bronze, plainly a woman's grave, and two Viking carved bone objects. The defences must have crumbled away gradually. A bypass to the west eventually took the traffic to the new bridge at Boroughbridge and Aldborough, still confined by its defences and with access only at its Roman gates, ceased to be of any importance.

Notes

1. J. N. L. Myres, K. A. Steer and Mrs A. M. H. Chitty, 'The defences of Isurium Brigantum', *Y.A.J.*, xl (1959), 1–77.
2. *J.R.S.*, li (1961), 169; lv (1965), 204; lvi (1966), 200; lviii (1968), 180.
3. Dimensions taken from R. G. Collingwood and I. A. Richmond, *The Archaeology of Roman Britain* (1969), 95–6.
4. H. Eckroyd Smith, *Reliquiae Isurianae* (1852), 13, pl. xxii, fig. 1.
5. Miss Mary Lawson-Tancred kindly showed me an early eighteenth-century map in her possession, showing the road before the bend was made.
6. *J.R.S.*, lv, 204; *Y.A.J.*, xl, 9.
7. Eckroyd Smith, *op. cit.*, 18, pl. v.
8. *Y.A.J.*, xl, figs. 6, 13, 20.
9. Mr David Dymond, who cut this section for the R.C.H.M., has kindly allowed me to use his notes and section. Note in *J.R.S.*, li, 169.
10. *Y.A.J.*, xl, fig. 13.
11. *ibid.*, fig. 6.
12. *ibid.*, fig. 7, 6.
13. I am indebted to Mr B. R. Hartley for his report on the samian.
14. J. S. Wacher (ed.), *The Civitas Capitals of Roman Britain* (1966), 65; S. S. Frere, *Britannia* (1967), 250.
15. Wacher (ed.), *op. cit.*, 60.
16. *Y.A.J.*, xl, 55–8.
17. *J.R.S.*, xlv (1955), 204.
18. Smith, *op. cit.*, 14.
19. *Ant. J.*, xlvii (1967), 188–90.
20. *Y.A.J.*, xl, 60. Dr J. P. C. Kent kindly re-examined this coin. Its condition has deteriorated but he agrees that it could be Julia Domna and is confident that it is no earlier than this.

21. J. P. Gillam, *Types of Roman coarse pottery vessels in Northern Britain*, 2nd edition (1968).
22. *Y.A.J.*, xl, 64.
23. *ibid.*, 68.
24. Frere, *op. cit.*, 252
25. *RIB* 1280, 1281.
26. *Y.A.J.*, xl, 29–30.
27. Frere, *op. cit.*, 256.
28. Mrs Jones kindly allowed me to see her plans and notes.
29. *Y.A.J.*, xl, 25.
30. *ibid.*, 47–9.
31. Wacher (ed.), *op. cit.*, 96.

J. S. WACHER

Yorkshire towns in the fourth century

The word 'town' has been in recent years increasingly used to denote a settlement which was fortified by either a bank or a wall at some time in its history, as distinct from a fort on the one hand and an unfortified settlement on the other, and without regard either to its size or function.[1] If York, with its closely defined civic status as a *colonia*, is disregarded, there are three sites in Yorkshire which, according to the above definition, can be loosely described as towns. There are also perhaps a dozen or more other nucleated, but apparently unfortified, settlements. Little information is available on most of these, but a few appear to be *vici* attached to forts. It is the purpose of this paper to examine some of these sites at a time when each might be expected to show the maximum development, when, in the North, the distinctions between fort and town have often become blurred, and to see if the above definition is justified.

The three sites normally called towns are Aldborough, the civitas capital of the Brigantes; Brough-on-Humber, usually assumed to be the civitas capital of the Parisi, and Catterick. *Vici* are known outside the forts at Malton (Norton), Brough-by-Bainbridge, Ilkley, Doncaster, Templeborough and probably Adel. Other settlements are known at Millington Bridge, Cleckheaton, Tadcaster, Thornton-le-Street and Healam Bridge: still others no doubt remain to be found. Too little is known about the majority for useful generalizations to be drawn, but excavations and chance finds at Aldborough, Brough-on-Humber, Catterick and Malton (Norton) allow some tentative conclusions to be made about the function of these sites in the fourth century.

There is no doubt about the genuinely civilian bias in the fortified town of Aldborough. Although not much is known of the street plan, a number of houses have been encountered, as well as a number of isolated mosaics.[2] Indeed it is possible that it was the centre for a firm of mosaicists (*pace* Smith[3]).

The situation at Brough-on-Humber appears rather different and the writer has already attempted to show elsewhere[4] that what has long been thought a walled town was primarily a naval base in the third and fourth centuries. In addition to the history of the defences, which tend to follow a purely military chronology, none of the buildings so far excavated inside the fortified area find parallels with the houses and shops normally to be seen in a town. That being so the question may be asked what was the fate of the *vicus* attested by the theatre inscription, *RIB* 707. It would seem that after the early-Hadrianic fort had been abandoned, the *vicus* was developed along lines already well established elsewhere to be the civitas capital of the Parisi. If a theatre was built, even if it was connected with a temple, of which so far there is little hint, then presumably there were other more essential public buildings also. No recognizable trace of any of them has yet been found inside the fortified area, although, admittedly, not all parts have yet been examined. This gives rise to a number of questions: 1) if a properly regulated civitas capital was planned, did it embrace a larger area than that subsequently walled; 2) were all the normally essential public buildings, such as a forum or bath-house, ever built, or, if started, ever finished; 3) did they lie wholly outside the later walled area; and lastly, but most important, 4) what happened to cause the apparent dissolution of the *vicus*? The first question can, in part, be answered by considering the earliest defences (Period V). Belonging to the late Hadrianic or early Antonine period, they are themselves exceptional for a town in Britain at that time, and a possible reason for their construction has already been discussed elsewhere.[5] However, it is clear from the excavations that they were intended to take in a much larger area than the later defences. It is possible that they were intended solely for the naval base, with the *vicus* being left unfortified. Bearing this in mind it will be seen that the scope of the enquiry can be enlarged, being no longer restricted to the walled area. Consequently it may be necessary to look for the principal town buildings outside it. It is worth remembering that the foundations of a masonry building have been found as far north as the golf-course, although no date can be ascribed to them.[6] The apparent scarcity of urban theatres in Britain might suggest that the theatre at Brough was only erected after more necessary public buildings had been completed. Yet such buildings, had they still been in everyday use, would hardly have been left outside the stone fortifications, when these were built at the end of the third or early in the fourth century. It might be argued that the civitas capital would have possessed its own walled enclosure separate from, but perhaps adjacent to, the naval base, as occasionally happened elsewhere when military and civilian sites existed together, as at Corbridge (and see p. 172 below). However it should be emphasized that no evidence to support such a conclusion has been found at

Brough. Both the north-east and south-east corners of the known enclosure have been examined. It would be at these corners that a junction would be most likely to occur.[7] Corder thought that the theatre inscription had been re-used in the wall of a later building,[8] which means that yet another suggestion can be considered. The second-century *vicus* of Petuaria as attested by the theatre inscription, and the πόλις of Ptolemy,[9] both with their hints of a civitas capital, may have become a 'failed' town if there were no good reasons for survival. The whole concept of urbanization when applied to the civitas capitals was essentially artificial. No matter how much help was given initially by the central government, the town would fail unless there was local support and a sound economic reason for its continued existence. If there had been no successors to men like M. Ulpius Ianuarius, the theatre would eventually have shut its doors for the last time, along with the other public buildings, and it has long been recognized that the main wealth of the Parisi remained firmly in the countryside, suggesting a lack of support by the local inhabitants. Had this happened then it is more than likely that any disused buildings would have been robbed of their masonry when the stone fortifications were constructed, along with much other new building, in the late third and early fourth centuries (fig. 23). This would certainly account for the re-use of the theatre inscription in another building. It is of course possible that the inscription was badly executed and never used, but there is nothing to suggest that the surviving portion was in any way erroneous.

It might be argued under the circumstances postulated above that at least some trace by way of robber trenches or mortar spreads would have been observed, either during the excavations in Bozzes Field or during commercial excavations in regions outside the walled area. But such traces need not have survived,[10] and, even if they had, they would be exceedingly difficult to interpret in a small scale excavation. Clearly there is room for a careful re-investigation. In the meantime, while there is no good reason to doubt the one-time existence of the *vicus* and civitas capital, it would seem unwise to continue to call the fortified area at Petuaria a 'town', in the sense used in the opening paragraph, when its obvious bias towards naval or military matters is recognized.[11]

The nature of the walled settlement at Catterick (fig. 24, plates 6, 7) is, in some ways, even more difficult to resolve since there is a complete absence of inscriptions dealing with the civilian settlement. Since the final report on the 1959 excavations has not yet been published, a brief summary of the results is given here.[12]

The earliest fort at Catterick would seem to have been established by Agricola, at the end of a spur of land with extensive views to north and east. The excavations in 1959 were however confined to a strip, about 700ft long and 200ft wide, beyond

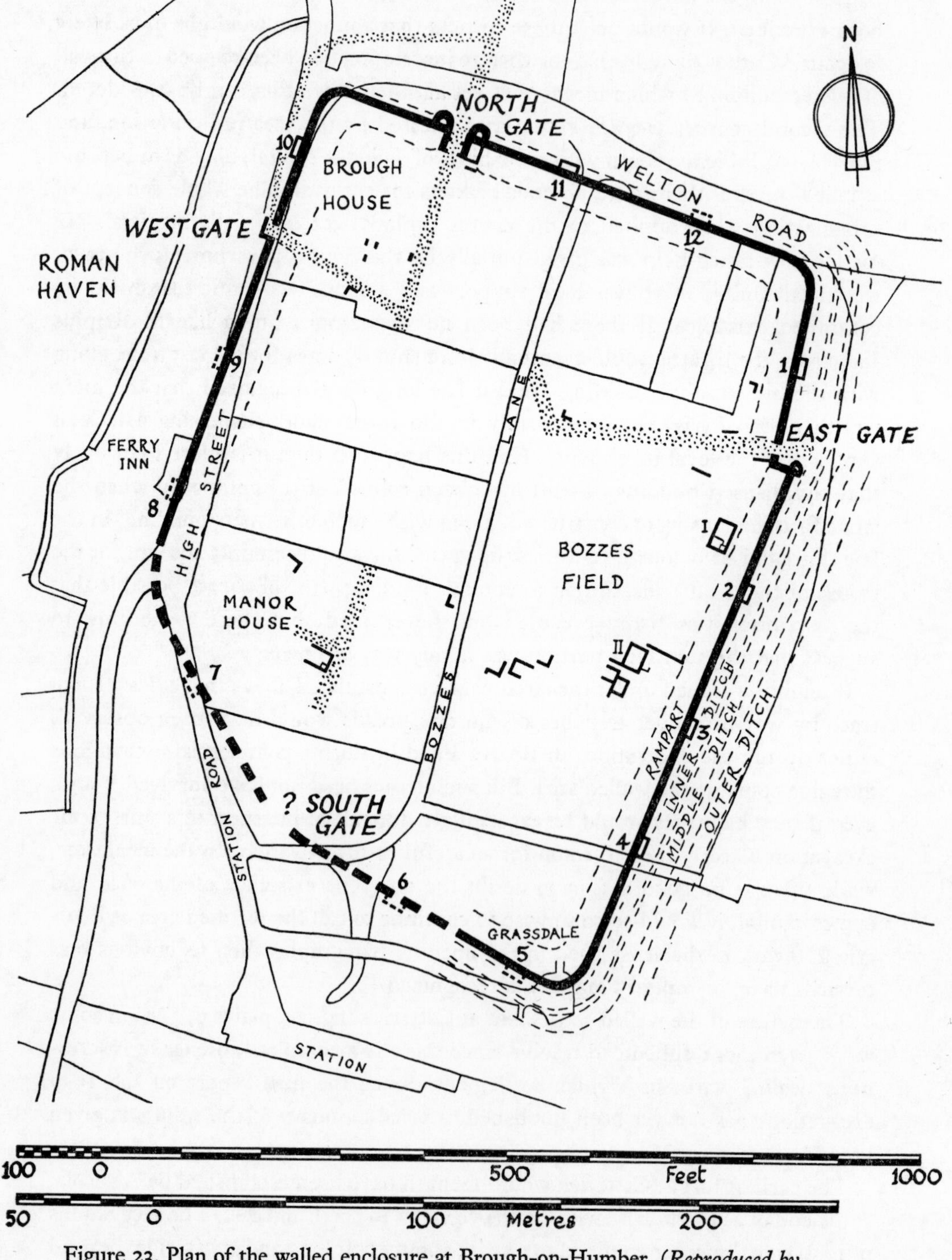

Figure 23. Plan of the walled enclosure at Brough-on-Humber. (*Reproduced by permission of the Society of Antiquaries*)

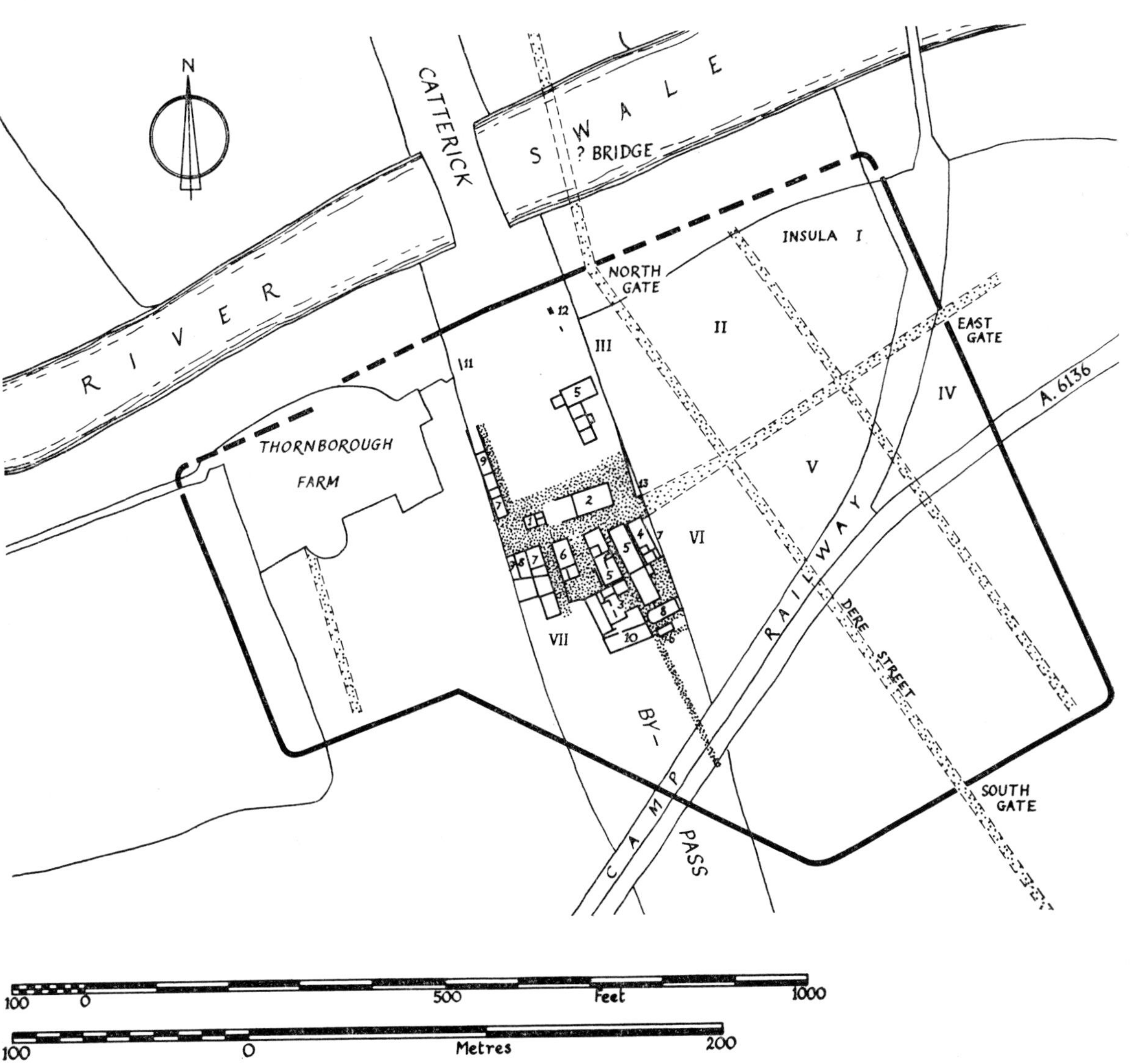

Figure 24. Plan of the walled enclosure at Catterick. (*Crown copyright*)

the eastern limits of the fort, and only its outer ditch was encountered. The fort was probably associated with a military tannery which was in part situated on the downhill slope to the east; a bath-house was also constructed on this slope but nearer to the River Swale. A large midden was connected with the tannery and covered nearly an acre of ground to a maximum depth of about 5ft. It lay south of the bath-house and the other structures associated with the tannery.

This fort appears to have been evacuated *c*. A.D. 120. Any civil settlement which may have grown during its occupation was probably too ephemeral to survive the removal of its chief reason for existence, as a scarcity of site finds dating to the earlier Hadrianic period was noted.

However, after the fort was evacuated, a large and complex building, interpreted as a *mansio*, was constructed in and around the area of the fort bath-house, which was rebuilt on a larger scale to serve as the baths for the new building. In addition to the large bath wing, the *mansio* contained a series of rooms which were arranged in two main suites, each with its own principal room and piped water-supply; it was entered through a small south-facing portico flanked by columns. A stone inscribed COH VIIII[13] had been set at a low level in the wall of one room; it implies that the building was constructed by, or under the control of, a ninth cohort. No such high numerals are known among auxiliary cohorts in Britain and a legionary cohort is inferred, which at this date would probably be the ninth cohort of Leg. VI from York.

The fort was almost certainly reoccupied *c*. A.D. 160, and with it a civil settlement now grew up south of the *mansio*, which was itself dismantled before the end of the second century. However, no sign of wholesale destruction, which could be related to the invasion and rebellion of A.D. 196, was observed during the excavations, and the *vicus* continued to prosper throughout the third century.

It is not known if, or when, the fort was finally evacuated, and excavation is required to settle the point. The stone wall defences surrounding the *vicus* (fig. 24) were probably erected towards the end of the third or early in the fourth century and appear, from the aerial photographs (plates 6, 7), to include the area occupied by the fort, so giving rise to the unusual shape of the enclosure. A similar conjunction can be observed at London,[14] and to a less marked degree, at Heddernheim.[15] The defences at Catterick present a number of problems. The stone wall was 7ft 6in. thick, although it sat on a clay and cobble foundation 13ft thick, suggesting that a wider wall was originally envisaged. There was no trace of a rampart behind the wall and only a single, wide ditch lay beyond it. The angles of the wall, with the exception of the re-entrant angle, appear to be rounded. No bastions were found and none are visible in Dr St Joseph's exceptionally clear aerial photographs (plates 6, 7). It would seem from these features that the defences represent a transitional stage in the development of castrametation. The absence of a rampart and the presence of a single, wide ditch belong typologically to defences of the fourth century, while the comparatively thin wall and the rounded angles are both characteristic of an earlier period. The lack of bastions is more difficult to explain, but a suggestion is made below (p. 172).

It would appear likely that part of the regular pattern of streets, which can be seen in the aerial photographs (plates 6, 7), was laid out at the same time as the defences were constructed. The site is interesting because, as one of the 'small towns' of Britain, it has an apparently regular layout of *insulae*, being probably, with Corbridge, among the last examples of co-ordinated town-planning to take place.

Many of the excavated buildings inside the town were also rebuilt during the opening years of the fourth century. The majority of them were shops fronting the streets, but chief among the new buildings was a small bath-house[16] constructed on the same site as, but on a less ambitious scale than, the bath-wing of the second-century *mansio*. Unfortunately it was never completed; it was left a roofless shell, with no floors, wall-jacketing or hypocausts and was soon partly filled with domestic refuse.

In about A.D. 370 or soon after, a major rebuilding programme appears to have taken place, which radically changed the nature of the existing buildings (fig. 25). Almost all the shops fronting the street on the north side of Insula VII were rebuilt on different alignments and the total number was increased (Buildings VII, 7, 8, 9). Moreover, instead of having open fronts as before these were now closed in with masonry. A new street was also made, running north over ground originally occupied by the *mansio*, to sub-divide Insula III, and was lined on its west side by buildings (Buildings III, 7, 9) similar to those in Insula VII. In the north-east corner of Insula VII a group of buildings (Buildings VII, 5, 6) were also closed in to form a unified complex grouped round an L-shaped courtyard. A great gate with an arch spanning about 9ft gave entrance to this court from the north. Similarly, immediately south of this new complex, an amalgamation took place to form yet another small courtyard house (Buildings VII, 3, 10). In the north-west corner of Insula VI, the open fronts of more shops were blocked, and one (Building VI, 8) was closed by an apse. For the first time the standard of masonry declined, and although deep and adequate cobble foundations were used, much of the superstructure consisted of rough lumps of hard, white limestone, replacing the earlier and more carefully worked local sandstone. Only in the gate leading into the north compound was a reasonable standard maintained, and here large ashlars and massive voussoirs were found.

These alterations would seem to point to a radical change in the nature of the settlement, which involved the apparent closure of shops, and their conversion to other uses. The two new complexes of buildings in Insula VII should, by the monumental nature of the gate, be more appropriately related to government service rather than to private enterprise. The date at which these changes took place and the position of Catterick near the mouth of Swaledale on one of the major routes to the North, might suggest that the town was caught up in the reorganization by Count Theodosius of the British defences.

The two zoomorphic buckles which E. J. W. Hildyard found in 1952 on the floor of Building III, 1[17] and part of what may be another similar buckle, together with a miscellaneous collection of weapons and equipment (figs. 26, 27) from the 1959 excavations, might well be taken as evidence for the presence of a detachment of the army in the years after A.D. 370, a suggestion already made by Professor E. Birley.[18] If so, then the converted shops might be seen as barracks or store-rooms and the two complexes of buildings perhaps as the *principia* and *praetorium*. Moreover such military buckles were often used by *gentiles* and *laeti*, who would be independent of the duke's command and so would not be listed in the relevant chapter of the Notitia Dignitatum. How large the detachment was, how much of the town was taken over and what happened to the civilian occupants cannot be said until much more excavation has been done. It is possible that the civilians were herded together in another part of the town, and there would certainly seem to be more than enough room with 15½ acres inside the walls; alternatively they may have been completely removed. There is however one point in favour of suggesting that Catterick became more a fort than a town, and that is the absence of bastions. It is probable that it was Theodosius who gave the orders for external towers to be added to town walls, but few, if any, auxiliary forts were provided with them, even among those rebuilt after A.D. 369. Here then might be the explanation for their absence at Catterick. If the site became a fort after this date it would have helped in the protection of the Vale of York. Harking back to a strategy first used in Britain by Agricola to seal off the Scottish Highlands, a fort at Catterick would have controlled egress from Swaledale and so filled the gap which existed between the fort at Piercebridge controlling Teesdale and that at Brough-by-Bainbridge controlling Wensleydale.

The subsequent history of Catterick is soon told. It is not possible to state how

Figure 26. Weapons from the late levels at Catterick: 1, 4 and 5 from the region of the bath-house (III, 5); 2 from Building VII, 5; 6 from near Building III, 2. (1) a large spear-head; (2, 3) light spear-heads; (4, 5) light, barbed javelins; (6) a heavier, square-sectioned lance-head. Scale ½. (*Crown copyright; drawn by D. S. Neal and P. A. Broxton*)

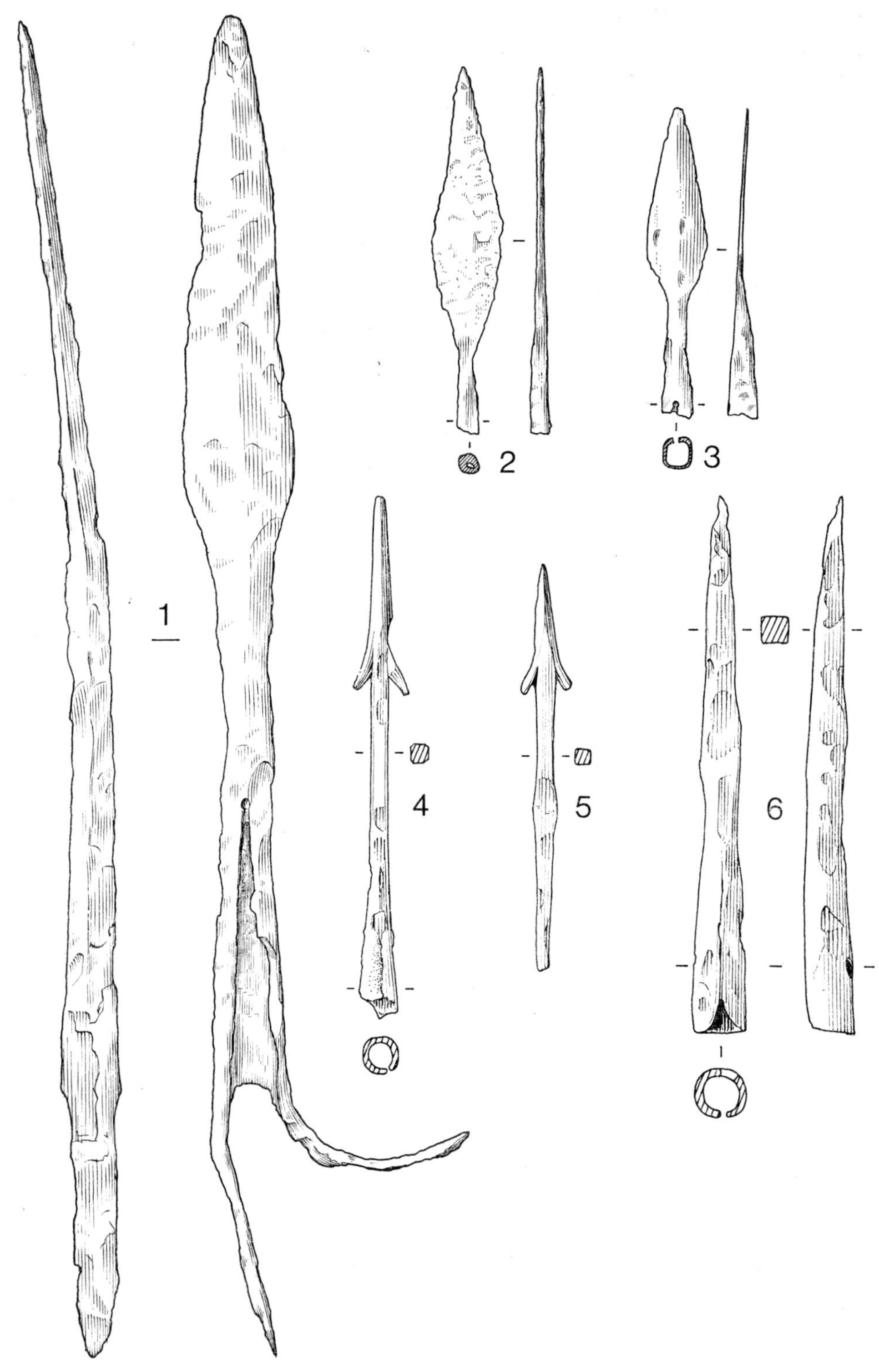
1
2
3
4
5
6

long this army unit remained there. But suffice it to say that, after its evacuation, the part at least of the walled area which was excavated remained vacant, the buildings in many cases becoming ruinous and often obscured by earth and vegetation. Only then did further rebuilding take place, and often in such a way as to suggest that earlier building lines had been completely lost. Moreover the buildings themselves were of timber construction with posts or sleeper beams supported on large boulders and blocks of stone. This reoccupation, probably now of civilian character, came before the main waves of Anglo-Saxon settlers reached this part of Yorkshire, as only five sherds of Saxon pottery were found in the 3½ acres of ground covered by the excavations. It probably dates to the very end of the fourth or more likely to the early part of the fifth century.

The last site to be considered is the fort at Malton and its associated *vicus*, which extended from close to the south-east side of the fort across the River Derwent to Norton.

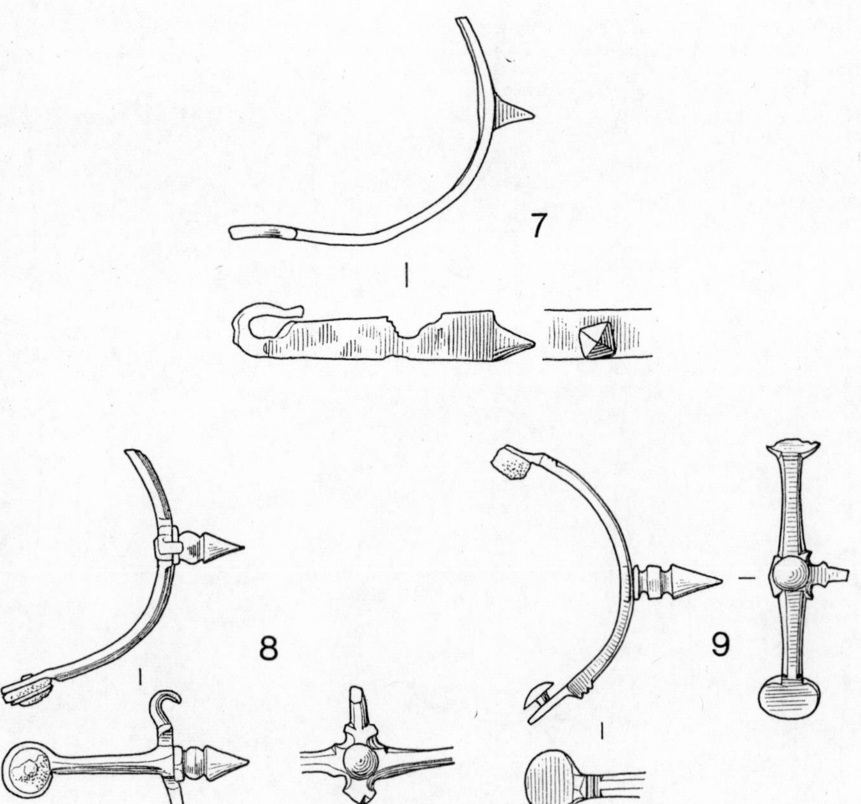

Figure 27. Three spurs from the late levels at Catterick: 7 from Building VII, 5; 8, 9 from the bath-house (III, 5). (*Crown copyright; drawn by D. S. Neal*)

Excavations have shown that the fort at Malton was extensively rebuilt in the late third or early fourth century (Period 5). Considerable modifications also took place about A.D. 370 (Period 6), which Corder attributed to the work of Theodosius. He recorded that poorly executed alterations and reconstructions took place in the northern angle of the fort. This had followed an obvious decline in military standards during the preceding period (Period 5), when 29 infant burials had been deposited in buildings of the same area.[19] Limited excavation in the *vicus*[20] close to the south-east gate of the fort has also shown that the first part of the fourth century was a period of apparent prosperity, with luxurious houses being built. The excavator considered that some of these buildings met a violent end soon after the middle of the fourth century. In addition he suggested that emergency defences were erected round part of the *vicus* at the time of the Picts' War, the ditch connected with them cutting through the buildings which had earlier been destroyed. Finally, he concluded that occupation in the enclosed part of the *vicus* ceased soon after this event.

How are these results to be interpreted and how can the information from the fort be correlated with that from the *vicus*? The writer and Mr R. S. O. Tomlin have already attempted to show elsewhere that the unit (*numerus supervenientium Petueriensium*), named in the Notitia Dignitatum as being stationed at Malton, was transferred there from Petuaria soon after the middle of the fourth century and certainly before A.D. 370.[21] It is not known how many men this *numerus* contained, but it seems certain that by itself it could never have filled completely the 8.4 acres enclosed by the fort defences.[22] Its arrival at Malton in Period 5 was probably marked by the collapse of the strict military standards noted above.[23] It is not impossible that it was at first brigaded with another unit in this overlarge fort, but certainly, if such a unit existed, it had been moved by the time the first part of the duke's list in the Notitia was compiled.[24] A more likely explanation though is that, from the time of this unit's arrival at Malton, civilians were moving inside the fort. The process was almost certainly accelerated by the events of A.D. 369–70, culminating apparently in the virtual abandonment of a large part of the *vicus*, for the safety provided by the fort. To this period probably belonged the substandard buildings of Period 6, and the whole is reminiscent of many of the forts on Hadrian's Wall after the Theodosian reorganization.

In sum then what can one say of Yorkshire towns of the fourth century? In only one, Aldborough, does the civilian character seem to have been maintained throughout the period. At Brough-on-Humber, the chronology for the defences emphasizes its essentially military, or better, naval character, until the evacuation soon after the middle of the fourth century, when part at least seems to have reverted to civilian use. Catterick, starting as a *vicus*, ultimately became a walled town by the early fourth century, only to revert to a military-type occupation after A.D. 369. Like Brough, it also returned to civilian life after the army had gone. At Malton there was a reversal of events, with civilians, at first gradually, later almost entirely, taking over the fort, so that it must have ended its life more like a walled town. The main conclusion to be drawn is that care must be taken before a dogmatic classification is laid down for any type of site, especially in the fluid conditions obtaining in the fourth century. In the words of W. S. Gilbert: "things are seldom what they seem".

Notes

1. This is not the place to discuss the accuracy of such a statement, which in many ways is unsatisfactory as a definition. See J. S. Wacher, *The Towns of Roman Britain* (forthcoming).
2. H. Eckroyd Smith, *Reliquiae Isurianae* (1852); Lady Lawson-Tancred, *Guide Book to the Antiquities of Aldborough and Boroughbridge* (3rd edition, 1948); *Y.A.J.*, xl (1962), 1–77; *J.R.S.*, li (1961), 169; lii, 166; lv, 204, lvi, 200; lvii, 179; lviii, 180.
3. D. J. Smith in *La Mosaïque Gréco-Romaine* (1965), 96, and also in A. L. F. Rivet (ed.), *The Roman Villa in Britain* (1969), 102.
4. J. S. Wacher, *Excavations at Brough-on-Humber, 1958–61*; Research Report of the Society of Antiquaries of London no. xxv (1969), *passim*.
5. *ibid.*, 26–7. Only a short section of these defences could be uncovered.
6. *ibid.*, 73.
7. South-east corner: *ibid.*, fig. 15; north-east corner: P. Corder and T. Romans, *Excavations at the Roman Town at Brough, E. Yorkshire, 1935* (1936), 11. Prof. J. E. Bogaers considers, however, that the civil centre would be perhaps a little distance away from the fortified area and not connected to it, with possibly a cemetery between them. There is no immediate candidate on this basis, but the site at North Ferriby should not be forgotten.
8. P. Corder and T. Romans, *Excavations at Brough-Petuaria, 1937* (1938), 36–40.
9. *Geog.*, ii, 3, 10.
10. In the writer's experience of excavation at Brough, this could easily have happened, due to the very thorough robbing and later cultivation, which occurred in many places.
11. During the first and second centuries, when a civitas could not govern itself, a *praefectus* or *princeps civitatis*, either a Roman officer or a native person, was appointed. This certainly happened in Pannonia: *CIL* IX, 5363. *L. Volcacius Primus ... praef(ectus) ripae Danuvi et civitatium duar(um) Boior(um) et Azalior(um)*; B. Saria, *Burgenländische Heimatblätter*, xiii (1951), 4, no. 103; xiv (1952), 100: *M. Coc[c]eius Caupianus pr(aefectus) c(ivitatis) B(oiorum) ... pr(inceps)* could be read in place of *pr(aefectus)*; cf. A. Mócsy in *Historia*, vi (1957), 494.

   It is not known whether similar circumstances obtained in Britain, or, for that matter, what happened in the later Empire if a *civitas* proved incapable of self-government.

But such an officer, had one been appointed to the Parisi, might well have lived in a *praetorium*, so perhaps giving rise to the name Praetorium Petuaria. The juxtaposition of two so similar names could easily have caused the confusion which lead to the second being dropped and the site being called only Praetorium in the Antonine Itinerary. This is an alternative to the view already expressed by the writer in *Brough-on-Humber* (1969), 26 n. 2.

The writer is fully aware that the identification of Petuaria with the Praetorium of the Itinerary is not supported by Rivet (*Britannia*, i (1970), 41) but is nevertheless of the opinion that all different views should be put forward.

12. A short note and a plan appeared in *J.R.S.*, l (1960), 217.
13. *ibid.*, 237, no. 7.
14. W. F. Grimes, *The Excavation of Roman and Medieval London* (1968), fig. 2.
15. *Römische Funde in Heddernheim*, ii (1898), taf. 4.
16. *J.R.S.*, l (1960), pl. xxv, 3 for an illustration.
17. *Y.A.J.*, xxxix, 243.
18. *ibid.*, 246.
19. P. Corder, *The Defences of the Roman Fort at Malton* (1930), 67–8.
20. *Y.A.J.*, xli (1963), 209–61; *J.R.S.*, lviii (1968), 182.
21. Wacher, *op. cit.*, 54, 74.
22. Compare the numerus fort at Eining, which only occupies a small corner of the earlier cohort fort: W. Schleiermacher, *Der römische Limes in Deutschland* (1961), 59.
23. Nine infant burials were found during the Brough excavations. All belong to the period suggested for the occupation of Petuaria by this unit: Wacher, *op. cit.*, 233.
24. After A.D. 383 according to Frere, *Britannia* (1967), 234.

The writer records his thanks to the University of Leicester for a grant received for travelling expenses incurred in the preparation of this paper.

H. G. RAMM

The end of Roman York

The title of this paper has been chosen to parallel that of Professor Frere's paper on the end of towns in Roman Britain,[1] and my aim is to produce for York evidence for the same period for which Professor Frere gave the evidence from Canterbury and other towns without the necessity for repeating his general thesis.

In view of the more limited objective the title is perhaps question-begging. In one sense Roman York still survives today. The great west-angle bastion of the fortress is a direct physical survival of the Roman fabric of York, but a more powerful and pervasive influence is that of the town plan. In its major outlines this plan is still the Roman one and it is possible to trace its continuous development from A.D. 71 to the present. Inundations in the fifth and sixth centuries caused major alterations but the most drastic changes are to be associated with tenth-century expansion and the disastrous events of 1069. The city defences show a development from Roman times to the seventeenth century linked with that of the town plan, and although their history reflects troubled times between the fourth and the ninth centuries it does not demonstrate an end and a beginning.

The possibility of continuous occupation and of more gradual change shifts the emphasis of the question raised by the title – not so much when or how did Roman York end but when or how did it cease to be Roman. Fundamental changes may well have taken place before the withdrawal of the Roman army and administrative machinery. The late Sir Ian Richmond interpreted certain burial evidence from York as implying "social revolution" and "a complete rupture in tradition" which he associated with the reorganization of the army under Diocletian and the destruction of A.D. 296.[2] Nevertheless the new fortress H.Q. built in the early fourth century is still completely Roman, with plaster painted to imitate marble and a Latin graffito scrawled on it.[3] After A.D. 350 a town house new built in the *colonia* with its suite of heated rooms still belongs firmly to the

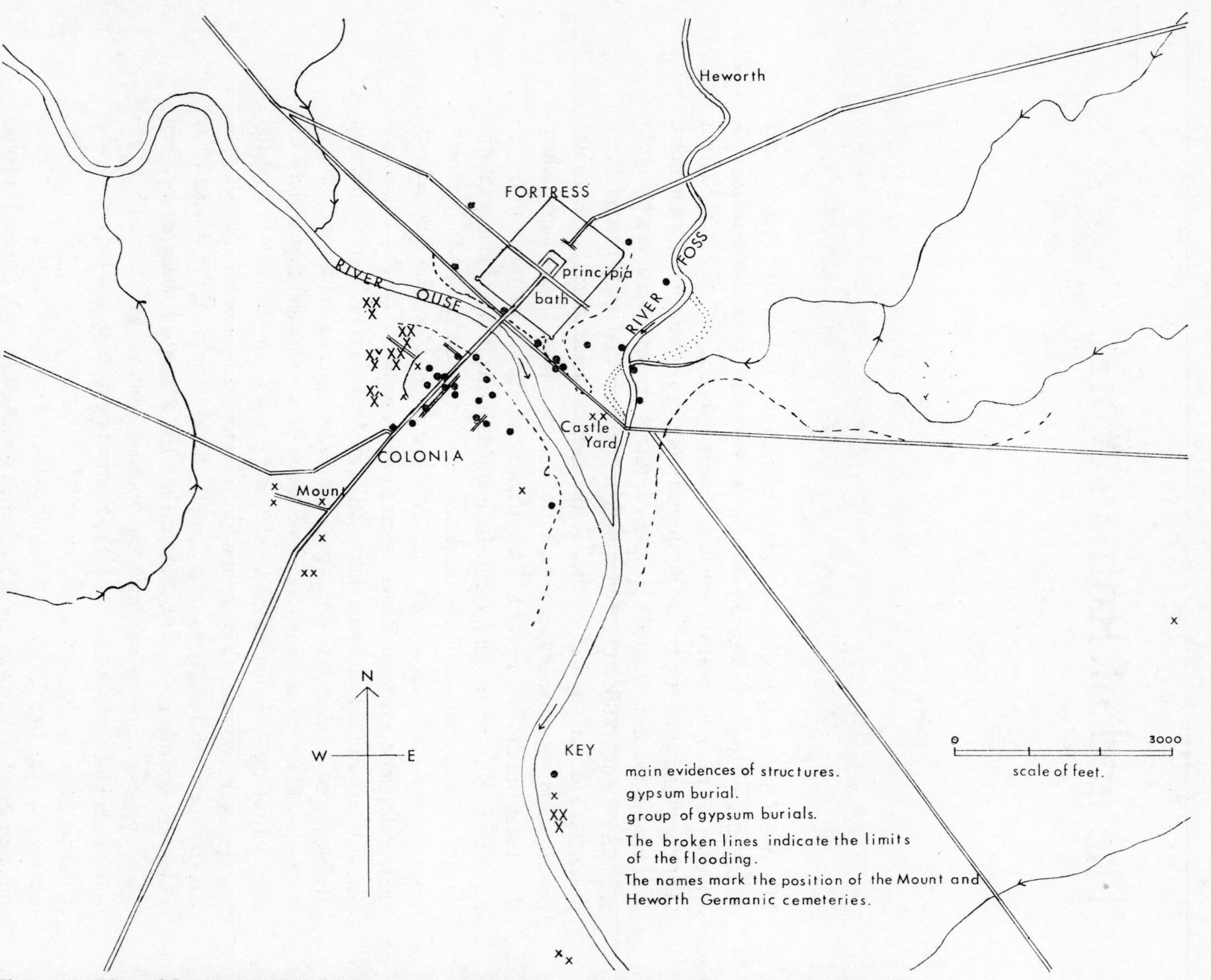

Figure 28. Plan of fourth- to fifth-century York, showing occupation, flood levels and gypsum burials.

world of Roman Britain.[4] The burial evidence with its indications of a break in tradition and its introduction of the first purely Germanic pottery illustrates the strains and stresses of fourth- and early fifth-century York rather than marking an end.

The most serious obstacle facing fifth-century archaeology in York as elsewhere is the disappearance of dateable artifacts,[5] which indeed remain scarce until the ninth century. Throughout the seventh and eighth centuries, when we know from written record that York was a great and prosperous centre, the archaeological record is incredibly thin;[6] for the fifth and sixth centuries, when the written record is almost non-existent, the difficulty is so much the greater. This end of abundant pottery and small finds is in itself significant and archaeologically marks the end of Roman York, but it makes it extremely difficult to discover what in human terms actually did happen in York in the fifth and sixth centuries. If fourth-century York is still firmly Roman, seventh- and eighth-century York are equally certainly English. In this paper I cannot provide any answer as to how or when the transition occurred or to any of the more general problems, and propose to limit myself to three separate strands of evidence, the evidence for severe flooding in the fifth and sixth centuries, the structural histories of individual buildings from the fourth century onwards, and finally the burial evidence.

The floods

In Hungate on the banks of the Roman course of the River Foss excavations for a new Telephone Exchange in 1951–2 revealed the remains of a wharf and massive foundations of what had probably been a crane, which had become buried under a bank of silt.[7] The conditions of the excavation did not allow the immediate stratigraphy of these structures to be closely examined but the levels corresponded to those of an adjacent scientifically excavated trench, where Roman layers of the late third to mid-fourth century were succeeded by an accumulation of alluvial sands of which the last two or three feet "must represent a considerable lapse of time during which sporadic flooding continued".[8] This flooding had begun in late Roman times, since strata "containing Roman material were seen to be interleaved with water-laid silty sand such as would be deposited by the seasonal overflowing of the river".[9] The next structures above the sand deposit represented systematic drainage and the construction of a riverside embankment in the late ninth or early tenth century. On a low riverine site evidence for flooding need not cause much comment, although the complete abandonment and silting over of what must have been a principal wharf in the main Roman harbour without reinstatement until the late ninth or early tenth century is clearly relevant to our subject. At Hungate the average Roman level seems to have been about 20ft O.D., with the top of the wharf at 17½ft and of the silt bank at 23ft O.D.

In Castle Yard the natural soil is a hard, reddish clay with pockets of sand. Under the Norman motte excavations in 1902 showed that this had been "overlaid by a bed of lacustrine marl of very variable thickness, apparently deposited by a tidal river in pools. In this marl was discovered a wooden boatstay, evidently of great age, with an iron nail sticking into it."[10] A few yards east of the motte the contents of two coffins buried into the clay in late Roman times (see below) had been subject to periodic inundation destroying the shape of gypsum casts that might otherwise have formed round the bodies. The basal marly layer immediately above the Roman layer sealing the graves I interpreted at the time of discovery as the throw-up from the ditch surrounding the motte but it could well have been the same layer found by G. Benson under the motte in 1902. The Roman level here is at 30ft O.D., that is 10ft above the average Roman level at Hungate, and a flood deposit at this level is clearly of much greater significance. This site too was reoccupied in late Saxon times since a complete shire of the city was said to have been *vastata in castellis*,[11] but a hanging bowl (discussed below) suggests that this higher site was reclaimed at an earlier date than Hungate.[12]

Miss Richardson in her report on the Hungate excavations drew attention to parallels with another site excavated by G. Benson in 1902 in High Ousegate, which he recorded "has been subject to floods, warp being deposited, and vegetation growing between times to be entombed by warp with recurring floods. The district was a swampy one; the leg bones of a stork or heron were found. The area had been raised by warp deposits. . . . The depth of the warp deposit has not been reached, though penetrated three feet below the present level of digging."[13] The lowest level of warp reached was probably about 35ft O.D. The Roman level under the bank at the corner of Ousegate and Nessgate, and on the opposite corner between Ousegate and Spurriergate varied from 33 to 36ft O.D. The flood level observed by Benson was under a wicker stockade related by Miss Richardson to the Hungate embankment[14] and probably part of the Danish defences. Outside the Roman south-angle bastion it is possible that a deposit of about 2ft of loose grey earth may represent the flood horizon – but the area had been disturbed by pits (Roman level at 34ft O.D.).[15] Certainly in Coney Street close to the south-west gate of the fortress and also near to tower S.W.3 no traces of flooding were found in recent exposures of Roman levels (38ft O.D. in both cases).[16] A critical level of *c.* 35ft O.D. would seem to be implied for the flooding. Additional evidence at 27ft O.D. comes from Tanner Row [17] with three feet of silt, and outside the city from Fulford East Moor, near Bleak House Farm, at *c.* 30ft O.D., where the Roman road was covered by 1ft of sand and 2ft of clay just north of Germany

Beck.[18] At the Friends' Meeting House between Clifford Street and Castlegate, finds mainly of Viking date but including a seventh-century bronze bowl were made in 1884. The ground here had a marked slope on which under the finds "was heather and ling" indicating an open site in what had been the middle of the closely packed civilian area south of the fortress.[19] Heath is the vegetation that might be expected to grow over the silt left behind after the floods had receded.

The evidence for an encroachment of the sea in the Humber area during the Dark Ages with the possibility of high spring tides reaching to between 15 and 20ft O.D. has recently been summarized.[20] Such high tides combined with a high river flow would produce considerable backing of water and would be consistent with flooding up to 35ft O.D. The dating of the flood horizons in the peat on the Hatfield Moors is dated by carbon 14 to *c.* A.D. 550 and by pollen analysis to *c.* 450.[21] At York the areas that had suffered from flooding were fully reclaimed by the early tenth century. Ninth-century finds occur within the flood area in Tanner Row, and the bronze bowls from Clifford Street and Castle Yard may indicate an end to the flooding in the seventh century or earlier. The evidence from Hungate implies that on that low-lying site flooding had already begun in the late Roman period.

On the plan (fig. 28) the Roman 35ft contour is marked, and it is clear that although the area of the fortress and much of the *colonia* was above flood level, the effect of annual winter flooding on the scale implied by the silting would have been little short of disastrous on a town already weakened economically by the break-up of Roman government and the devastations of raiders. York had suffered and recovered from destruction before, and was to recover from far worse destruction in the seventh, late ninth and eleventh centuries. Conquest, sacking and rebuilding then was not to affect her long-term commercial position, but the effects of the flooding struck at what Professor Frere has called "the compulsion of communications or other economic factors".[22] To this period we must attribute the disappearance of the Roman bridge, and a consequent division of the town into two except for the more tenuous communication by ferry or ford. The destruction of Roman harbour and wharfage facilities beyond recovery is illustrated by what happened at Hungate. In whatever form life continued at York, it was not until the eighth century that she recovered her position as an international trading centre and port.

Structural history

A comparison between the present and Roman plans of York demonstrates the surviving influence of the latter only in those areas above the flood level. The majority of known Roman structures are to be found above this level because of the greater depth at which those below it are buried and their consequent comparative immunity from penetration by excavation. An examination of the fourth-century and later structural history of buildings above the floods does indicate the possibility of a continuing if less prosperous occupation of the site.

The defences are normally the best place to read the history of a defended town. At York little is known of the Roman defences of the *colonia* on the south-west side of the Ouse and nothing about how they developed into the surviving medieval wall. On the north-east side of the river the evidence is fuller. Here was the Roman legionary fortress and north-west of it a further fortified enclosure or annexe. On the north-east, north-west and that part of the south-west side in Museum Gardens the Roman defences survive on the medieval line for the most part buried in the earthen rampart on which the city wall stands. The south-east side, although remains survive underground, has left no trace on the plan of the city, except for the convergence of Colliergate and the Shambles onto the site of the old south-east gate. The south-west side is marked by property and parish boundaries reflecting a later date for its abandonment than the south-east side. The Danes renewed three sides of the fortress, omitting the south-east side, by covering the Roman wall and mound with an earth bank on which they erected a timber stockade.[23] To the south-east they extended the north-east side along the line of the present medieval wall as far as the great re-entrant angle opposite Jewbury. From this angle a parish boundary marks the line to St Anthony's Hall, and another takes the line south-west from there to link with the Danish river embankment found in Hungate,[24] which is structurally analogous with another bank between Ousegate and Coppergate on an alignment that links with the south-west side of the fortress at the south angle.[25] The Danish treatment of three sides of the Roman defences has preserved them for us in the state they had reached at the end of the ninth century. Some of the damage that they display could well have been incurred in 867 when the walls were broken,[26] yet evidence of other repairs implies earlier damage and a far from uneventful intervening history. On the south-west side, south-east of the *porta praetoria*, the wall had been reduced to a height of 8–9ft and the evidence of an excavation in 1955[27] was that it had already been reduced to this height before the Danish refortification. In Museum Gardens the wall still survives almost to its full height and here the evidence derives from the ditch system. The Constantian ditch was 23ft wide by 6½ft deep separated from the wall by a 17ft berm. A layer of soil 18in. thick overlay the berm and thickened over the filled Constantian ditch. A new ditch was dug into this layer with revetments of turf and stone, 23ft wide and 6½ft deep separated from the wall by a 12ft berm. After this ditch in its turn had filled in the rubble footings of a rectangular timber building were erected over it.[28] All this had taken place before the Danish refortification, implying a period of some duration when the ditches of the early fourth-century defences were allowed to silt up, followed by a refortification, and then again by a period when the defences were so much out of use that buildings were allowed to crowd them on the outside. The same sequence is implied by the evidence from J. Radley's 1969 excavation of the chamber discovered in the nineteenth century behind the north-west wall. Here a vaulted defensive tower in coursed oolitic ragstone had been inserted into a breach in the Constantian wall. This tower had already begun to collapse when the Danes covered all with their bank.[29] At the point where Miller cut across the north-west defences further to the north-east he also recorded a rough stone repair to the upper part of the wall[30] which must also be pre-Danish. At the east angle of the defences, where the Danish bank like its successors continued south-east, whilst the Roman wall curved south-west, the latter had been reduced to the level of its plinth and footings. "Following the outer curve were a series of wooden stakes a foot apart. This timber patching was of post-Roman date. The thick deposit which covered it, however, represented a considerable period of accumulation and was in turn covered by the tail of the early medieval bank."[31]

At separate places the defences produce a similar story. The Roman wall, damaged and breached, suffers a period of neglect and is then refurbished before again being neglected until the Danes refortify. The second period represents peace and prosperity at York, and peace rather than emptiness may be the cause of the first period of neglect. There is little clue to the dating of the middle period when York felt the need for refortification although it is tempting to link it with the events of King Edwin's reign.

Within the fortress the major building to demonstrate a history beyond the fourth century is the cross-hall of the Headquarters Building. Originally filling the whole of the north-east side of the *principia*, the cross-hall had in the early fourth century been shortened, and the north-west end was occupied by small rooms divided by both stone and lath and plaster partitions. Moreover a portico that had flanked the street running alongside the north-west side of the *principia* was now incorporated into it and the painted plaster already referred to graced the wall of one of the resultant rooms. These rooms at the north-west end of the new cross-hall had a thick occupation layer including quantities of late fourth-century wares. Thereafter the lath and plaster walls disappeared and were partly replaced by crude stone walls. The earlier stone walls continued to serve but underwent many repairs of sometimes a rather rough nature. New floors were inserted, some of flags resting on a thick rubble base whilst others were of a kind of imitation *opus signinum*, a hard white mortar containing lumps of broken tile and dusted on the surface with powdered tile to give it the correct red appearance.

Plaster remained intact on many of the Roman walls, but where it did not it was replaced with a coarser monochrome plaster of which there was sometimes more than one layer. The techniques are still Roman but the standard of workmanship is debased.

The new building did not occupy all the rooms at the end of the cross-hall, and part was now in the open air. A precinct wall was built which to the north-west and north-east overlay the Roman street. That the new occupation was domestic is implied by an open cooking hearth with an ingeniously devised chimney cut into the wall behind it. The building was finally destroyed and the thick layers of ash in the levelling up above indicate a great conflagration. The date of this destruction is uncertain although a sherd of imported Frankish ware of the early seventh century was found in or beneath the rubble of destruction.

The fourth-century cross-hall remained intact to a much later date and its final destruction was probably the result of the Danish attack on York in the late ninth century. A thin layer of silty soil was the only clue to its immediate post-Roman history.[32]

Another major building in the fortress was the legionary bath-house in St Sampson's Square, also rebuilt in the early fourth century.[33] The pottery in the lowest layer of the debris resulting from the destruction of its hypocaust dated from the last 30 years of the fourth century. This represented the material from the last occupation on the floor above collapsed into the basement. It certainly indicated that the building was in use at the end of the fourth century, but need not imply, as the excavator thought, the destruction of the hypocaust *c.* A.D. 395, in view of the general scarcity of dateable finds immediately successive to those fashionable in the late fourth and possibly continuing into the fifth century. The building was crudely repaired at a time when it had ceased to perform its original function. The plunge bath was deliberately filled with large blocks of sandstone, probably at the same time as wall repairs in a similar material. The absence of finds dating these repairs may well imply that they belong to the period after the disappearance of the late fourth-century types of pottery and before it became common again in the ninth century.

The barrack blocks from Davygate also had a late fourth-century occupation and only pottery of this date was found in their destruction layer. A deposit of black occupation soil immediately overlay the destruction level, and the next structural finds were the rough stone foundations of timber houses similar to the foundations over the ditches in Museum Gardens. The excavator dated those in Davygate to the ninth or tenth century, but the evidence was not strong and they may well be earlier. Time must have elapsed after the destruction of the Roman buildings for the deposit to have accumulated, and an earlier date must be given to the destruction of these barracks than to that of the two larger buildings we have so far considered.[34]

In the *colonia*, excavations on the site of the church of St Mary, Bishophill Senior, revealed a house with a suite of heated rooms which had been completely rebuilt after A.D. 350. The debris that had collapsed into the hypocaust channels showed that this building, too, had had a heavy late fourth-century occupation. It is not always clear when or why the floor collapsed but in places it was certainly the result of grave digging of a much later date. What is certain is that the hypocaust system had become obsolete and disused before the occupation of the building had ceased. Small rooms added to the south-east side of the house overlay the spread and destroyed remains of the furnaces serving the hypocaust, one of which had been considerably altered and repaired on more than one occasion before it went out of use. The masoncraft of the new rooms was still Roman, but small finds to date them were absent. A bone spindle and whorl from one of the rooms suggest the use to which they were put.[35]

The evidence from all these sites is of a heavy late fourth-century occupation, after which some of the buildings continue to have a history but with a deterioration in building technique and sophistication, although still in the Roman tradition. Hypocausts are dispensed with, and baths are no longer used for their original purpose. Cooking is done over an open hearth but what vessels were used is a mystery.

Burials

As already noticed the discussion of the burial evidence must begin with the fourth-century burials from Castle Yard which Sir Ian Richmond regarded as indicating a "social revolution" and "a complete rupture in tradition". This he associated with the reorganization of the legions under Diocletian and the destruction of A.D. 296. That tombs were indeed disturbed at that date is demonstrated by tomb fragments built into the north-west gateway of the fortress[36] and possibly also the north-east gateway.[37] A fragment of an inscribed tombstone[38] built into the foundation of the Norman Minster had been re-used as a building stone in the Roman period, probably, from its position, in the *principia*, when rebuilt in the early fourth century. There is, however, all the difference in the world between the requisitioning of tombstones by a ruthless central government for military purposes and the robbing of tombs by private individuals. The evidence, moreover, from Castle Yard suggests the possibility of a later date for the burials there. The bracelet (iv) from burial (4)[39] has a close parallel in a late fourth-century bracelet from Shakenoak[40] and is generally similar to those from Lydney,[41] while the apparent snakehead terminal to bronze bracelet (iii) is the broken hook of a bracelet similar to other late fourth-century bracelets from Lydney[42] and Richborough.[43] Burial (4) and by implication the stratigraphically later burial (3) belong to the late rather than the early fourth century. Both burials had been in shallow graves, the one in a wooden coffin and the other in a revetted grave. The re-used stone and associated lead coffin adjacent, both containing gypsum burials, were buried somewhat more deeply but nevertheless there does not seem any valid reason for making these burials any earlier than the other two. In its original use the inscribed coffin cannot be put earlier than the second half of the third century.

There is other evidence from York of inscribed stone coffins re-used in the fourth century, including that of a centurion's infant daughter, Simplicia Florentina,[44] and that of Aelia Severa, *honesta femina* and therefore probably the wife or daughter of a decurion.[45] The latter had for its lid the tombstone of Flavia Augustina,[46] wife of a VI Legion veteran, and both burials came from the Mount. There was also another re-used centurion's coffin from the Castle Yard[47] and two from the Railway cemetery belonging to a decurion[48] and the wife of a sevir,[49] where re-use, although suspected, is not absolutely proven. The re-use of coffins belonging to the civil magistracy demonstrates that more than the reorganization of the legions lay behind the "social revolution", although the reorganization would explain how a continuing body like the centurionate was not able to look after its own.

The re-use of these coffins is difficult to date closely, since except for the gold ring on the finger of the body in the decurion's coffin none of the new interments had recorded grave goods or adornments, but they were all found in areas where there were other fourth-century burials in close proximity. The coin evidence from both earlier and later discovered burials[50] near Simplicia Florentina's coffin indicates that this area was in use for burial throughout the fourth century. Aelia Severa's coffin was 700ft nearer the Mount, close by another stone coffin and other inhumations as well as a cremation cemetery in Anglo-Frisian urns.[51] Burials in the area began in the second century and probably by the third century the main road had begun to be lined by monumental tombs. It is these tombs in use or building through the third century which have fallen into decay and from which coffins were being rifled and tombstones torn from the walls. In the new interments the coffins are buried in the ground and no longer accessible to view. Both these re-used coffins from the Mount as well as one from Castle Yard contained gypsum burials, a type of burial which on present evidence should be dated to the fourth century.

In gypsum burials a greater or lesser amount of this substance is packed round the body and its main effect, apart from preserving a cast of the body if sufficient gypsum were used, would be to help dry out the body and prevent some of the more unpleasant liquid effects of decay. Its use may have resulted from a belief that it had preservative properties which it did not possess and may be an attempt to save the body from decay altogether. At York the custom is relatively frequent: at least 49 examples have been discovered. Others come from the Aire valley along the route by which the stone sarcophagi were brought to York, and, outside Yorkshire, from London and the Home Counties (particularly Kent), and Dorchester, Dorset (see Appendix). At Poundbury near Dorchester the burials are from a fourth-century Christian cemetery with mausolea.[52] At York 17 out of the 49 examples are of fourth-century date and in only one case has an earlier date been argued for.[53] Two of the Aire examples also date from the fourth or even fifth century.[54]

In the Rhineland under the church of St Maximin at Trier was a small Christian cemetery of about 50 burials in sandstone coffins associated with a small mortuary chapel. Several of the skeletons had a thin surviving layer of lime (*kalkschicht*) over them preserving the impression of their clothes.[55] This fourth-century chapel and cemetery suffered neglect as a result of the many Frankish sackings of the town in the first half of the fifth century. Anthropological examination of skeletal material has suggested at Trier a community of non-Germanic origin deriving from the Mediterranean region (Iberian peninsula, North Africa, Asia Minor), a picture apt to the varied mixture of race to be found in a late Roman cosmopolitan city. London and York were the two most important and cosmopolitan centres of Roman Britain, and the racial mixture of York compared with other parts of Roman Britain has also recently been illustrated by an examination of skeletal material.[56] The fact that gypsum burial is attested mainly in relation to these cosmopolitan centres implies that it is not a custom of native origin in Britain or on the Rhine.

The custom originated in north Africa. In a cemetery dating from the third to the first century B.C. at Saint-Leu, Algeria, the bodies had been wrapped in a simple shroud occasionally coated with a thin layer of cast lime (*enduit quelquefois d'une mince couche de chaux coulée*), an ancient African method of burial of which the earliest examples occur at Carthage.[57] A later example of Roman date occurs at Constantine where two sarcophagi contained bodies buried in lime (*enfouis dans la chaux*). These were in a cemetery built over after A.D. 365.[58] At Tipasa, in the cemetery associated with the fifth century basilica of St Salsa, many of the thickly crowded stone coffins still sealed with lead contained the skeleton clothed in a shroud on a bed of lime.[59] In the apse of a small Christian chapel, one of four, at Bou-Takrematem was a burial with the skeleton drowned in gypsum (*noyé dans le plâtre*).[60] At Timgad a group of burials associated with the fourth-century Donatist cathedral were in makeshift sarcophagi with the interior filled with lime,[61] but more impressive was the very large Christian cemetery on a hill to the south-west of the town, where more than ten thousand burials have been exposed, some in coffins or slab tombs, but mostly under inclined tiles[62] as often too in York. Almost all of these were gypsum burials with the shrouded bodies completely clothed in lime (*enrobés totalement dans la chaux*).[63] One example where the cast preserved the folds of the shroud, was in a tomb central to the nave of the small church, built of re-used materials including pagan tombstones, that stood in the middle of the cemetery.[64] In this cemetery were also found several of the vessels from which the liquid lime or gypsum had been poured.[65]

In Algeria an ancient but not common native burial custom suddenly and in a Christian context becomes almost the only burial rite in some cemeteries in the fourth and fifth centuries. Its spread to Britain and the Rhineland must reflect the presence of Africans in those provinces, a deduction confirmed in the case of Trier by analysis of skeletal material. At Poundbury and Trier as in Algeria the burials are Christian and by analogy they should also be so at York. This is difficult to prove in individual cases, particularly where alignments follow roads rather than ritual requirements, and there are no inscriptions. At Trier the orientation was north-west–south-west and not strictly west–east although the head was at the more westerly end. In Castle Yard of the six burials whose alignment we know, four were parallel to an adjacent road, north-west–south-east, and two at right angles, south-west–north-east, but in each case the head was at the more westerly end, looking in the more easterly direction. Two of the Castle Yard burials were in gypsum, one in lead and one in a re-used stone coffin, another without gypsum was in a re-used coffin, and two others were dated to the late fourth century. This cemetery could well be Christian, and this would give added significance to the hanging bowl found in the nineteenth century in poorly recorded circumstances.[66] If this represents part of the furnishings of an early seventh-century church on the site of a late Roman Christian burial ground, then we would indeed have evidence of a continuity of tradition, in spite of an intervening period of flooding and silting.

There are however two cases in York where the burial is deliberately aligned north–south, and one case where a child cremation is contained in the same coffin. Not all gypsum burials are Christian or the Christianization is only partial. In the fourth century in York gypsum is the fashionable and expensive form of burial. After Christianity became the official religion of the Roman Empire converts were to be found among the wealthier classes in the administrative centres of Gaul and Britain. In any event the change in burial custom and the re-use of earlier coffins reflects a change in the attitude to the dead and in the general religious climate of the time, a social revolution but not a complete rupture in tradition. In Roman sepulchral law the dedication *dis manibus* had the effect of making a tomb an inviolable *locus religiosus*.[67] In fourth-century York we have the wholesale violation of tombs. The same attitude is reflected in the re-use of an altar as a building stone,[68] or the fragment of another as rubble in a cairn to mark a grave,[69] and possibly the heap of stones including a cult statue and three altars above burials in Nunnery Lane may have been another cairn marking a fourth-century grave.[70]

Another type of burial in cists, probably also fourth-century, links York with the limestone belt south-west and north-west of Malton, where similar cists date to the fourth and fifth centuries and possibly continue into Anglian times, graves lined with thin slabs of oolitic limestone, sometimes packed with rubble, covered by other slabs. In the Howardian Hills they have been found at Crambe, associated with a late fourth-century farm;[71] at Crambeck, where two of five were dated to the late fourth or early fifth century;[72] at Easthorpe, where the grave-goods sound Anglian; and a group at Yearsley thought by Greenwell to be Anglian.[73] From the north side of Ryedale, one has been found at Nawton,[74] and two not far from a late fourth-century farm at Spaunton.[75]

In York a cist of oolitic stone from the Howardian Hills differed in using rubble walling rather than slabs to line the grave.[76] Such thin slabs as were readily available in the limestone areas were friable and barely worth the trouble of transporting to York. Where slab cists occur at York the stone is likely to be gritstone and to contain gypsum burials.[77] A cist recorded from Castle Yard with a crouched burial may be prehistoric[78] but crouched burial does occur in Roman times in York.[79]

Cremation is rare in fourth-century York but isolated examples have been recorded, particularly of infants whose ashes had been kept for burial with their parents.[80] The sole use of cremation by the people who buried their dead in urns of Germanic type on the Mount and at Heworth is as remarkable as the pottery itself. This is mainly Anglo-Frisian but includes some types which imply that the cemetery was in use before A.D. 400 and the burials are of mercenaries paid with land to defend the Romano-British settlements.[81] Germanic mercenaries or levies were no new thing at York[82] but earlier levies presumably Romanized have left no trace in the archaeological record. At Canterbury traces were found of huts built to house similar levies.[83] But at York neither traces of huts nor sherds of domestic pottery have yet been found. The two York cemeteries do not, like the similar cemeteries at Sancton and Driffield, show evidence of continuity into the sixth and seventh centuries.[84]

In addition to these two cremation cemeteries there are slight hints of other burials, e.g. a well-known fifth-century glass bowl comes from an unspecified site on the Mount[85] but two cremations in urns recorded from the ruins of a Roman building at the junction of Parliament and Market Streets[86] must be later Pagan Saxon after flooding had made this a waste area.

Finally we must briefly consider the Christian inhumation cemetery on Lamel Hill, south-east of the city. Dr John Thurnam in 1846–8 excavated what is now a landscaped garden feature but before that had been a windmill mound.[87] The original ground surface was marked by a seam of moist black material from one to two inches thick. Below this was a series of burials aligned west–east and a storage jar of seventeenth-century date.[88] The whole of the mound is therefore seventeenth-century and probably raised as a battery during the civil wars.[89] The burials are much older and in heaping up the mound many of the burials were disturbed, since the mound is full of disturbed skeletal material. Dr Thurnam thought that the ground into which the undisturbed burials had been dug was made-up and part of a low tumulus or tumular cemetery but the soil he describes with calcareous matter amongst clay, gravel, and stones under the undisturbed skeletons is typical of the glacially deposited material that is the natural soil of the area; we are dealing with a flat cemetery on a hill and the appearance of a mound has been accentuated by the removal of adjacent soil. The burials had been laid out as regularly as in a churchyard and the rarity of overlapping burial implies that the burials were marked above ground, and the cemetery not in use over a very extended period. No medieval church is known from this site nor is one probable. The burials were in wooden coffins and the metal fittings similar to those from the Anglian cemetery in Garton parish in the East Riding which also has west–east burials[90] and like Lamel Hill is at the boundary of the settlement it served.[91] Lamel Hill belongs to a later period than that immediately post-Roman and probably as late as the seventh century.

Appendix

Gypsum Burials

From York and district

CASTLE YARD

1. Thin coating gypsum in linen. Lead coffin. North-west–south-east. Fourth-century.[92]
2. Gravel below gypsum over body. Stone coffin. North-west–south-east. Fourth-century.[93]

OLD STATION: AREA (a)

3. Child coated gypsum. Wood coffin in lead. Within built-up area.[94]
4. Encased in gypsum. Wood coffin in brick vault. Outside *colonia* wall.[95]

RAILWAY: AREA (b)

5. Gypsum-coated. Lead coffin with infant's cremation. Fourth-century.[96]
6. Several gypsum-coated. Stone coffins.
7. Gypsum-coated. Lead coffin.
8. Gypsum-coated. Stone coffin. 6–8 form a probably near contemporary group with 5.[97]
9. Gypsum-filled coffin. Hair preserved. Wood coffin in brick vault.[98]
10. Several gypsum-coated in slab cists.[99]
11. Gypsum-coated in stone coffin.
12. Gypsum spread over body. Stone coffin. Suite of jets, including one datable to fourth century.[100]
13. Several "containing lime". Stone coffins.[101]
14. Several "laid in lime". Stone coffins.

ROYAL STATION HOTEL: AREA (c)

15. Good gypsum cast. Stone coffin, lid sealed with red cement.

16–18. Three gypsum burials in stone coffins, a contemporary group with 15.[102]

19. Good gypsum impression. Body had rested on a bier. Stone coffin, lid sealed with red cement. Grave-goods including fourth-century glass.[103]
20. Child's gypsum burial, without coffin, associated with 19.
21. Gypsum burial. Stone coffin. North–south.[104]
22. Thinly coated in gypsum. Stone coffin. North–south.[105] 21–2 part of group of fourth-century burials.
23. Gypsum cast of legs only. Stone coffin. North-west–south-east. One of a pair of burials, the other late third–fourth-century.[106]

THE STATION: AREAS (d) AND (e)

24. Good cast of body with hair preserved. Decorated lead in stone coffin. South–north. Late-third–fourth century.[107]
25. Cast of child. Stone coffin.[108]

26–7. Adult with child above, both gypsum, in separate stone coffins.[109]

28. Child. Gypsum coated. Lead coffin.[110]
29. Adolescent. Cast. Lead coffin.[111]
30. Gypsum under legs. Stone coffin. Associated with other fourth-century burials.[112]

31. Cast. Wood coffin in large cist.[113]
32. Cast. Stone coffin.[114]

RAILWAY, NORTH OF STATION: AREA (f)

33. Coated with gypsum. Narrow stone coffin. Associated with other fourth-century burials.[115]
34. Laid on gypsum. Lead coffin.[116]
35. A little gypsum. Stone coffin.[117]

NEAR MICKLEGATE BAR

36. Cloth preserved, ? gypsum burial. Stone coffin. Cloth of Germanic type.[118]

THE MOUNT

37. Male coated with gypsum in Aelia Severa's re-used coffin. [119]
38. Well preserved in gypsum. Stone coffin.[120]
39. Head and feet in gypsum, rest in gravel. Stone coffin. North–south.[121]
40. Laid on and covered with "white composition". Simplicia Florentina's re-used stone coffin.[122]

TRENTHOLME DRIVE

41. Gypsum-coated body of 14-year-old boy in stone coffin. North–south. Dated by excavator before A.D. 270.[123]
42. Isolated lump of gypsum from a disturbed burial.[124]

CLEMENTHORPE

43. Good cast of mother and child in stone coffin.[125]

NEAR MIDDLETHORPE

44–5. Two gypsum burials in stone coffins.[126]

HESLINGTON

46. Fine gypsum cast. Stone coffin. Suite of adornments. Fourth-century.[127]

HEWORTH

47. Gypsum burial in lead coffin.[128]
48. Thin layer of gypsum. Stone coffin. North–south. Late-third–fourth century pottery in grave fill.

POPPLETON

49. Burial with clotted hair, ? gypsum burial. Stone coffin.[129]

From the West Riding

BIRKIN

50. Calcareous mud. ?gypsum burial. Stone coffin.[130]

CASTLEFORD

51. Body completely covered with gypsum. Pegs for some kind of wood frame round gypsum. Stone coffin. East–west. Late-third- or fourth-century.[131]

LEEDS

52. "Plaster" cast. Stone coffin. Mirror glass (? fourth-century).[132]

POLLINGTON

53. Thin covering gypsum, body on sand. Stone coffin. West–east. Said to be fourth–fifth-century.[133]

From London

54. Boy, 10–12 years, with a quantity of lime. Lead coffin in stone. East–west. Late third–fourth-century. Coin of Valens sometimes associated with burial.[134]
55. Lime. ?cast of face. Lead coffin in wood.[135]
56. Embedded in lime. Lead coffin.[136]
57. In lime. Stone coffin. East–west.
58. In lime. Purbeck stone coffin. North–south.[137]
59. With lime. Lead coffin. Late-third- or fourth-century.[138]

From Ware, Herts

60–61. Bodies in lime or white mortar, in one case with cloth impression, both in wooden coffins inside stone ones. Both east–west. Coin of Constantine or Constantius in grave fill of one coffin.[139]

62. Young female. Overspread white plaster. Cast of face. Hair preserved. Stone coffin.

From Kent

CANTERBURY

63. On bed of lime and packed with clay. Lead coffin. North–south.[140]

CHATHAM

64. Embedded in lime. Cast of shoulder. Hair preserved. Lead coffin in wood case. Fourth-century.[141]

MILTON-NEXT-SITTINGBOURNE

65. Masses of calcareous matter. Beard preserved. Lead coffin in wood frame. Fourth-century glass.[142]
66. Masses of calcareous matter. Female. Lead coffin.

SITTINGBOURNE

67. Child's skeleton. ?gypsum. Calcareous deposit on jewellery. Decorated lead in wooden coffin. West–east. Gold and jet adornments. Fourth-century.[143]

From Poundbury, Dorchester, Dorset

68. Adult packed in gypsum. Wood coffin in lead. West–east.
69. Packed in gypsum. Wood coffin in lead. West–east.
70. Poorly preserved gypsum burial in stone coffin. West–east.[144]
71. One burial of a pair, covered in gypsum, in wood in stone coffin. East–west.[145]
72. Poorly preserved burial with traces of gypsum in a stone coffin. West–east.
73. Female burial with remains of a bone comb and gypsum retaining cloth impressions in a stone coffin. West–east.[146]

An article of 1870 by Albert Way[147] discussed gypsum burial in relation to a Saxon interment in an inscribed third- to fourth-century Roman coffin at Westminster Abbey. This contained carbonate of lime, which may have survived from the original Roman burial. He cites additional examples of gypsum burial besides those described in the above list – from Sutton Valence near Maidstone, Kent, and from Great Chesterford, Essex, as well as possible French examples at Bordeaux and Puy-de-Dôme.

Notes

1. Wacher (ed.), *Civitas Capitals of Roman Britain* (1966), 87–100.
2. R.C.H.M., *York*, xxxiv.
3. York Minster, excavations by H. G. Ramm and D. Phillips, 1967 proceeding.
4. Bishophill Senior, excavation by H. G. Ramm, report forthcoming.
5. Wacher (ed.), *op. cit.*, 91.
6. Cramp, *Anglian and Viking York* (1967), pl. iv, for a distribution map of Anglian finds.
7. R.C.H.M., *York*, 64; *Arch. J.*, cxvi (1961), 51ff.
8. *ibid.*, 56.
9. *ibid.*, 53.
10. *Y.P.S.R.* (1902), 71.
11. *V.C.H.*, *Yorks.*, II, 191–3.
12. Cramp, *op. cit.*, 5 and pl. iii.
13. *Y.P.S.R.* (1902), 65.
14. *Arch. J.*, cxvi (1961), 61.
15. *Y.A.J.*, xxxix (1958), 519–21.
16. *Y.A.J.*, xli (1966), 581ff.; *Y.A.J.*, xlii, pt 166 (1968), 118, full report forthcoming.
17. information from J. Radley.
18. *Y.A.J.*, xli (1966), 559; additional information from J. Radley.
19. *Y.M.H.* (1891), 216.
20. Eyre and Jones (ed.), *Geography as Human Ecology* (1966), 106–7.
21. *Radiocarbon*, iv (1962), 64–5; *New Phytologist*, lvii (1958), 19.
22. Wacher (ed.), *op. cit.*, 87.
23. Coney Street, 1955, excavation by H. G. Ramm, medieval material unpublished. Behind York Public Library, 1969, excavation by J. Radley.
24. O.S. (1952), for obsolete parish boundaries, *Arch. J.*, cxvi (1961), 61, for medieval reference to a dyke.
25. *Y.P.S.R.* (1902), 64–5.

26. *V.C.H., City of York*, 10.
27. See 23 above.
28. R.C.H.M., *York*, 23–5; *Y.P.S.R.* (1963), 17.
29. information from excavator.
30. *J.R.S.*, xviii (1928), 86.
31. *A.N.L.*, 6 (Oct. 1948), 12–14.
32. see note 3 above.
33. R.C.H.M., *York*, 42–3. Y.A.Y.A.S., *Procs.*, i (1933), 3ff.
34. *Y.A.J.*, xl (1962), 507ff.
35. excavations, 1964, by H. G. Ramm, report forthcoming.
36. R.C.H.M., *York*, 131–3, nos. 122, 126, 127 and 135.
37. *ibid.*, 132, no. 128.
38. *J.R.S.*, lviii (1968), 208.
39. *Y.A.J.*, xxxix (1958), pl. iv.
40. Brodribb, Hands, and Walker, *Excavations at Shakenoak*, i (1968), 88–9, fig. 30, no. 21.
41. Wheeler and Wheeler, *Excavations of . . . site in Lydney Park* (1932), 82–3, fig. 17.
42. *ibid.*, fig. 17, no. 56.
43. Cunliffe (ed.), *Fifth Report on . . . Roman Fort at Richborough* (1968), pl. xli, no. 155.
44. R.C.H.M., *York*, 130, no. 108.
45. *ibid.*, 128, no. 103.
46. *ibid.*, 122, no. 77.
47. *ibid.*, 128–9, no. 104.
48. *ibid.*, 85–6 (ix).
49. *ibid.*, 86, g (i); 130, no. 106; 131, no. 110.
50. *ibid.*, 100–1, (xxi); *Y.A.J.*, xxxix (1958), 2.
51. R.C.H.M., *York*, 99 (vi); *Y.A.J.*, xxxix (1958), 427ff.
52. R.C.H.M., *Dorset*, ii, 572, 583–5. The Christian nature of the cemetery has since been confirmed by C. J. S. Green's excavations of 1968–9, exposing a rectangular mausoleum or perhaps chapel, Dorset N.H. & A.S., *Procs.*, xci (1969), 83ff.
53. Wenham *et al.*, *The Romano-British Cemetery at Trentholme Drive, York* (1968), 40.
54. Castleford; *J.R.S.*, lvii (1967), 179; Pollington; *Y.A.J.*, xxxvii (1951), 526.
55. Kramer (ed.), *Neue Ausgrabungen in Deutschland* (1958), 360–2.
56. Wenham *et al.*, *op. cit.*, 157.
57. Christofle (ed.), *Rapport sur les travaux de fouilles et consolidations effectuées en 1933–6 par le service des Monuments Historiques de L'Algérie* (1938), 131, 147.
58. *ibid.*, 256.
59. *ibid.*, 77.
60. *ibid.*, 295.
61. Courtois, *Timgad, antique Thamugadi* (1951), 67 with plate.
62. Ballu, *Les Ruines de Timgad. Sept Années de Descouvertes (1903–10)* (1911), 35.
63. Christofle (ed.), *op. cit.*, 380.
64. *ibid.*, 369–70.
65. *ibid.*, 380.
66. Cramp, *op. cit.*, 5–6.
67. Gaius, *Inst.*, 11.4.6. Mommsen, *Gesamellte Schriften* iii, 198ff. For pillage of tombs elsewhere in the fourth century compare Ostia. (Meiggs, *Roman Ostia* (1960), 466, 146.)
68. R.C.H.M., *York*, 116, no. 33.
69. *ibid.*, 83 (x); 116, no. 34.
70. *ibid.*, 94 (iv); 115, no. 30; 118, nos. 38–9; 120, no. 59; *Y.P.S.R.* (1880), 48.

71. *Y.P.S.R.* (1966), 28.
72. Corder, *Roman Pottery at Crambeck, Castle Howard* (1928), 10–14, 18–20.
73. Whellan, *York and North Riding*, ii (1859), 210; Greenwell, *British Barrows* (1877), 550–1.
74. *Y.A.J.*, xl (1962), 307.
75. Home, *Evolution of an English Country Town* (1905), 46–7; *Y.A.J.*, xl (1962), 310.
76. Wenham *et al.*, *op. cit.*, 42.
77. R.C.H.M., *York*, 81 (v), (viii); 84, (xiii).
78. *ibid.*, 69, note 1.
79. e.g. *ibid.*, 105.
80. e.g. *ibid.*, 81 (ii).
81. Myres, *Anglo-Saxon pottery and the settlement of the English* (1969), 73ff.
82. R.C.H.M., *York*, xxxiv.
83. Wacher (ed.), *op. cit.*, 91–3.
84. Cramp, *op. cit.*, 3.
85. *Y.P.S.R.* (1927), 7; *Y.A.J.*, xxxix (1958), 430; Harden (ed.), *Dark Age Britain* (1956), 142, pl. xvi, g.
86. Hargrove, *New Guide . . . to York* (1838), 52–3.
87. *Arch. J.*, vi (1848), 27ff.
88. The dating is based on a re-examination of the pot at the Retreat, York, and a comparison with two similar pots in the Yorkshire Museum.
89. *Arch. J.* vi (1848), 30–1.
90. Mortimer, *Forty Years Researches . . .* (1905), 254–7, burials, 31–60.
91. For the boundary; *Y.A.J.*, xli (1966), 585. For relationship between burials and boundaries; *W.A.M.*, lxi (1966), 25.
92. R.C.H.M., *York*, 67.
93. *ibid.*, 67–8.
94. *ibid.*, 80 (i).
95. *ibid.*, 80 (viii).
96. *ibid.*, 81 (ii); 140.
97. *ibid.*, 81 (v).
98. *ibid.*, 81 (vi).
99. *ibid.*, 81 (viii). (See also for no. 11.)
100. *ibid.*, 81 (ix); 143.
101. *ibid.*, 81 (x). (See also for no. 14.)
102. *ibid.*, 82 (iii).
103. *ibid.*, 82 (iv); 141.
104. *ibid.*, 82 (vii).
105. *ibid.*, 82 (viii).
106. *ibid.*, 82 (x).
107. *ibid.*, 83 (i).
108. *ibid.*, 83 (ii).
109. *ibid.*, 83 (viii).
110. *ibid.*, 83 (ix).
111. *ibid.*, 84 (xi).
112. *ibid.*, 84 (xii).
113. *ibid.*, 84 (xiii).
114. *ibid.*, 84 (ii).
115. *ibid.*, 85 (iv).

116. *ibid.*, 85 (vi).
117. *ibid.*, 85 (vii).
118. *Y.M.H.*, (1891), 138; *Y.P.S.R.*, (1951), 22.
119. R.C.H.M., *York*, 99 (vi).
120. *ibid.*, 97 (x). For gypsum: Pearson, *Roman Yorkshire* (1936), 155.
121. R.C.H.M., *York*, 100 (xv).
122. *ibid.*, 100 (xviii). For gypsum: *York Courant*, 7 June 1838.
123. Wenham *et. al.*, *op. cit.*, 40–2.
124. *ibid.*, 45.
125. R.C.H.M., *York*, 108.
126. *ibid.*, 108.
127. Wellbeloved, *Eburacum* (1842), 108–9; *Y.M.H.* (1891), 116. Small finds in Yorkshire Museum, H323, 1–14.
128. *Y.P.S.R.* (1967), 50–60. (See also for no. 48.)
129. *Yorkshire Gazette*, 2 Feb. 1833.
130. *Handbook, Old Leeds Exhibition* (1908), 4n.
131. *J.R.S.*, lvii (1967), 179.
132. Parson and White, *Annals, History and Guide of Leeds and York* (1830–1), i, 274.
133. *Y.A.J.*, xxxvii (1951), 526.
134. R.C.H.M., *Roman London*, 157, Minories.
135. *ibid.*, 164 (2); *Gents. Mag. Lib.*, *R.B.*, i, 181, implies cast of face.
136. R.C.H.M., *Roman London*, 164 (3). (See also for no. 57.)
137. *ibid.*, 165, Notting Hill.
138. *ibid.*, 169, Battersea.
139. *Gents. Mag. Lib.*, *R.B.*, i, 136–7. (See also for no. 62.)
140. *ibid.*, 143–4.
141. *V.C.H.*, *Kent*, iii, 149; *Arch. Cant*, xii, 420; xiii, 168.
142. B.M., *Roman Guide* (1922), 102; *Gents. Mag. Lib.*, *R.B.*, i, 155. (See also for no. 66.)
143. Payne, *Collectanea Cantiana* (1893), 54–7.
144. R.C.H.M., *Dorset*, ii (1970), 584–5, no. 225 (h).
145. *ibid.*, 583–4, no. 225 (e).
146. *ibid.*, 584, no. 225 (g).
147. *Arch. J.*, xxvii (1870), 191–4.

Index

York and
the Roman Occupation of
northern England
(*based on R.C.H.M.* York, *fig. 1*,
by permission of
the Royal Commission on
Historical Monuments)

Key

A Adel
B Birrens
Ba Brough by Bainbridge
Bf Burton Fleming
Bn Brough on Noe
Bo Bowes
C Carlisle
Ca Castleford
Cb Carrawburgh
Cd Crawford
Cl Cleckheaton
Cm Cowlam
Co Corbridge
Cr Carkin Moor
Ct Catterick
D Doncaster
F Fremington
G Greta Bridge
H Healam Bridge
I Ilkley
M Millington Bridge
N Newstead
Nk Newton Kyme
P Piercebridge
R Ribchester
Ri Risingham
S Stanwick
Sc Scalesheugh
T Tadcaster
Ts Thornton le Street
W Wilderspool